Inequality Around the World

This is IEA conference volume no. 134

Inequality Around the World

Edited by

Richard B. Freeman

Ascherman Professor of Economics, Harvard University

palgrave macmillan

in association with

International Economic Association

First published 2002 by
PALGRAVE MACMILLAN
Houndmills, Basingstoke, Hampshire RG21 6XS and
175 Fifth Avenue, New York, N.Y. 10010
Companies and representatives throughout the world

PALGRAVE MACMILLAN is the global academic imprint of the Palgrave Macmillan division of St. Martin's Press, LLC and of Palgrave Macmillan Ltd. Macmillan® is a registered trademark in the United States, United Kingdom and other countries. Palgrave is a registered trademark in the European Union and other countries.

ISBN 0–333–77354–3 hardback
ISBN 0–333–77355–1 paperback

This book is printed on paper suitable for recycling and made from fully managed and sustained forest sources.

A catalogue record for this book is available from the British Library.

A catalog record for this book is available from the library of Congress.

10 9 8 7 6 5 4 3 2 1
11 10 09 08 07 06 05 04 03 02

Printed and bound in Great Britain by
Antony Rowe Ltd, Chippenham and Eastbourne

Contents

Part III Understanding Micro-Behaviour and the Broad Economy of Inequality

The International Economic Association

A non-profit organization with purely scientific aims, the International Economic Association (IEA) was founded in 1950. It is a federation of some sixty national economic associations in all parts of the world. Its basic purpose is the development of economics as an intellectual discipline, recognising a diversity of problems, systems and values in the world and taking note of methodological diversities.

The IEA has, since its creation, sought to fulfil that purpose by promoting mutual understanding among economists through the organization of scientific meetings and common research programmes, and by means of publications on problems of fundamental as well as current importance. Deriving from its long concern to assure professional contacts between East and West and North and South, the IEA pays special attention to issues of economies in systemic transition and in the course of development. During its 50 years of existence, it has organised more than 100 round-table conferences for specialists on topics ranging from fundamental theories to methods and tools of analysis and major problems of the present-day world. Participation in round tables is at the invitation of a specialist programme committee, but 12 triennial World Congresses have regularly attracted the participation of individual economists from all over the world.

The Association is governed by a Council, comprising representatives of all member associations, and by a 15-member Executive Committee which is elected by the Council. The Executive Committee (1999–2002) at the time of the Buenos Aires Congress was:

President:	Professor Robert Solow, USA
Vice-President:	Professor Vittorio Corbo, Chile
Treasurer:	Professor Jacob Frenkel, Israel
Past President:	Professor Jacques Drèze, Belgium
Other members:	Professor Bina Agarwal, India
	Professor Maria Augusztinovics, Hungary
	Professor Eliana Cardoso, World Bank
	Professor Gene Grossman, USA
	Professor Seppo Honkapohja, Finland
	Professor Valery Makarov, Russia
	Professor Andreu Mas Colell, Spain

Sir Austin Robinson was an active Adviser on the publication of IEA Conference proceedings from 1954 until his final short illness in 1993.

The Association has also been fortunate in having secured many outstanding economists to serve as President:
Gottfried Haberler (1950–53), Howard S. Ellis (1953–56), Erik Lindahl (1956–59), E. A. G. Robinson (1959–62), Ugo Papi (1962–65), Paul A. Samuelson (1965–68), Erik Lundberg (1968–71), Fritz Machlup (1971–74), Edmund Malinvaud (1974–77), Shigeto Tsuru (1977–80), Victor L. Urquidi (1980–83), Kenneth J. Arrow (1983–86), Amartya Sen (1986–89), Anthony B. Atkinson (1989–1992), Michael Bruno (1992–95) and Jacques Drèze (1995–99).

The activities of the Association are mainly funded from the subscriptions of members and grants from a number of organizations, including continuing support from UNESCO, through the International Social Science Council. Specific support from the latter was received for the Buenos Aires Congress under its Project R4/CAR.

Acknowledgements

The Twelfth World Congress of the International Economic Association (IEA) was held in Buenos Aires on August 23–27, 1999, at the invitation of the Asociación Argentina de Economia Politica (AAEP). The IEA is deeply grateful to the AAEP for its willingness to host the congress, and above all for superbly handling the local arrangements. The 1,260 registered participants undoubtedly feel equally grateful.

The congress was dedicated to the memory of the late Michael Bruno, President of the IEA 1992–95, as a tribute to his valuable contributions to economics, and in particular to the IEA.

The Organising Committee consisted of Enrique Bour, president, Rolf Mantel, vice-president, Victor Beker, executive secretary, Marcela Cristini, Maria Echart, Marcos Gallacher and Javier Ortiz. It is very sad that Rolf Mantel died prematurely in February 1999. He had been a productive researcher and an influential member of the Latin American scientific community. He was an exceptionally fine person. The IEA joins Mrs Mantel and Rolf's numerous friends in treasuring his memory.

Special thanks go to Enrique Bour, former AAEP President, who shouldered much responsibility as president of the Organizing Committee. He showed exceptional dedication, ability and congeniality.

Financial support towards the local organization came first from Banco Central de la República Argentina, soon complemented by Banco de la Nacion Argentina, Banco de la Provincia de Buenos Aires, Banco Hipotecario, Ministerio de Relaciones Exteriores, Comercio Internacional y Culto, Secretaría de Industria, Comercio y Miniera and Secretaría de Programacíon Económica y Regional. Their support is gratefully acknowledged.

The logistics of the congress were handled with competence by the staff of Maria Graziani y Asociados of Buenos Aires and by IEA administrative assistants Marie David and Véronique de Labarre.

The scientific programme included two series of invited lectures, one on 'Macroeconomics' organized by Jacques Drèze (Université Catholique de Louvain) and one on 'Inequality' organized by Richard Freeman (Harvard University and London School of Economics). These lectures appear in the present proceedings volume and in Volume 1. The rest of the programme comprised 310 contributed papers, selected from a still larger number of submissions by a 30-member Programme Committee ably and diligently chaired by David de la Croix (Université Catholique de Louvain). From these fifteen important papers dealing with Latin American issues constitute Volume 3, edited by Enrique Bour, Daniel Heymann and Fernando Navajas. Maureen Hadfield and Michael Kaser supervised the editorial process, and for this volume Jennifer Amadeo-Holl (NBER) is particularly thanked for marshalling the papers and copyright assignments. The IEA expresses its gratitude to all participants in their efforts for both programme and publication.

Some 100 authors of invited papers, in particular authors from emerging countries, received travel grants to Buenos Aires. These grants were funded by the World Bank, the World Bank Institute, the Inter-American Development Bank, the Asian Development Bank and the European Investment Bank. Their support is gratefully acknowledged.

The main credit for the success of the congress goes to the authors of invited lectures and contributed papers. They supplied a rich intellectual material, incompletely but representatively covered in these three volumes.

List of Contributors

Kenneth J. Arrow, Stanford University, USA
Dwayne Benjamin, University of Toronto, Canada
Elizabeth Brainerd, Williams College, Massachusetts, and Harvard University, USA
Loren Brandt, University of Toronto, Canada
Samuel Bowles, University of Massachusetts, USA
Fatma El-Hamidi, University of Pittsburgh, USA
Armin Falk, University of Zurich, Switzerland
Urs Fischbacher, University of Zurich, Switzerland
Richard Freeman, Harvard University and National Bureau of Economic Research, Cambridge Mass., USA, and London School of Economics and Political Science, UK
Paul Glewwe, University of Minnesota, USA
Robert G. Gregory, Australian National University, Australia
Marianne Hilgert, Inter-American Development Bank, Washington, DC, USA
Guo Li, The World Bank, Washington, DC, USA
Marco Manacorda, London School of Economics and Queen Mary College, University of London, UK
Remco H. Oostendorp, Free University, Amsterdam, Netherlands
Miguel Székely, Office for Regional Development Presidency of the Republic, Mexico
Katherine Terrell, University of Michigan, USA

List of Abbreviations and Acronyms

2SLS	two-stage least squares
AEEP	Asociación Argentina de Economia Politica
ANC	African National Congress
ANOVA	analysis of variance
CEPR	Centre for Economic Policy Research (UK)
CHNS	China Health and Nutrition Survey
COLA	cost-of-living adjustment (US)
coop	cooperative
CPI	consumer price index
d.f.	degree of freedom
EBRD	European Bank for Reconstruction and Development
GDP	gross domestic product
GLS	generalized least squares
Goskomstat	State Statistical Committee (Russia)
HRS	Household Responsibility System (China)
HSEU	Household Survey of Employment and Unemployment (Costa Rica)
ICP	International Comparison Project (UN Statistical Office)
IDB	Inter-American Development Bank
ILO	International Labour Office/Organization
ISTAT	Istituto Nazionale di Statistica (Italy)
IV	instrumental variable
LSMS	Living Standards Measurement Survey (World Bank)
MIT	Massachusetts Institute of Technology
MSR	money supply rules
NBER	National Bureau of Economic Research (US)
NNCLSS	North and Northeast China Living Standards Survey
nd	no date
OLS	ordinary least squares
OECD	Organization for Economic Cooperation and Development
OWW	Occupational Wages around the World (ILO)
PPP	purchasing power parity
PRC	People's Republic of China
RLMS	Russian Longitudinal Monitoring Survey

RMB	renminbi (Chinese yuan)
SHIW	Survey of Households' Income and Wealth (Bank of Italy)
SM	Scala Mobile (Italy)
SSB	State Statistical Bureau (China)
SSHRC	Social Science and Humanities Research Council (Canada)
TVE	township and village enterprise (China)
UNESCO	United Nations Educational, Scientific and Cultural Organization
WHO	World Health Organization

1
Introduction

Richard B. Freeman
Harvard University and NBER, USA, and Centre for Economic Performance, London School of Economics, UK

Increases in inequality within countries and between countries is one of the most disturbing developments at the beginning of the twenty-first century. The rise of inequality runs counter to much standard economic thinking. Trade and capital flows are, after all, supposed to reduce economic differences between countries and, while they may increase earnings differentials in advanced countries, are supposed to reduce those differentials in less developed countries. The increase in educational attainment within countries should reduce inequality within countries as well. But the facts tell a different story.

This volume reports on a variety of studies covering patterns of change in income inequality around the globe and particular factors that contribute to this. The focus is on developments in parts of the world that have not received the attention given to the US and UK in analyses of rising inequality – China (Benjamin, Brandt, Glewwe and Li); Russia (Brainerd), Australia (Gregory), Latin America (Székely and Hilgert; El-Hamidi and Terrell); Italy (Manacorda) – and to ideas about inequality that go beyond arguments over the impact of technological change and globalization on inequality (Falk and Fischbacher; Bowles; and Arrow). In addition, the volume describes a new data set for examining inequality in wages by occupation around the world, the files of which are available on the web (Freeman and Oostendorp).

By selecting areas and topics that lie outside much current work on inequality, the volume makes a distinct contribution. There is new information, new data, and new ideas that help illuminate this troubling world development.

Part I

International Patterns and Advanced Countries

2
Wages Around the World: Pay across Occupations and Countries

Richard B. Freeman
Harvard University and National Bureau of Economic Research, USA, and Centre for Economic Performance, London School of Economics, UK

and

Remco H. Oostendorp
Free University, Amsterdam, and Amsterdam Institute for International Development, Netherlands

1 Introduction

Consider the wages of workers in two occupations in two countries: say a labourer and software engineer in India and a labourer and software engineer in Germany. There are three useful contrasts one can make with these wages:

1. The percentage (or absolute) differential between the wages of more skilled and less skilled workers within each country. All else the same, this *skill differential* reflects the return to human capital and the degree of inequality in the wage structure in the countries.
2. The ratio of the wages of workers in the same occupation between the countries, measured in a common currency through exchange rates. All else the same, this *cost differential* reflects the different cost of producing goods with these workers.
3. The difference in wages for workers in the same occupation, measured in purchasing power parity (PPP) units. All else the same, these *living standard differentials* measure differences in the economic well-being of similarly skilled workers.

With data for many occupations and countries, one can examine generalizations of these relations: the variance of occupational earnings within countries; the dispersion of cost differentials among countries; and inequality in living standards for similarly skilled workers around the world. With data over time, one can further examine changes in these measures and the tendencies, if any, toward equalization of pay across occupations and countries.

Labour economists have traditionally focused on the pattern of skill differentials (Reder (1962)). Their chief generalization is that differentials are lower in advanced countries and decline over time with economic development, because of more plentiful supplies of skilled workers.[1] In Tinbergen's 'race' between education-induced increases in the supply of skills and technology-induced increased in demand for skills, the shift in supply has dominated, reducing differentials (Tinbergen (1974)).

Trade economists focus on differentials in the cost of comparable labour across countries. The major issue is the extent to which trade produces factor price equalization. In its strongest form, the Samuelson–Stolper theorem predicts the same pay for workers with the same skills around the world. Still, trade theory allows the wages of similarly skilled workers to differ if countries operate in different cones of diversity or use different technologies.

Development economists focus on how economic growth affects living standards and thus on wages deflated by PPP price indices. They worry whether growth raises the living standards of the poor in the early phases of development; whether an effectively infinite supply of labour from the traditional sector keeps real wages down; or if urban bias in wage-setting creates excessive rural–urban migration and unemployment.

In short, wage differentials around the world are central to various economic questions and theories about the operation of the labour market. Despite this, there are no generally accepted international data on occupational wages. The most widely used cross-country data on wages are the International Labour Organization's annual *Yearbook of Labour Statistics* manufacturing wages which does not differentiate occupations or skills. Studies of occupational wage structures treat a single country or a small number of countries or the wages of workers in specific occupations across countries. Psacharapoulos' data on earnings by education cover many countries but rely on many different sources and are of dubious quality or comparability.[2]

This study examines wages in 161 occupations around the world using the new *Occupational Wages around the World* (OWW) file. This is a data file that we developed by standardizing wages from the most far-ranging survey of wages, ILO's October Inquiry Survey, into a consistent series of pay across occupations, countries, and time. Using the OWW to examine skill differentials, cost differences, and living standard differentials from 1983 to 1998, we find:

1. Skill differentials vary inversely with gross domestic product *per capita*. During the 1980s–1990s, they fell modestly in advanced countries; fell more sharply in upper middle income countries; and rose markedly in countries moving from communism to free markets and in lower middle income countries.
2. Wages in the same occupation vary greatly across countries measured by common currency exchange rates and measured by PPP. Cross-country differences in pay for comparable work increased, despite increased world trade.
3. The principal forces that affect the occupational wage structure around the world are the level of gross domestic product *per capita* and unionisation/wage-setting institutions.

2 Standardizing the ILO October Inquiry Survey

2.1 The ILO October Inquiry Survey

Since 1924 the ILO has conducted an 'October Inquiry' to obtain data on pay by occupation across the world. The ILO sends a questionnaire to national governments asking for wages in detailed occupations within particular industries. Table 2.1 shows the coverage of the October Inquiry by occupation and country over time. In 1924 the survey gathered data on male earners in 18 occupations in 15 countries. In ensuing years the ILO expanded the number of countries and occupations. Country coverage increases fairly steadily so that the 1983–98 Inquiry data files on which we focus had wage statistics for 156 countries in at least one year and wages on up to 76 countries in any given year. The number of occupations increased from 30 occupations in 1929, to 41 in 1951, to 48 in 1953, and then to 161 in 1983.[3]

To assure comparability of occupational definitions across the countries, the ILO specifies in detail the work involved in each occupation. To get a flavour of the specificity consider the following description of a clicker cutter in the footwear industry:

> *Clicker cutter (machine). Operates press machine which cuts out upper parts of footwear; lays material on the table of machine; selects cutting dies; arranges dies on material to cut it economically and avoid weaknesses; cuts out show part by lowering press onto dies; removes cut-out parts from material.*

Or this (abbreviated) description of an accountant in a bank:

Accountant. Plans and administers accounting services and examines, analyses, interprets and evaluates accounting records for the purpose of giving advice on accountancy problems or preparing statements and installing or advising on systems of recording costs or other financial and budgetary data:...keeps record of all taxes, fees, etc. to be paid by the bank... conducts financial investigations on suspected fraud...prepares and certifies financial statements for presentation to the board of directors, executives, shareholders...

If each country obtained wages from a nationally representative survey based on ILO definitions, the October Inquiry would be the ideal source for comparing the pay of comparable labour across countries. Clicker cutters, accountants, economists, whomever from Pakistan or Romania or Germany or the US would have essentially interchangeable skills, so that one would truly be comparing equivalent labour.

But the October Inquiry data fall short of ideal. To the contrary, the Inquiry data has so many problems that the survey is one of the least widely used sources of cross-country data in the world. The main problem is that countries respond to the ILO in inconsistent ways. Recorded wages are not directly comparable across countries, in the same country

Table 2.1 Development of the ILO October Inquiry Survey, 1924–98

	Number of occupations	*Number of countries reporting*	
		In given year	*Cumulative reporting*
1924	18	15	15
1925–28	18	16–19	20
1929	30	17	20
1930–50	30	16–37	69
1951	41	19	69
1952	41	48	77
1953	48	47	82
1954–82	48	54–103	181
1983	161	56	182
1984–97	161	48–76	194
1998p	161	14	194

Source: International Labour Office, *October Inquiry Survey*, 1983–98 from computer data files; earlier years from published reports:
1924–50: *International Labour Review* (vols 10–54).
1935–57: *ILO Yearbook of Labour Statistics* (issues X–XVIII).
1951–63: *International Labour Review – Special Issue of the Statistical Supplement* (vols 66, 70, 72, 74, 76, 78, 80, 82, 84, 86, 88, 90).
1964–82: *Bulletin of Labour Statistics* (1965–83).

over time, or even among occupations in a country at a point of time, in part because countries report data from differing national sources rather than conducting special surveys to answer the ILO request. Some countries report average earnings in an occupation from an employer survey, others report legislated minimum wages, yet others report collectively bargained wages, while others give hourly wage rates. In 1995 the US reported median weekly earnings from a household survey; Germany reported minimum collectively bargained hourly, daily, weekly, and monthly wage rates, depending on the occupation; India reported minimum daily and monthly wage rates; Nigeria reported average monthly wage rates and average monthly earnings. Some countries give wages for men in some occupations. Others report wages for men and women. Others report wages for women in some occupations. And so on.

Another problem is that countries do not report consistently from year to year. In the 1983–98 period 156 countries reported wages in at least one year, but just 11 countries reported wages 15 or 16 times (effectively every year given that we have only preliminary data for 1998), 31 reported 10–14 times, 45 reported five–nine times, and 47 reported one–four times and 22 reported just once. Looking across the years, in 1983, 56 countries reported wages, in 1985, 70 reported wages, in 1990, 73 reported, in 1992, 61 reported, in 1995, 76 reported, in 1997, 48 reported.

A third problem is that the Inquiry fails to obtain information on all supplementary labour costs. The ILO asks that countries include cost of living adjustments and other guaranteed and regularly paid allowances in their reports on wages and asks that countries include paid vacation and holidays as well in earnings. But the Inquiry excludes employer contributions to social security, pension funds, severance pay, irregular bonuses, including such important payments as the annual or bi-annual bonuses paid in Japan and some other Asian countries, and contributions to health insurance. To the extent that social charges are proportionate to wages, this will not affect estimates of relative wage structures in countries, but it will underestimate differences in labour costs or living standards across countries.

A fourth problem is that even with the ILO's detailed specification of skills, the work performed in an occupation will vary across countries. Even in a country, skills differ within the narrow ILO categories. The skill of cooks working in restaurants and hotels (an ILO occupation) in Great Britain range widely, depending on the size of an establishment, cuisine, and number of stars in the guidebooks. Such differences are likely to be even greater across countries. To the extent that differences in skills within occupations are associated with education, workers are likely to be more skilled in advanced countries than in less advanced countries.

Finally, the changing numbers of occupations over time makes comparisons between the post-1983 period and earlier years difficult. In addition, some countries do not in fact provide national data but data from particular regions, such as major cities or urban areas.

Table 2.2 gives a detailed description of information in the Inquiry files from the 1983 to 1998 period on which we focus. The complicated structure of the data makes it clear why few researchers use these data to analyse wages around the world.

Panel A gives information on the size of the sample. It shows the maximum conceivable number of observations that the Inquiry would contain if each country reported a single wage statistic for each occupation yearly: over 400,000 pieces of data.[4] The actual number of observations is smaller, largely because most countries do not report statistics in many years. On average, countries report wages for 6.3 years out of 16 possible years. Even if we ignore 1998, which has preliminary data for only 14 countries, more than half of country year observations are empty. In addition, countries do not report data for every occupation in the years when they do report. The bottom line is that there are 74,056 country × year × occupation cells with wage data in the 1983–98 file.

But there is a further complication. Many countries report more than one wage for a single occupation. Some give hourly wage rates *and* average earnings. Others give wages for men *and* wages for women. Others give wages for one gender and for both genders. Nearly half of the observations (46.3 per cent) contain multiple wage figures. While this will help us calibrate the data to a single form, it makes the raw data difficult to use in cross-country comparisons, particularly since different countries report pay differently. Including multiple wages, we have 124,016 pieces of data.

Panel B shows the frequency distribution of countries by the number of occupations they report; and the frequency distribution of occupations by the number of countries that report statistics on them. The distribution of countries by number of occupations shows that in most countries there are sufficient occupations with wage data to get a good measure of the overall wage structure. It also shows, however, that different countries report on different numbers of occupations, which creates problems in comparing wage structures across countries. The distribution of occupations by country shows that many occupations

Table 2.2 Observations in the October Inquiry Survey computer files, 1983–98

A SAMPLE SIZE	
Maximum conceivable observations	**401,856**
Observations missing because country did not report in given year	242,466
Observations missing because occupation missing in year country reported	85,344
Actual year/country/occupation observation	**74,056**
Observations with multiple figures	34,262
Multiple figures	49,960
Total, including all multiple observations	**124,016**

B COUNTRIES AND OCCUPATIONS WITH AT LEAST ONE REPORTED WAGE STATISTIC	
Countries with reported wage statistic for different numbers of occupations	
Number of occupations	*Number of countries (total: 156)*
<30	11
30–59	21
60–79	24
80–99	18
100–119	34
120–139	15
140+	33
Occupations with one reported wage statistic for different numbers of countries	
Number of countries reporting on occupation	*Number of occupations (total: 161)*
<59	17
60–79	28
80–99	42
100–119	53
120+	21

C ACTUAL OBSERVATIONS	
Pay concept	
Wages (141 countries)	81,869
Earnings (93 countries)	42,147
Averaging concept	
Mean	83,766
Minimum	28,541
Maximum	4,515
Prevailing	4,596
Median	1,803
Other	148
Missing	647

Table 2.2 (*Continued*)

C ACTUAL OBSERVATIONS	
Period concept	
Monthly	75,882
Hourly[a]	22,775
Weekly	15,184
Daily	6,359
Annual	2,444
Fortnight	1,197
Other	133
Missing	42
Gender	
Males	53,605
Both	44,707
Females	25,704

Note:[a] The hourly figures include a small number for whom the data state to be related to hours paid for and another small number for whom the wages relate to hours worked.
Source: Tabulated from ILO October Inquiry Survey, files, 1983–98.

have wage data for large numbers of countries, which will allow us to contrast labour costs and living standards for workers in the same occupation around the world.

Panel C shows the diverse way in which countries report wages. Most countries report wage rates, presumably from employer surveys or collective bargaining contracts or legislated pay schedules. However, many report earnings, which may come from household surveys. Most give statistics in the form of averages[5] but 23 per cent report minimum wages, some from collective bargaining contracts. Some countries report maximum wages. Others give prevailing wages. The US reports median weekly earnings for most occupations (from individual reports on the Current Population Survey). The time period to which the pay refers also varies. The most common period is the month, followed by the hour, but some countries report weekly pay, others give daily rates for some occupations, and so on. There is also variation by gender: 43 per cent of the observations relate to male workers, 36 per cent to all workers, and 21 per cent to female workers.

2.2 Standardizing the data

Combining all of these different variants, the vast majority of the Inquiry statistics are non-comparable. Just 5.8 per cent relate simultaneously to the most common pay concept (wages), use the most common averaging (mean), cover the most common time span (monthly), and relate to the most common gender (male).[6] How is one to make a valid contrast of pay across country lines when the US reports median weekly earnings for both genders and China reports average monthly wages for females and males separately and Germany gives collectively bargained minimum wages for different time periods? Is it possible to put the Inquiry data into a form that researchers can readily use?

The principal contribution of this chapter is to demonstrate that the answer to this question is 'yes'. It is possible to transform the Inquiry data into a usable form by calibrating the diverse statistics into a normalized wage or earnings rate. To see how we standardized the data, consider each observation W to be the sum of a standard rate W^*, which we take to be the most common form of data in the Inquiry – monthly average wages for male workers[7] – and a data type adjustment term, W^a, where a reflects the deviation of the observed wage from the most common type, and an error term, v:

$$W(i,j,o,t) = W^*(j,o,t) + W^a(i,j,o,t) + v(i,j,o,t) \qquad (1)$$

where i measures the data type; j refers to the country; o is the occupation; t is the time period

The calibration problem is to estimate W^* for observations where data is reported in non-standard form – that is, to find adjustment coefficients that measure how non-standard forms of data diverge from W^* for different countries, occupations, and time periods. Let $X(i,j,o,t)$ be a row vector of dummies for data type, which takes the value one if the observation is of the particular data type and $B(i,j,o,t)$ be a column vector of deviations of a particular type of data from the normal. Then we write (1) as:

$$W(i,j,o,t) = W^*(j,o,t) + X(i,j,o,t)\,B(i,j,o,t) + v(i,j,o,t) \qquad (2)$$

The natural way to estimate the B coefficients is to regress the $W(i,j,o,t)$ on $W^*(j,o,t)$ and the dummy variables for observations with both standard and non-standard rates using the observations in which there is data for both the standard form and the non-standard form:

$$W(i,j,o,t)' = W^*(j,o,t)' + X(i,j,o,t)'\,B(i,j,o,t)' + v(i,j,o,t)' \qquad (3)$$

where the observations $(i,j,o,t)'$ are those for which we have both standard and non-standard wages and where v is a residual term with $E(v) = 0$.

Given the estimated *B*s, we can predict $W*$ for observations that did not have both types from the following equation:

$$PW*(j,o,t) = W(i,j,o,t) - X(i,j,o,t)\,PB(i,j,o,t) \tag{4}$$

where *P* before a term reflects the predicted or estimated value.

The extent of variation in the Inquiry data complicates this standardization exercise. The big problem is that there are many different types of data. There are two types of earnings, three types of data by gender, three forms of data by time span that cannot be standardized by dimensional analysis;[8] and five distinct forms of averaging. This gives us 90 ($= 2 \times 3 \times 3 \times 5$) different potential combinations of data types. In addition, there are possible differences in *B* coefficients by country, occupation, or time. There is insufficient overlap of observations for all the different possibilities to estimate a full set of *B* coefficients.

To cut through this morass, we must simplify the *X* vector in various ways – for instance, by assuming that different data types affect wages separately rather than interactively (reducing the dimension of *X* from 90 to 12); or by assuming that *B* is time invariant or independent of occupation or country. These simplifications put some of the deviation of $W(i,j,o,t)$ from $W*(j,o,t)$ into the error term, introducing heteroscedasticity.

Unfortunately the variation in the Inquiry data is too 'thin' to limit the estimation of *B* to the observations (i,j,o,t) for which we have both standard and non-standard rates. In principle this would give us 19,010 observations, except that many of the data types occur rarely in conjunction with a standard data type. This happens because in most circumstances these data types are reported in lieu of the normalized data type. Only the wage/earnings and male/female wage differentials can be estimated with any precision in this manner.

For this reason we choose to estimate the normalized wage as well, running the following regression on the entire sample:

$$\begin{aligned} W(i,j,o,t) = D(j,o,t)A(j,o,t) + X(i,j,o,t)B(i,j,o,t) \\ + \theta(j,o,t) + v(i,j,o,t) \end{aligned} \tag{5}$$

where $D(j,o,t)$ is a row vector of country, occupation and time dummies (including possible interaction terms), $A(j,o,t)$ a column vector of coefficients, and $\theta(j,o,t)$ the random component of the normalized wage not captured by the country, occupation, and time dummies. The predicted *B* can be used to predict $W*(j,o,t)$ using (4).

The most troublesome aspect of our standardization process is that there is no natural single way to simplify the vector of *B* coefficients. We run the risk that one method of simplification, for instance assuming that the *B* coefficients in less developed countries are the same as those in advanced countries could yield sufficiently different estimated wages from another simplifying assumption, say that advanced and developing countries have different *B* coefficients. To take an example, if gender differentials fall by level of development and we adjusted female wages to the male monthly standard using an adjustment parameter estimated for both advanced and developing countries, we would understate male wages in particular occupations in the developing countries and overstate male wages in the advanced countries. The only way to solve this problem is to try several standardization procedures and examine the difference among them in final outcomes.

Even for any given standardization procedure, a multiplicity of predictions or calibrations for the normalized wage will arise if there is more than one wage reported for any given country, occupation and year. If the variance–covariance structure of the error term $v(i, j, o, t)$ is known, optimal weights can be calculated to derive a weighted prediction with minimal sampling variance. In practice these optimal weights are difficult to derive and different weighting schemes can be used to examine their impact.[9] Alternatively, (5) can be estimated as a random effects regression model with heteroscedasticity, and a unique prediction of the normalized wage can be derived as:

$$PW^*(j, o, t) = D(j, o, t)\ PA(j, o, t) + P\theta(i, j, o, t) \qquad (6)$$

Prima facie, this direct procedure is more efficient, but potentially less robust because it assumes more knowledge about the variance–covariance structure of the regression model.

In Freeman and Oostendorp (2000), our Appendix shows that each of the above calibrations, with alternative simplifications for the coefficient *B*, different weighting schemes, or different estimation procedures gave similar results, with correlations ranging from 0.9745 to 0.998 for the predicted wages, and from 0.9650 to 0.9987 for the dispersion measures used in this paper.

Using the above standardization or calibration procedure, what can the OWW tell us about the determination of wages and operation of labour markets around the world? By itself, the new file allows us to examine occupational wage structures within countries over time and the cost of comparable labour and living standards of similarly skilled workers across countries. In conjunction with other data sets it allows us to examine the determinants of wages in comparable occupations around the world and the effect of those wages on other economic phenomena.

3 Skill differentials

The OWW is a huge country–occupation–time matrix of wages with many missing elements. Elements are missing because countries report on different occupations in different time periods. New Zealand, for instance, reports wage data continuously from 1984 to 1991, but not earlier or afterwards. It gives wages for 84 occupations in 1984, 131 occupations in 1985, 143 in 1986, and 135 in 1991. Hungary gives wages for 26 occupations in 1987 and wages for 130 or so occupations in 1995, 1996, and 1997, but gives no figures in other years. And so on. To obtain manageable and comprehensible statistics about skill differentials, we must collapse the OWW matrix into consistent summary measures of the spread of pay among occupations. We compress the data in three ways.

First, for every country we calculated the standard deviation of the log of pay and the ratio of the wages in the occupation in the 90th percentile of the occupation wage distribution to the wages in the occupation in the 10th percentile of the distribution for *all of the occupations* reporting in a given period.[10] This comparison uses the maximum amount of data but it compares different numbers of occupations across countries, so that the measured spread of wages may be affected by the number of occupations that enter the summary statistic. The most natural way to deal with this problem is to compute measures of skill differences for exactly the same occupations for all countries. But countries give wages for different occupations, so that this common denominator strategy would greatly reduce the sample size.

Instead, we have chosen a different way of compressing the data. This is to treat observations as samples from the distribution of occupational wages for each country, rather than as estimates of wages for a specific occupation.[11] We then estimate the decile distribution of wages by occupation and calculate measures of dispersion from this distribution. Specifically, we ordered occupations by their wage in each country time period; divided the ordering into deciles, and took the mean wage in each decile as that decile's wage in the country.[12] This gives us 10 wages for each country, from which we calculate measures of dispersion. For instance, if the top 10 per cent paying occupations in the US consisted of eight occupations, we would use the mean wage among those eight to represent the top decile in the US, whereas if the top 10 per cent in India had wages only for three occupations, we would use those three wages to estimate the top decile in India. It turns out that the measures of dispersion of pay based on all this decile analysis and measures based on all of the data are highly correlated, which implies that the number of occupations problem is not a serious one in our data. Accordingly, most of the results we report are from analysis of the maximum number of occupational data points, with countries that report on 25 or more occupations, rather than from analysis of the derived decile distribution.

Third, to compare changes in wage structures over time, we limit our analysis to *the same occupations in each country*. If Argentina reports 100 occupations in one year and 56 in another, and just 50 of the occupations overlap, we compare the wages of those 50 occupations over time. If Mexico reports consistently on 30 occupations over time, we use wages in those 30 occupations. In this case we opt for comparability over time rather than comparability in numbers of occupations or in the quantile distribution of occupations.

Table 2.3 presents our measures of the dispersion of wages by occupation for the mid-period in our data, 1988–92, organized by the level of development of countries. To obtain the maximum number of comparisons over this period, we report the figures for the year in the interval which gave the most data. Columns (1) and (2) give the statistics based on all of the occupations reporting in the peak year, while columns (3) and (4) give the statistics based on our estimated decile earnings in the occupation–earnings distribution. Both calculations show that skill differences or wage inequality is smaller in the more advanced countries, and is particularly small in the communist countries. Since these facts are well known from more limited country comparisons, this can be viewed as broadly validating the OWW file.

Figure 2.1 shows the inverse relation between skill differentials and level of economic development in a somewhat different way. It graphs the standard deviation of ln wages by occupation in a country against the level of GDP *per capita* in the country for the year for which the highest number of occupations were reported. While there is considerable variation in occupational wage inequality for countries with the same level of GDP *per capita* – for instance, the US and UK have high levels of inequality for advanced countries – the scatter diagram shows clearly the inverse relation between income per head and the spread of wages among occupations.

Table 2.3 Measures of the occupational wage structure within countries, 1988–92

High Income Economies		*Sd Ln* W		p90/p10	
	No. occup	*All*	*Decile*	*All*	*Decile*
AT – Austria	144	0.33	0.33	2.30	2.45
AU – Australia	149	0.24	0.24	1.71	1.90
BE – Belgium	42	0.17	0.17	1.49	1.52
DE – Germany	159	0.37	0.35	2.56	2.59
DK – Denmark	57	0.19	0.19	1.57	1.67
FI – Finland	124	0.24	0.24	1.80	1.90
GB – United Kingdom	50	0.28	0.26	2.04	2.01
HK – Hong Kong	52	0.41	0.38	2.34	2.74
IT – Italy	144	0.27	0.25	1.76	1.92
JP – Japan	41	0.35	0.30	1.96	2.25
NL – Netherlands	70	0.15	0.13	1.43	1.41
NO – Norway	31	0.18	0.17	1.68	1.56
NZ – New Zealand	136	0.35	0.31	2.25	2.30
SE – Sweden	130	0.20	0.17	1.55	1.57
SG – Singapore	121	0.54	0.50	3.72	3.77
US – United States	86	0.34	0.34	2.31	2.45
Upper Middle Income Economies		*Sd Ln* W		p90/p10	
	No. occup	*All*	*Decile*	*All*	*Decile*
AR – Argentina	133	0.75	0.71	7.46	6.95
GA – Gabon	60	0.62	0.63	4.96	5.39
KR – Korea, Republic of	129	0.39	0.40	2.45	2.92
MU – Mauritius	89	0.50	0.49	4.19	3.74
MX – Mexico	46	0.18	0.11	1.44	1.35
PR – Puerto Rico	48	0.34	0.31	2.37	2.24
TT – Trinidad and Tobago	118	0.56	0.52	3.29	3.95
UY – Uruguay	45	0.50	0.50	2.70	3.79
VE – Venezuela	142	0.44	0.41	2.91	2.92
Lower Middle Income Economies		*Sd Ln* W		p90/p10	
	No. occup	*All*	*Decile*	*All*	*Decile*
BO – Bolivia	117	0.65	0.62	4.89	5.49
CI – Côte d'Ivoire	134	0.66	0.67	5.34	6.38
CM – Cameroon	51	0.71	0.74	6.77	6.49
CO – Colombia	41	0.65	0.59	5.12	4.82
DZ – Algeria	135	0.33	0.31	2.57	2.37
JO – Jordan	105	0.43	0.38	3.12	2.81
PH – Phillipines	36	0.14	0.15	1.33	1.46

SN – Senegal	73	0.44	0.40	2.87	3.00
SV – El Salvador	138	0.54	0.54	3.70	4.38
TH – Thailand	125	0.49	0.49	3.68	3.72
TN – Tunisia	67	0.16	0.10	1.21	1.23
TR – Turkey	45	0.27	0.26	2.07	1.97

Low Income Economies		*Sd Ln* W		p90/p10	
	No. occup	*All*	*Decile*	*All*	*Decile*
BD – Bangladesh	133	0.48	0.44	3.10	3.33
BF – Burkina Faso	110	0.43	0.43	2.90	3.11
BI – Burundi	69	0.76	0.77	6.11	7.62
BJ – Benin	72	0.74	0.72	6.72	6.65
CF – Central African Republic	91	0.78	0.78	6.05	7.97
EG – Egypt	81	0.36	0.34	2.18	2.50
HN – Honduras	109	0.56	0.56	4.53	4.72
ID – Indonesia	33	0.29	0.29	1.96	2.10
IN – India	92	0.60	0.52	4.09	3.73
LS – Lesotho	106	0.69	0.71	5.61	7.08
ML – Mali	112	0.60	0.58	4.42	4.85
MM – Myanmar	138	0.29	0.28	2.09	2.14
MZ – Mozambique	117	0.45	0.45	3.19	3.48
NP – Nepal	32	0.41	0.36	2.20	2.13
RW – Rwanda	126	0.70	0.72	6.85	7.01
SD – Sudan	130	0.42	0.35	2.35	2.59
SL – Sierra Leone	102	0.59	0.57	2.93	4.79
TD – Chad	91	0.76	0.77	6.13	7.25
TG – Togo	39	0.52	0.50	3.40	3.60
ZM – Zambia	132	0.56	0.53	3.87	4.23

Economies with Small Populations		*Sd Ln* W		p90/p10	
	No. occup	*All*	*Decile*	*All*	*Decile*
AG – Antigua and Barbuda	64	0.41	0.42	2.53	3.12
AI – Anguilla	56	0.37	0.34	2.59	2.46
AN – Netherlands Antilles	47	0.40	0.36	2.64	2.69
BB – Barbados	97	0.44	0.46	3.11	3.43
BH – Bahrain	84	0.54	0.51	3.67	3.98
BM – Bermuda	46	0.42	0.38	2.11	2.54
BS – Bahamas	39	0.47	0.51	3.25	3.66
BZ – Belize	100	0.56	0.55	3.23	4.23
CY – Cyprus	112	0.47	0.44	3.43	3.25
FK – Falkland Islands (Malvinas)	65	0.39	0.34	2.33	2.49
GF – Guyane, French	63	0.37	0.33	2.45	2.41

Table 2.3 (*Continued*)

Economies with small population		*Sd Ln* W		p90/p10	
	No. occup	*All*	*Decile*	*All*	*Decile*
GI – Gibraltar	32	0.30	0.28	1.91	2.05
IM – Isle of Man	58	0.33	0.32	2.26	2.40
KM – Comores	74	0.55	0.54	4.01	4.37
LC – St Lucia	97	0.54	0.56	3.61	4.51
PF – Polynesia, French	87	0.46	0.44	3.40	3.23
PM – Saint-Pierre-et-Miquelon	67	0.30	0.32	2.10	2.40
SC – Seychelles	58	0.39	0.40	3.28	3.06
SR – Suriname	57	0.53	0.49	3.71	3.87
VI – Virgin Islands	70	0.40	0.40	2.79	2.93

Communist and Ex-Communist Economies		*SD Ln* W		p90/p10	
	No. occup	*All*	*Decile*	*All*	*Decile*
BG – Bulgaria	112	0.28	0.25	1.88	1.97
CN – China	81	0.24	0.23	1.77	1.85
CU – Cuba	129	0.28	0.26	2.00	1.90
CZ – Czech Republic	110	0.20	0.20	1.61	1.73
RO – Romania	160	0.24	0.24	1.88	1.89
RU – Russian Federation	41	0.28	0.28	2.05	2.19
SI – Slovenia	57	0.34	0.35	2.93	2.58
SK – Slovakia	110	0.20	0.20	1.61	1.73
YU – Yugoslavia	159	0.36	0.36	2.40	2.69

Note: In some tabulations we allocate the small economies or communist economies to their appropriate income class.

We pursue the link between GDP *per capita* and the occupational wage structure in Table 2.4 through regression analysis of a pooled cross-section time series file for all of the years and countries in the OWW. Columns (1)–(3) record the results of regressions that link the occupational wage structures to the level of GDP *per capita* in a country. Each regression includes dummy variables for the year of the observation so that the estimates reflect solely the cross-section relation between the variables. Since we do not have observations for every year for countries, the file is unbalanced. We report robust standard errors to correct for clustering.

Regression 1 (column (1)) confirms the tendency for skill differentials to fall with rising income *per capita* and for countries with communist

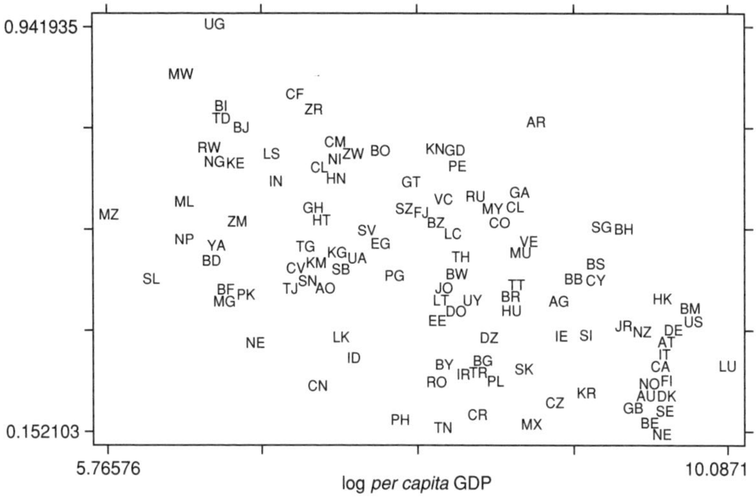

Figure 2.1 Standard deviation of ln occupational wages vs log GDP *per capita*, by country

Note: Countries included are:
AO–Angola; AG–Antigua and Barbuda; AR–Argentina; AT–Austria; AU– Australia; BB–Barbados; BD–Bangladesh; BE–Belgium; BF–Burkina Faso; BG–Bulgaria; BH–Bahrain; BI–Burundi; BJ–Benin; BM–Bermuda; BO–Bolivia; BR–Brazil; BS–Bahamas; BW–Botswana; BY–Belarus; BZ–Belize; CA–Canada; CF–Central African Republic; CI–Côte d'Ivoire; CL–Chile; CM–Cameroon; CN–China; CO–Colombia; CR–Costa-Rica; CV–Cape Verde; CY–Cyprus; CZ– Czech Republic; DE–Germany; DK–Denmark; DO–Dominican Republic; DZ–Algeria; EE–Estonia; EG–Egypt; FI–Finland; FJ–Fiji; GA–Gabon; GB–United Kingdom; GD–Grenada; GH–Ghana; GT–Guatemala; HK–Hong Kong; HN–Honduras; HT–Haiti; HU–Hungary; ID–Indonesia; IE–Ireland; IN–India; IR–Iran, Islamic Rep.of; IT–Italiy; JO–Jordan; JP–Japan; KE–Kenya; KG–Kyrgyzstan; KM–Comores; KN–Saint Kitts and Nevis; KR–Korea, Republic of; LC–St.-Lucia; LK–Sri Lanka; LS–Lesotho; LT–Lithuania; LU–Luxembourg; MG–Madagascar; ML–Mali; MU–Mauritius; MW–Malawi; MX–Mexico; MY–Malaysia; MZ–Mozambique; NE–Niger; NG–Nigeria; NI–Nicaragua; NL–Netherlands; NO–Norway; NP–Nepal; NZ–New Zealand; PE–Peru; PG–Papua New Guinea; PH– Philippines; PK–Pakistan; PL–Poland; RO–Romania; RU–Russian Federation; RW–Rwanda; SB–Solomon Islands; SE–Sweden; SG–Singapore; SI–Slovenia; SK–Slovakia; SL–Sierra Leone; SN–Senegal; SV–El-Salvador; SZ–Swaziland; TD–Chad; TG–Togo; TH–Thailand; TJ–Tajikistan; TN–Tunisia; TR–Turkey; TT–Trinidad and Tobago; UA–Ukraine; UG–Uganda; US–United States; UY–Uruguay; VC–St.Vincent and the Grenadines; VE–Venezuela; YA– Yemen; ZM–Zambia; ZR–Zaire; ZW–Zimbabwe.

regimes to have particularly low levels of skill differentials. The estimated coefficient on income *per capita* is sizeable, implying that much of the difference in the wage structure between more/less advanced countries is attributable to differing levels of income per head. The inclusion of the squared term in regression 2 provides, moreover, some support for the existence of a Kuznets-type curve linking inequality to development. Inequality rises as GDP *per capita* rises (positive coefficient on GDP *per capita*), then falls with GDP *per capita* (negative coefficient on GDP *per capita*^{2}). The turning point occurs at a relatively low level of GDP *per capita*. Regression 3 records coefficients based on a median regression (which finds the coefficients that minimize absolute differences between predicted and actual values rather than squared differences). The case for a Kuznets inverse U-shaped curve pattern is stronger than in regression 2, with the estimated effects of both GDP *per capita* and GDP *per capita* squared on inequality higher, and the level of GDP where increases reduce inequality rises.

4 Trends in skill differentials

Figure 2.2 turns to the trend in skill differentials over time. It gives summary statistics on the spread of wages within countries for *fixed numbers of occupations* over time.[13] It covers three periods, 1983–88; 1989–92; and 1993–98. In each of these periods we picked the year that gave us the maximum number of comparable occupations over time. The figure shows little change in the dispersion of wages among advanced countries as a group, though the underlying data show increased dispersion in the US, Great Britain, and Italy, among others, consistent with the picture in other data sets (Freeman and Katz (1994)). Taken individually, the dispersion of occupational wages rises in eight of the advanced countries for which we have data and falls in eight countries. Figure 2.2 also shows a sharp rise in inequality in the transitional countries (Russia, Romania, the Czech Republic and Slovakia),[14] again reassuring given the evidence of increased inequality in those countries. In the lowest income countries for which we have comparable data, the decline in dispersion shown in the figure is somewhat misleading. This is because the most striking pattern in the individual country data is one of divergence in skill differentials. Inequality falls sharply in two economic disaster countries, the Sudan and Myanmar, but rises sharply in Egypt and Sri Lanka. Overall, seven of 12 of the less developed countries have falls in skill differentials while five have rises. The coefficient of variation in the standard deviation of ln wages in the least developed countries was 1.10 in 1993–98 compared to 0.88 in 1983–87.

Columns (4)–(7) in Table 2.4 pursue this analysis of trends in skill differentials for all of the countries in our sample. Each of these

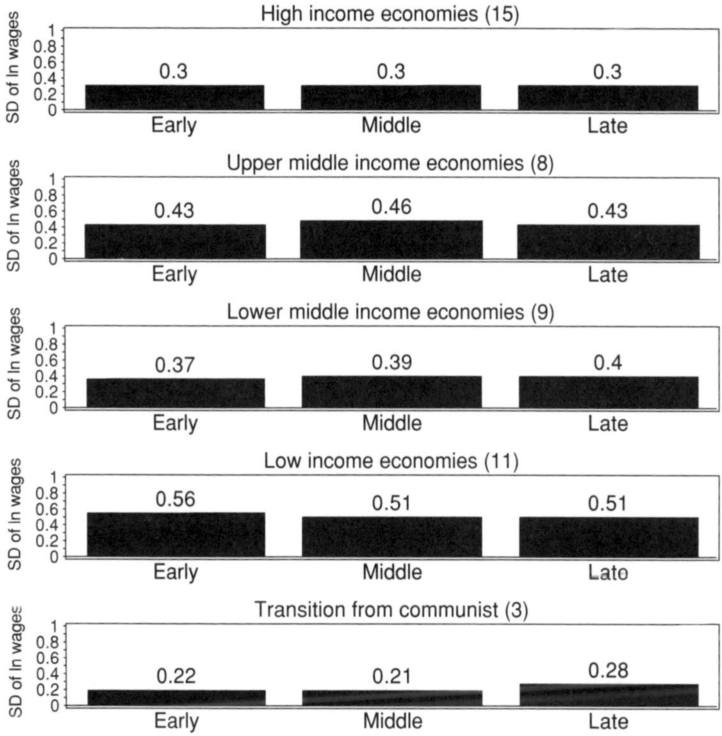

Figure 2.2 Trends in skill differentials, by groups of countries (based on consistent occupations within countries over time)
Notes: This analysis is limited to countries that reported 30 or more occupations. The results are comparable if we include countries with less than 30 occupations as well.

regressions include country dummies, which subsume cross-section patterns, and thus focus on changes within a country over time. Regression 4 replaces the year dummies in the earlier regressions with a linear trend to identify more easily the direction of change over time. Looking across all countries, the coefficient on trend in regression 4 is small and lacking statistical significance, implying that there was little change in occupational wage structures in the 1980s–1990s, on a global scale. Regression 5 gives separate trend coefficients for countries in different income classes; it shows that skill differentials fell in advanced countries and more sharply in upper middle income countries while rising in lower middle income countries. In low income countries, there is a modest but insignificant downward trend in inequality.

Table 2.4 Regression estimates of the effect of *per capita* income and trend on standard deviation of log occupational wages (standard errors in parenthesis)

	Cross-section				*Time series*		
	OLS (1)	*OLS* (2)	*MEDIAN* (3)	(4)	(5)	(6)	(7)
Log GDP *per capita*	−0.098	0.135	0.413			−0.064	
	(0.011)	(0.186)	(0.261)			(0.031)	
(Log GDP *per capita*)^2		−0.014	−0.031				
		(0.011)	(0.016)				
Communist (1 = comm. years)	−0.19	−0.20	−0.23	−0.11	−0.05	−0.08	−0.10
	(0.02)	(0.02)	(0.03)	(0.02)	(0.03)	(0.02)	(0.03)
Trend			−0.0010				
				(0.0008)			
Trend, by income level							
High income					−0.002		
					(0.001)		
Upper middle income					−0.006		
					(0.002)		
Lower middle income					0.007		
					(0.002)		
Low income					−0.002		
					(0.002)		
Log GDP *per capita* by income level							
High income							−0.068
							(0.054)
Upper middle income							−0.174
							(0.046)
Lower middle income							0.072
							(0.049)
Low income							−0.085
							(0.062)
Country dummies				√	√	√	√
Year dummies	√	√	√			√	√
Constant	√	√	√	√	√	√	√
No. of obs.	652	652	652	830	830	652	652
R^2	0.424	0.431	0.291	0.84	0.84	0.88	0.88

Notes: These regressions used dispersions based on raw data for countries that reported on 30 or more occupations. Regressions based on standard deviations of wages based on estimates of decile wages gave nearly identical results. Standard errors are corrected for clustering. Standard errors for median regression are based on (clustered) bootstraps with 1,000 replications.

That there is no world trend in occupational wage inequality does not mean that increases in GDP *per capita* do not reduce skill differentials. Regression 6 includes both year and country dummies, so that it identifies the effect of changes in GDP over time on inequality within a country. The coefficient on GDP *per capita* is negative, though smaller than in the cross-section regression of column (1). Since this calculation includes controls for both country and time, it implies that within the same country, greater growth of GDP was associated with reduced inequality of wages. Regression 7 decomposes the GDP *per capita* term into separate GDP *per capita* effects for countries with differing levels of income. It shows that, conditional on trend, GDP *per capita* has its largest impact in reducing skill differentials in upper middle income countries, while having a positive impact in lower middle income countries.

5 Cost of labour differences across countries

To analyse differences in the cost of skills across countries, we have deflated the wages for each country-year-occupation by exchange rates for the US dollar. The resulting dollar measure shows great variation across countries in the cost of labour. A carpenter in construction in India, for example, earns $48 per month, while one in Sweden earns $2,481 per month and one in Argentina earns $206 per month on average in the 1988–92 period. Even among the advanced countries, there are considerable differences in labour costs: a kindergarten teacher in Italy earns $1,786 per month; a kindergarten teacher in the US earns $1,501 per month; while a teacher in Japan earns $1,268; and one in Germany earns $2,484 per month, on average over the 1988–92 period.

Figure 2.3 displays the variation in pay across countries for five occupations in the 1988–92 period: a high-wage occupation (general physician); a low-wage occupation (logger); a white collar occupation (insurance agent); a blue collar occupation (clicker cutter); and a high-tech occupation (computer programmer). For ease of presentation, we have standardized the wages relative to the highest wage in the category. That is, the wage in the highest wage country in a given occupation is scaled as 1.0 and the wages of workers in that occupation in other countries are fractions between 0 and 1. The frequency distribution shows the number of countries with given wages relative to the highest paying country in each occupation. As a summary of the variation in each occupation, we record the ratio of the wage in the country at the median of the distribution relative to the wage in the country with the highest wage. This is not a common measure of dispersion, but it is an easily interpreted statistic:[15] the smaller the median wage relative to the maximum wage, the further from the maximum wage are occupational wages in other countries. The median wage/maximum wage for all five occupations is relatively

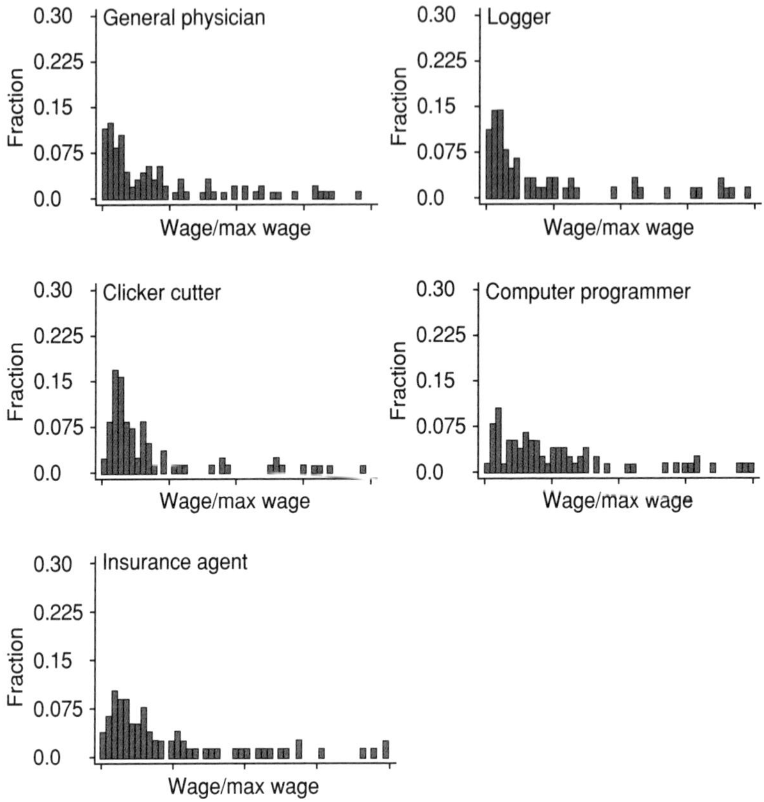

Figure 2.3 Variation in wages around the world in five occupations, 1983–98

low – it ranges from 0.050 to 0.159 – implying huge differences in the cost of nominally comparable labour across the world. We also report the standard deviation of ln pay for each occupation across the reporting countries. The standard deviation is also large, compared, say, to the standard deviation of ln wages among occupations within a country.

Panel A in Figure 2.4 extends this analysis to all 161 occupations. For this figure, we calculated the ratio of the wage in the median wage country in each occupation divided by the wage in the highest wage country and the standard deviation of ln wages across countries in each occupation. We then took the average of these statistics for all the occupations for which there are at least 25 countries reporting (145 occupations). The figure confirms the evidence in Figure 2.3 that there are huge differentials in the cost of nominally comparable labour across countries: the average median/max wage is just 0.10 while the standard deviation of the ln wage is 1.21.

The bottom parts of panel A present comparable statistics for countries with different income levels and for occupations disaggregated by skill level. The statistics for the wage in the median paying country/ maximum wage shows that advanced countries have occupational wages reasonably close to the highest wage (which of course is in an advanced country, though usually a different one). The average median/ maximum wage for less developed countries pay show a much wider spread from the maximum wage. In addition, these data show that higher skilled occupations have modestly less spread in pay than lower skilled occupations.

The standard deviation of ln wages in Figure 2.4 give the standard deviation in the ln wage around the average *within each country grouping*, rather than around the average for all countries. These standard deviations thus show the variation in wages within income classes. Within groupings, the advanced countries have less cross-country variation in occupational pay than do the less advanced countries and more skilled occupations have less cross-country variation than the less skilled occupations.

To what extent, if at all, did the economic developments of the 1980s and 1990s, such as increased globalization and the spread of technology, reduce differences in wages across occupations?

One way to answer this question is to regress measures of the country dispersion of pay in occupations on trend variables. Table 2.5 presents estimates of these trend effects, with individual occupation dummy variables included in each regression to eliminate cross-occupation variation in dispersion. The regressions show that variation in wages across countries rose over this period using either our median country wage/ maximum country wage measure of the spread of pay within an occupation (column (1)) or the standard deviation of ln wages in the occupation (column (3)). To see if this pattern differs according to the skill or wage level in an occupation, we ranked occupations by their rate of payin a single country, Germany,[16] giving the lowest paying occupation a one and giving the highest paying occupation a 161. Then we interacted the rank with the time trend. The results, given in columns (2) and (4) of Table 2.5, show that for both the median/max pay and standard deviation of ln pay, wages became more dispersed across countries in the higher skilled occupations.

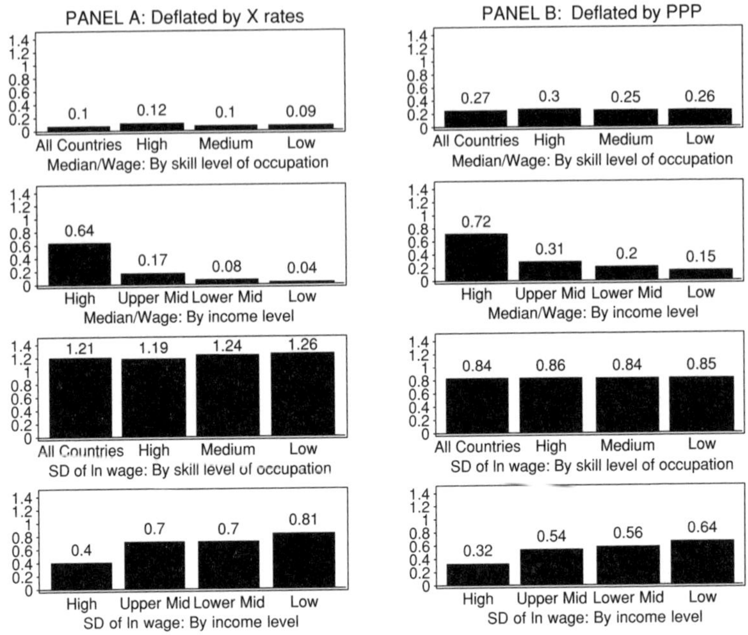

Figure 2.4 Cross-country variation in wages for workers in the same occupation
Notes: Panel A based on 45 countries, with 11 in the high income group; 10 in the upper middle income group; nine in the lower middle income group; and 15 in the low income group. Occupations classified as high, medium, and low skill based on 1992 German occupational wage distribution, with high skill defined as top 30 occupations in terms of wages, low skill defined as the bottom 30 in terms of wage, and the medium skill defined as the 30 occupations in the middle of the distribution (around the median) in terms of wage.
Panel B based on 38 countries, with 11 in the high income group; six in the upper middle income group; seven in the lower middle income group; and 14 in the low income group. Standard deviation of logs for the country groups are standard deviations within those groups.

Similar results are obtained if we restrict the countries to those for which we have PPPs.

The pattern for rising country differentials of occupational wages in a period of increased globalization suggests that factors beyond trade pressures greatly affected the dispersion of pay across countries. Determining what those factors were – The debt crisis of the 1980s? The deterioration of African economies? Smaller absolute increases in schooling in less developed countries than in more developed countries? Brain drains? – lies beyond the scope of this chapter.

Table 2.5 Estimates of differences in wages in occupations across countries (applying exchange rates)

	Median/Max wage		*Sd Ln wage*	
	(1)	*(2)*	*(3)*	*(4)*
Trend	−0.011 (0.004)	−0.006 (0.0005)	0.023 (0.002)	0.011 (0.003)
Occupation dummies	√	√	√	√
Rank by skill × trend (1 = least skilled)		−0.000056 (0.000005)		0.00016 (0.00003)
Constant	√	√	√	√
R^2	0.69	0.72	0.62	0.64
No. of obs.	1,416	1,416	1,416	1,416

6 Comparing living standards

If exchange rates reflected differences in the cost of goods across countries, wages deflated by exchange rates would suffice to measure living standards for similar workers. But exchange rates invariably overstate the cost of non-tradable goods and vary wildly on foreign currency markets for reasons having little to do with real economic conditions. Accordingly, to compare standards of living for comparably skilled workers across countries, we deflate observed wages by the PPP prices in the Penn World Tables.[17] PPP prices diverge greatly from exchange rate prices. Virtually all less developed countries have higher purchasing power for their currency than exchange rates show. Summers and Heston show that the ratio of PPP to the exchange rate rises with GDP from below one to levels above one, and that the divergence is particularly sharp for non-tradables (Summers and Heston (1991), Table 1). The magnitude of the increase in PPP/exchange rates is sizeable, ranging from 0.38 in low income countries to 1.17 in high income countries in 1988.

The lower cost of living in low income countries implies that the variation in wages across countries will be lower when we deflate wages by purchasing power parity prices than when we deflate by exchange rates. Panel B in Figure 2.4 shows that this is the case. Here we calculate our two measures of the dispersion of wages across countries using wages deflated by PPPs rather than by exchange rates and report the average across occupations of these statistics. With the PPP adjustment, the variation in wages among occupations is reduced considerably compared to what it was with the exchange rate adjustment. The median to maximum wage statistic rises from 0.10 to 0.27 while the standard deviation of ln wage drops by 0.37 ln points, from 1.21 to 0.84. Still, even with wages deflated by PPPs there remains huge cross-country variation in the payment to workers in the same occupation.

7 Determinants of wage structures

What factors beyond GDP *per capita* determine the spread of occupational wage structures and wages? We have analysed the impact of three potential determinants of occupational wages:

- The educational attainment of workers in the economy, which most analyses view as the primary cause for the lower level of differentials in advanced countries;
- The extent of institutional determination of wages and/or prices in a country, which most analyses view as reducing pay differentials;
- The link to the global economy, which is expected to reduce skill differences in less developed countries and raise them in more developed countries owing to the pressures of factor price equalization on countries with differing levels of skill among workers.

Our measures of these factors are crude, though no more so than in studies of cross-country growth rates, since we have simply imported some variables from the cross-country growth literature. Still, we view the results as tentative, subject to revision given better measures of the independent variables or more structured models or better specified empirical tests.

We measure *educational attainment* by years of schooling in 1985 from the Barro and Lee (1993) data set. For some observations, the attainment figures are based on UNESCO data on average years of schooling; for other observations, they are derived from historical enrolment data using a perpetual inventory method of transforming enrolment flows into educational stock. While the data surely distinguish between countries with very high and very low levels of schooling, they are subject to considerable error (Behrman and Rosensweig (1994)), which makes any analysis of changes a problem (Krueger and Lindahl (1999)). Ideally, we would want educational levels for occupations within a country for each of our three periods, but the current analysis is limited to cross-country differences using a single year's education for each country.

We have two types of measures of the role of *institutions in wage-setting*. First, we have obtained estimates of union density for a larger number of countries in 1990–95 from Visser (1997); these numbers are also subject to considerable measurement error. But perhaps the biggest problem with them is the union density does not necessarily translate into collective bargaining and wage determination. Some countries, such as the Netherlands or Austria have modest union density but near-universal collective bargaining. Other countries, such as the Ukraine or China have high union density, but little or no collective bargaining. Accordingly, we have modified the density data in two ways. For OECD countries, we have replaced unionism with OECD estimates of collective bargaining coverage from OECD (1997). For communist countries such as China and for ex-communist countries, where the union figures do not reflect free trade unions, we have coded unionism as zero.[18] Our second type of data are subjective evaluations of the extent of institutional intervention in an economy taken from the Heritage Foundation's Index of Economic Freedom. We have taken two indicators: the rank of country in its economic freedom scale, and the score given the country in the extent of wage/price interventions in the economy. As the economic freedom scale places market economies, including those that intervene significantly in wage-setting such as the Nordic countries, high in its ranking, it is less appropriate for analysing occupational wage dispersion than the more narrowly defined wage/price intervention scale. We have taken these variables from the 1998 Index of Economic Freedom, because this gives us the maximum number of country coverage.

For **trade** we chose two types of measures. We use the ratio of exports plus imports to GDP from the World Bank's *World Development Indicators* to indicate the extent to which a country is connected to the global economy. While some trade economists are dubious of quantity measures of the openness to trade, on the grounds that trade can have sizable effects on wages through prices, even with no trade flows, others argue that quantitative measures of trade may still affect wage and other outcomes, not least because it may reflect barriers such as tariff or non-tariff policies. [19] As our second indicator of the potential influence of trade on the structure of wages, we use the Heritage Foundation measure of trade policies from its economic freedom report. To the extent that this subjective measure ignores actual flows of goods and services to focus on presumably exogenous policy factors, it has particular merit for our analysis. Because trade is expected to have a differential effect on skill differentials in advanced and less advanced countries, raising dispersion in high income countries with relatively high levels of labour skill and lowering dispersion in low income countries with relatively low levels of labour skill, we have introduced both of these trade measures interactively with gross domestic product *per capita*.

Table 2.6 presents regression coefficients that link the standard deviation of ln occupational wages to these indicators of education, wage-setting institutions, and trade in a pooled cross-section analysis over all the years for which we have country data. The number of observations in the various regressions differs somewhat owing to the availability of measures for particular countries. Since the explanatory variables are from single years, we include year dummies in each regression and report robust standard errors that take account of the clustering of observations. Column (1) shows that countries with greater years of schooling have a smaller spread in skill differentials than other countries but that the country's rank by the Heritage Foundation economic freedom indicator has effectively no relation on the dispersion of pay. The negative estimated effect of education on differentials should not, however, be interpreted as an elasticity of relative wages to exogenous changes in schooling, since schooling will itself respond to the returns to skill. It is a reduced form estimate that understates the potential effect of exogenous changes in schooling on the spread of pay across occupations. The negligible relation between the broad economic freedom indicator and occupational differentials suggests that countries with differing reliance on market forces have considerable option to choose different levels of inequality – the Nordic countries, being the most notable case in point. Addition of log GDP *per capita* to the regression greatly reduces the effect of schooling on the occupational wage structure. This reflects the strong correlation between levels of schooling and levels of GDP *per capita* in cross-section country contrasts. It may also indicate that rises in GDP tend to reduce dispersion of pay through a broader set of mechanisms than increased schooling. In columns (3) and (4) we have dropped the economic freedom ranking and entered our measures of institutional wage-setting: unionism in market economies and the Heritage Foundation measure of wage/price regulation. The column (3) regression shows that unionism has a substantial reductive effect on the dispersion of occupational pay. This reflects the greater unionisation of lower skilled workers in many countries and the tendency for collective bargaining of various forms to improve the wages of the less skilled. The wage-price regulation index in column (4) takes on only five values, with lower scores reflecting greater market freedom in wage- and price-setting and higher scores reflecting greater regulation. It also obtains a negative coefficient, indicating that regulation reduces inequality.

Table 2.6 Regression coefficients and standard errors for factors which affect the standard deviation of ln wages across countries

	(1)	*(2)*	*(3)*	*(4)*	*(5)*	*(6)*
Economy wide						
GDP *per capita*		−0.071	−0.046	−0.054	−0.096	−0.062
		(0.036)	(0.034)	(0.032)	(0.030)	(0.039)
Years of schooling	−0.032	−0.017	−0.007	−0.013	−0.005	−0.003
	(0.006)	(0.010)	(0.012)	(0.011)	(0.010)	(0.013)
Economic freedom rank	−0.000	−0.001				
	(0.001)	(0.001)				
Communist	−0.112	−0.146	−0.202	−0.177	−0.186	−0.220
	(0.054)	(0.050)	(0.025)	(0.030)	(0.025)	(0.027)
Wage-setting						
Union			−0.173	−0.146		−0.161
			(0.052)	(0.043)		(0.052)
Wage-price regulations				−0.045		
				(0.027)		
Trade						
(X + M)/GDP × GDP *per capita* (× 1000)					0.046	0.020
					(0.025)	(0.028)
Year dummies	√	√	√	√	√	√
R^2	0.34	0.42	0.39	0.46	0.41	0.41
No. of obs.	522	459	401	386	503	389

The most problematic regressions in Table 2.6 relate to the impact of trade on the occupational wage structure. Our calculations using the Heritage Foundation's score for free trade showed no relation between the score and occupational inequality. But we obtained some fragile relations between the ratio of exports and imports to GDP and occupational wage dispersion. As column (5) shows, when this measure of trade × ln of GDP is included in the regression without the union and institutional wage-setting indicator, it obtains the anticipated positive effect, indicating that greater trade raises dispersion of pay more in high income countries. But column (6) shows that inclusion of unionism by itself reduces the measured trade effect substantially. The relation between the extent of trade and the occupational wage structure is sufficiently weak to be highly sensitive to inclusion of other variables and to the way we treat Singapore and Hong Kong, which are extreme outliers in terms of their reliance on trade. If trade has sizable effects on occupational wage structures, it will take a much more detailed analysis than ours to nail them down with any precision.

In short, the results in Table 2.6 suggest that within the limits of extant measures, institutional factors relating to wage-setting and the level of GDP *per capita* have the most pronounced impact on occupational wage structures across countries. While additional or better measures of the various potential determinants and extension of the analysis from cross-section to time series variation could alter this broad conclusion, it is sufficiently consonant with studies from more limited country samples (Freeman and Katz (1994)) that we expect the results to be fairly robust to further investigation.

8 Conclusion

Lack of an internationally accepted body of data on wages by skill has hampered analysis of occupational wage structures and of the wages of comparably skilled workers across the world. In this study we introduce the Occupational Wages around the World (OWW) data file, which gives consistent pay in 161 occupations in over 150 countries from 1983 to 1988 and propose this file as the best source of data by skill around the world. We developed the OWW by standardizing the diverse data in the rarely-used International Labour Office's 'October Inquiry' survey into rates of pay defined in the same units for workers by occupation in all countries and time periods. Variant standardizations yielded similar results, so that the OWW file is robust to plausible alternative ways of standardizing the Inquiry data. The OWW data file that we use can be extended back in time to at least the 1950s, though with less occupational detail.

Our analysis of the OWW shows that, consistent with extant wisdom, economic development was associated with smaller skill differentials, due in part to the difference in educational attainment between more and less developed countries but in larger part to institutional factors such as collective bargaining; but that contrary to extant wisdom and fears about the effects of globalization on wages, the disparity of pay for similar work across countries widened in both exchange rate and purchasing power parity (PPP) terms in the period studied.

The OWW offers a rich data set on the price side of the labour market. Combined with additional data from the quantity side of the labour market, such as the structure of employment or unemployment,[20] and with more refined measures of economic institutions and policies, we hope that it will illuminate important questions about the position of labour in the global economy in the future.

Notes

1 Since the supply of workers to education depends on the returns to schooling, however, this analysis requires some consideration of the determinants of those returns and such factors as public provision of schooling and technological change in education and the rest of the economy.
2 Psacharopoulos (1994). For an analysis of some of the data problems with these estimates see Bennell (1996).
3 The ILO actually asks for information on 159 occupations but it differentiates occupation 139, executives in the government, into three sectors: national, regional or provincial, and local governments.
4 The maximum is the multiplicand of the number of countries (156) times the number of occupations (161) times the number of years (16).
5 In a few cases the wages are in the form of ranges. We found the midpoint of the range and report it as the wage for the category.
6 The situation is not quite as dire as this statistic indicates because we can obtain some greater comparability by taking account of the natural time dimensions, such as turning yearly earnings into monthly figures by dividing by 12, turning weekly wages into monthly by multiplying by 4.3, or by multiplying hourly pay by hours worked reported on the survey. But even if we standardize using these procedures, only 16.9 per cent of the reported figures are directly comparable.
7 We can transform into any other scale, such as average earnings for women on a weekly basis. Choosing the most common, however, minimizes the noise introduced by the calibration procedures because it starts with a larger number of non-calibrated wages.
8 By dimensional analysis we mean simply changing the time units in well-determined ways, such as obtaining weekly pay by dividing annual pay by 52.
9 See the Appendix to Freeman and Oostendorp (2000).
10 For countries which reported at least 30 occupations in a given year.
11 As long as occupations have different numbers of employees, the distribution of occupational wages will differ from the distribution of individual wages. But as long as we are concerned with the *structure* of wages, treating occupations as units of observation is valid.
12 This procedure keeps the vast bulk of our country-year data since virtually all countries report on some occupations in a given grouping. Out of 990 country–occupation–year data points, 718 have information on each decile and an additional 104 have information on all but one decile.
13 The results with our decile measure show a somewhat different pattern: no change in the more advanced countries and an increase in inequality in the lowest income countries, so the patterns in the text should be viewed cautiously. Regression analyses for both sets of measures of inequality are consistent with the pattern in Figure 2.2.
14 We have compared the Czech Republic and Slovakia with Czechoslovakia when it was a single country.
15 The statistics of extremes can readily be applied to this analysis, as it deals with the relation between extreme values and the central tendency and dispersion of a distribution. See Gumbel (1958).

16 The reason is that Germany reported on almost all of the occupations. For the two occupations for which it did not include wages, we interpolated from the distribution of occupational wages in Australia.

17 The Penn World Tables' PPP prices are derived from data obtained by the International Comparison Project (ICP) of the UN Statistical Office, extrapolated to additional countries and time periods. The ICP divides GDP into 151 detailed categories, of which 110 are consumption items, 35 are investment goods, and five are government spending. Ideally, countries report national prices for 400–700 specific items within these categories, based on ICP detailed specifications of over 1,500 commodities, services, or inputs. The item prices are expressed as ratios to US prices and then averaged to yield 151 separate price parities. Prices for each of the three main parts of GDP are then estimated by taking weighted averages of the country basic parity prices, and used to calculate an international price for GDP.

18 In preliminary calculations we created a separate unionism variable, but because there were too few communist or ex-communist countries in our sample to get a reliable coefficient, we dropped the separate union variable from our final calculations. The calculations gave a negative coefficient to the separate communist union variable similar to that on unionism in market economies.

19 Edward Leamer has argued forcefully that only prices matter while Paul Krugman has argued that counterfactuals based upon factor content quantity calculations also have important implications for assessing the effect of trade.

20 Countries with more compressed structures of wages may end up with different distributions of occupations or industries. See Davis and Henrekson (1999) for studies of the effect of pay compression on employment structures.

References

Barro, R. J. and J.-W. Lee (1993) 'International Comparisons of Educational Attainment', NBER Working Paper, no. 4349 (April).

Behrman, J. and M. Rosensweig (1994) 'Caveat Emptor: Cross-Country Data on Education and the Labour Force, *Journal of Development Economics*, vol. 44, pp. 147–71.

Bennell, P. (1996) 'Rates of Return to Education: Does the Conventional Pattern Prevail in Sub-Saharan Africa?', *World Development*, vol. 24, pp. 183–99.

Davis, S. and M. Henrekson (1999) 'Wage-Setting Institutions as Industrial Policy: Swedish Experience Seen from a US Perspective', NBER Summer Institute Workshop in Labor Studies, Comparative Labor Markets Session (28 July).

Freeman, R. and L. F. Katz (1994) 'Rising Wage Inequality: The United States vs Other Advanced Countries', in Richard Freeman (ed.), *Working under Different Rules* (New York: Russell Sage Foundation for NBER), pp. 29–62.

Freeman, R. and R. Oostendorp (2000) 'Wages around the World: Pay across Occupations and Countries', NBER Working Paper, no. 8058 (December).

Gumbel, E. J. (1958) *Statistics of Extremes* (New York: Columbia University Press).

Krueger, A. and M. Lindahl (1999) 'Education and Growth in Sweden and the World', NBER Working Paper, no. 7190 (June).

OECD (1997) *Employment Outlook* (Paris: OECD) (July).

Psacharopoulos, G. (1994) 'Returns to Investment in Education: A Global Update', *World Development*, vol. 22, pp. 1325–43.

Reder, M. (1962) 'Industrial Wages', in *Aspects of Labor Economics*, Universities National Bureau Conference Series, no. 14 (Michigan: University Microfilms).

Summers, R. and A. Heston (1991) 'The Penn World Table (Mark 5): An Expanded Set of International Comparisons, 1950–1988', *Quarterly Journal of Economics*, vol. 106, no. 2, pp. 327–68.

Tinbergen, J. (1974) 'Substitution of Graduates by Other Labour', *Kyklos*, vol. 27, no. 2, pp. 217–26.

Visser, J. (1997) 'Global Trends in Unionisation: A Report to the ILO Task Force on Industrial Relations', Cesar Department of Sociology, University of Amsterdam, mimeo.

3

Australian Responses to Increases in Unemployment and Wage Inequality: Comparisons with the United Kingdom, New Zealand and the United States

Robert G. Gregory
Research School of Social Sciences
Australian National University, Australia

1 Introduction

Over the last 25 years three facts have dominated much of the discussion of the macro labour market in the United States (US): constant or falling average real wages, the large increase in wage inequality, and strong employment growth. These three facts, tied together by simple models of labour demand and supply, have had a profound effect on labour market policy in some English-speaking countries which have experienced slow employment growth and high unemployment rates since 1975. Policy in these countries – Australia, United Kingdom (UK) and New Zealand (NZ) – has been strongly influenced by the idea that to achieve faster employment growth for the young and unskilled it is necessary to move towards a US-style less regulated labour market which is capable of generating slower real wage growth, greater wage inequality and more jobs. Hence the UK introduced a number of labour market reforms during the early Thatcher years (Schmitt (1995)). Australia began to deregulate the labour market from 1989 and is continuing down this path. NZ introduced large-scale reforms under the Employments Contracts Act 1991 (Maloney (1997), Silverstone *et al.* (1996)).

These institutional changes in the way labour markets operate are not trivial and they may have very large effects on employment, wages, and income distribution. To prepare the ground for the discussion, Section 2 describes labour market outcomes in the US and Australia in the 1960–75 period and briefly explains the centralized Australian wage setting system. Section 3 offers a brief discussion of US and Australian macro employment outcomes since 1975 and their relationships to average real wages, wage inequality and changing Australian policy towards labour market institutions. Since the higher levels of unemployment dating from the mid-1970s, Australian policy moved first towards more centralized wage fixing, with a focus on average real wage control, and then to a more deregulated labour market with an emphasis on increased flexibility, greater wage inequality and a reduced role for trade unions. Unemployment is still high, by the standards of the 1950s, 1960s and early 1970s and, given the poor employment response to the policy changes, Australia is about to move further towards a US-style labour market with changes to industrial relations practices and law which further weaken unions, centralized wage fixing and arbitration. It appears as though a century-long Australian tradition of using labour market policy to bring about a more equal distribution of income is coming to an end. The changes that are being made will not be easily reversed. Unless there is a large employment response to the widening Australian wage differentials, the impetus for further deregulation will further widen the gap between the high and low paid.

Changing labour market institutions to create employment growth by encouraging a greater dispersion of wages and lower wages for groups with high unemployment rates has important implications for other economic and social policies, particularly for the design of the welfare system. Section 4 therefore discusses Australian welfare policy responses to widening wage differentials and high unemployment rates. The initial response was to adjust the welfare system to largely offset the income effects of increased wage inequality for those with dependent children. But this has led to many subtle and interesting changes in the overlap between the welfare system and increasing wage dispersion which were largely unforeseen and unintended. These changes seem to indicate that the current welfare policy of leaning against the wind is unsustainable, unless the trend towards increasing wage inequality is arrested.

The NZ and UK labour market reforms have been more radical and immediate than the more gradual evolution of Australian policy. Section 5 briefly compares NZ and UK labour market experiences with those of Australia and the US to see whether there are simple relationships between labour market deregulation, increased wage dispersion and faster employment growth. Section 6 offers concluding remarks.

2 Australian and US labour market institutions

2.1 Pre-1975 outcomes

Throughout the 1950s and 1960s Australian and US labour market institutions were very different. The Australian labour market was subject to extensive wage regulation generated by a centralized wage-setting system which produced more or less fixed relative wages for each occupation and skill level. The labour market rigidities created by wage regulation were held in place by strong unions. Each occupation had its own minimum wage for each level of skill and these legally-binding minima – there were many thousands – extended throughout Australia.

Despite rigid relative wages many labour market outcomes evolved in a remarkably similar way to those of the US where the labour market more closely approximated the unregulated labour market of the economic textbooks. Between 1960 and 1970 real wages (Figure 3.1) grew at much the same pace in each country and the relationship between the employment-population levels of each country (Figure 3.2) were relatively constant.

Given that the Australian labour market was thought of as relatively rigid, and the US labour market as very flexible, it is not easy for an economist to make sense of the similarities of labour market outcomes in the pre-1970 period. There were two analytical problems.

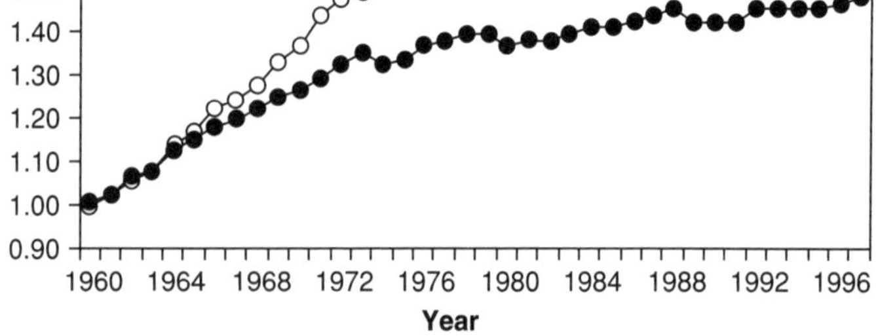

Figure 3.1 Real total compensation per employee, Australia and US, 1960–97
Source: *OECD Economic Outlook*.

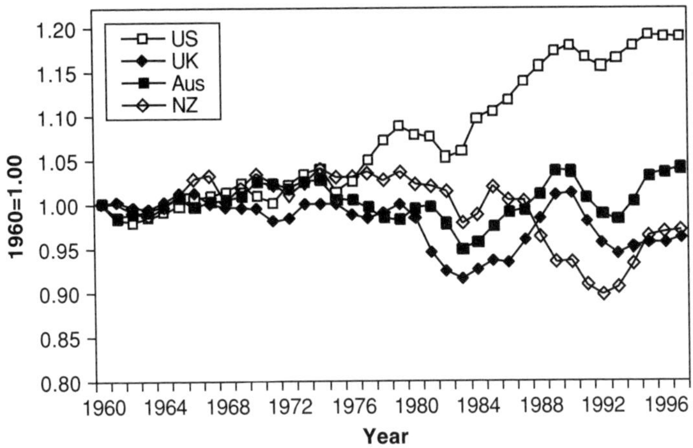

Figure 3.2 Employment/population indices, 1960–97
Source: *OECD, Main Economic Indicators* and *Economic Outlook.*

First, the Australian labour market, with inflexible relative wages, should have been less efficient at matching demand and supply. Yet Australian unemployment rates were typically 25 per cent of those of the US (Figure 3.3).[1]

Second, since Australian labour market institutions compressed wage structures, and raised the lowest wages relative to the median, it might be expected that significant unemployment might result among the least skilled. However, the unemployment pattern among different skill and demographic groups was much the same in both countries.

Given the similarity of employment and real wage growth, the lower Australian rate of unemployment and a similar pattern of unemployment, it appeared that Australian labour market institutions could compress the wage structure to contribute to social justice with very little efficiency cost. Australia could use government expenditure and taxes *and* labour market institutions to affect income distribution.[2] Furthermore, it was likely that labour market institutions were far more effective at lifting the income of the low-paid than the other two policy instruments.

The superior unemployment performance relative to the US, 'the better and more fair wage distribution' and the same employment and real wage growth over the 1950 to 1975 period suggested that there was no need to change Australian labour market institutions. Real wages were lower than those of the US but this could always be explained by

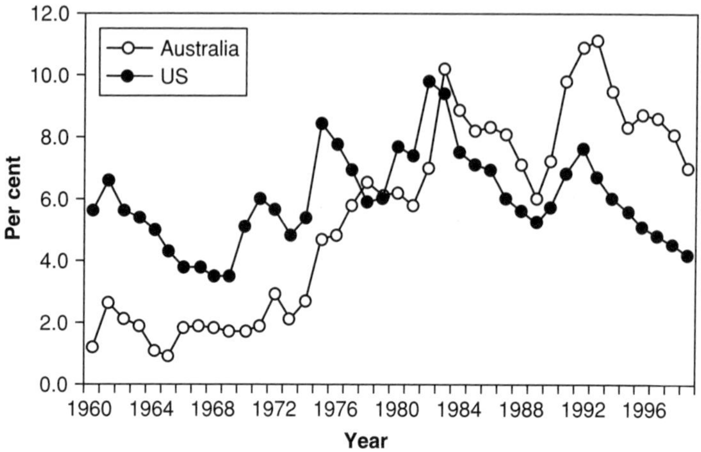

Figure 3.3 Unemployment rates, Australia and US, 1960–99
Source: *OECD, Main Economic Indicators* and *Economic Outlook*.

non-labour market factors – lack of scale economies, international trade barriers, lags in adopting overseas technology, and so on.[3] Why change institutions to accept a more unequal US wage distribution and higher unemployment? What was to be gained?

2.2 The post-1975 period

Since 1975, Australian and US employment outcomes have diverged considerably (Figure 3.2). The proportion of the population 15–64 years old employed in the US has increased 18 per cent. That in Australia has fallen 3 per cent. The divergence of full-time employment between the two countries is even larger. Although employment recessions are a little deeper in Australia, and the recoveries are less strong, different cyclical behaviour appears not to be the primary source of the growing employment gap, which seems to be the result of a break in the relative employment trends beginning in 1975.

The low rate of Australian employment growth since 1975 has been a major policy concern and has had a profound effect on particular groups. Consider three examples taken from families with dependent children. Since 1979, when the data first became available, the proportion of dependent children families with no parent employed has increased from 11 to 18 per cent. The proportion of dependent children families with no male employed has increased from 16.2 to 28.5 per cent. Finally, the proportion of dependent children families with no adult employed full-time is now 27.5 per cent. Some of these changes originate in shifting family structures and the growth of families with a female head, but lack of employment opportunities is an important contributor.

Government policy has reacted in two ways to the effects of insufficient employment growth: it has introduced labour market policies which it believes will generate faster job growth and it has extended the welfare system to increase the level of income support for families with children. These two policies are interrelated in a number of interesting ways which bear on the effects of increasing wage inequality.

3 Wages policy

3.1 The initial focus on centralised wage fixing and average wage outcomes

The post-1975 employment crisis was preceded by a large increase in Australian real wages. After 20 years of real wage growth, similar to the US, there was a marked divergence. Between 1973 and 1975 Australian real wages increased by approximately 15 per cent while those of the US remained largely unchanged.

The initial reaction to the employment crisis was to focus on these large real wage increases and to use existing labour market institutions to avoid further upward movements. With the implicit agreement of the unions, full wage indexation for price changes was introduced in 1975. In an environment of large nominal wage increases it was thought that this action would prevent real wages from increasing further. It was also hoped that the dividend from the normal rate of productivity gains over the following few years would translate into employment increases, rather than real wage gains, and that gradually productivity and real wages would be brought back into a balance that generated full employment.

The centralization of wage fixing that was necessary to index wages for price changes gradually produced labour market strains between unions and employers and was abandoned during the late 1970s. Almost instantly real wages increased again (Figure 3.3), to be followed by a major recession in the early 1980s as unemployment increased to 11 per cent. After the election of the Labor government in 1983, an explicit Accord was reached with the unions; wages were again indexed in response to price changes with the object of avoiding further real wage increases.

There was significant employment growth during the mid-1980s – as real wages fell slightly – but there was no clawing back of the employment loss relative to the US. Why might this be? It now appears in the US and Australia that there was a significant slowdown in the underlying rate of technical change. On average real wages appeared not to increase at all in the US between 1975 and the mid-1990s, and increased only marginally in Australia.[4] Hence, if full employment required re-establishing the old wage relativity with the US then real wage maintenance in Australia would not be sufficient. There must be some progress towards offsetting the large real wage increases during the early 1970s. In the absence of strong Australian productivity growth, the centralized wage setting system did not seem capable of moving real wages down to full employment levels.

By the end of the 1980s it had become clear that a different strategy was needed. The new focus was to move away from attempts to control average real wages and move towards using relative wages to encourage employment growth.

3.2 The new emphasis on decentralized wage setting

The new strategy, which was begun under a Labor government in 1989, was designed to weaken the centralized wage fixing system. Wage increases were to be negotiated enterprise-by-enterprise and linked more directly to firm profitability. Across-the-board nation-wide wage increases for all workers were abandoned. The new strategy opened the opportunity for greater wage dispersion.

After the defeat of the Labor government and the election of a Liberal–National Party coalition in 1996, Australia went further along the path of deregulating the labour market and introduced legislation that began to weaken further the centralized wage setting system and the union movement. Although never explicitly stated as policy, it was believed that weakening unions and the centralized wage setting system, would generate increased wage diversity and allow real wages to fall for groups with high unemployment rates. Australia was well on the way to producing a labour market more like that of the US.

Throughout this labour market reform process, the US employment–relative wage experience was thought to provide strong support for Australian policy. During the period of strong employment growth, wages at the bottom end of the US wage distribution had fallen considerably, particularly for men. In addition, US wage dispersion in each education and labour force experience category had increased and this too was thought to be partly responsible for the record rate of US employment growth.

As might be expected, Australian labour market outcomes were not as straightforward. Table 3.1 presents a brief summary of the male full-time relative wage structure for the US and Australia. The compression of the Australian wage structure, relative to the US, is readily apparent. In 1995, the US 90/10 ratio is 68 per cent higher than that of Australia. Most of the difference in the wage structure is accounted for by the 50/10 ratio, reflecting the greater wage compression at the bottom of the Australian distribution.

The Australian wage compression is also observed from a comparison of wages of the young with the wages of more experienced workers. In 1976, the ratio of the average full-time wage of a 15–19 year old to that of a 35–44 year old was 48 per cent in Australia and 38 per cent in the US.

It is interesting to note that despite the regulated nature of the wage-setting institutions and the long periods of centralized wage fixing, in many respects the Australian wage inequality over the post-1975 period

Table 3.1 Male full-time, full-week earnings ratios Australia, UK and US, 1976–95

Earnings ratios	*1976*	*1983*	*1995*
90/10 percentile			
Australia	2.26	2.43	2.76
UK	–	2.75	3.70
USA	3.36	4.00	4.64
NZ	–	3.06	3.45
10/50 percentile			
Australia	0.72	0.68	0.62
UK	–	0.62	0.50
USA	0.52	0.45	0.44
NZ	–	0.61	0.60
15–19 years/35–44 years			
Australia	0.48	0.46	0.40
UK	–	0.40	0.31
USA	0.38	0.33	0.31

Sources: Australia, *Weekly Earnings of Employees (Distribution)*, ABS Cat. No. 6310.0.
US, *Current Population Survey* (March).
UK, *General Household Survey*.
NZ, *Dixon* (1998).

appeared to increase at approximately the same rate as in the US. The percentage change in the 10/50 ratio between 1976 and 1995 is 16 per cent for the US and 24 per cent for Australia. The wage ratio of the young to the middle age groups fell 17 per cent in Australia and 18 per cent in the US.

Wage inequality began to increase in Australia before the new policy of labour market deregulation. And yet the growth of wage inequality, similar to the US, was not sufficient to generate fast growth in the employment–population ratio. How much more might low wages need to fall in Australia to generate employment growth comparable to the US? Indeed, will increased relative wage dispersion create significantly more jobs or just affect income distribution with wage falls for the low paid not being matched by employment increases?

Despite the lack of employment response, government policy is committed to further labour market deregulation and further falls in the relative wages of the low paid. The rationale is simple: if employment is too low then the wage must be too high.

4 Welfare policy

The second part of the strategy in response to growing wage inequality was to adjust the welfare system to increase the degree of income protection for families with dependent children.[5] This process has two important interrelationships between increased wage dispersion and the Australian welfare system. One interrelationship involves changes in the replacement ratio – a comparison of low wages with the level of welfare payments received when not employed. The other interrelationship, which we discuss first, is generated by the provision of government income support for those employed at low wages.

4.1 Relative wages and income support among the employed workforce

Table 3.2 summarizes some of the relationships between the wage distribution and the welfare system at August 1997. It lists government income support for different family types at the 10th percentile of the male and female full-time weekly earning distributions on the assumption that all welfare benefit entitlements are received.

Table 3.2 Wages, welfare payments, and taxation, 10th percentile, 1997

	F/T weekly earnings	*Gross income*	*Net income*	*Government income subsidy*		*Tax paid*	
	$	*$*	*$*	*$*	*(%)*[1]	*$*	*(%)*[2]
Male	414	414	345	0	(0)	69	(17)
Female	367	367	312	0	(0)	55	(15)
Family types							
Single with children, female							
1 Child < 13	367	505	474	138	(38)	31	(7)
1 Child < 13 & 1 Child 13–15	367	577	545	210	(57)	22	(4)
Married couple, no children							
One earner, Male	414	478	434	64	(16)	44	(10)
One earner, Female	367	464	426	97	(26)	38	(8)
With children, one earner							
Male with 1 child < 13	414	542	480	128	(31)	62	(11)
Female with 1 child < 13	367	525	475	158	(43)	50	(10)
Male, with 2 children < 13, 1 child 13–15	414	666	604	252	(61)	62	(9)

Notes: [1] As a per cent of gross F/T weekly earnings.
[2] As a per cent of gross income.
F/T = Full-time.
Source: Gregory, Klug and Martin (1999).

The range of entitlements varies considerably by family structure. Full-time weekly earnings at the 10th percentile are too high for a single individual to receive government income support but a married couple household with no dependent children, an employed wife (at the 10th percentile of the female full-time weekly earnings distribution) and an unemployed spouse can receive income support as high as 26 per cent of the wife's gross earnings. Among families with dependent children, income support is higher. For a married couple family with a dependent spouse and two dependent children, government income support at the 10th percentile of the male wage distributions can be as high as 61 per cent of the gross wage.

Table 3.2 also adjusts income levels for tax liabilities, which at the 10th percentile of the distribution of full-time weekly earnings range between 4 and 17 per cent of the gross wage, depending on family structure. For all groups, except single adults without dependent children, the government welfare subsidy exceeds taxation paid and has a very substantial impact on income distribution. Consider an employed female sole parent with two dependent children (Martin (1999)). Government income support, which effectively adds 57 per cent to her weekly earnings, lifts her gross income from the 10th to just over the 50th percentile of the female distribution of gross weekly earnings. Her after-tax income is just above that of a single female with no dependents at the 80th percentile of the net earnings distribution.

The very large wedge between gross earnings and net income that is created by tax and welfare policies has a number of important implications when labour market earnings change. If low-paid individuals increase their weekly earnings, government income support can be significantly reduced through additional taxation and reduced welfare payments. The welfare withdrawal rate can be quite large and extend well up the wage distribution (Table 3.3).

The combination of additional income tax and welfare withdrawal as income increases means that for many families the marginal effective tax rate – the percentage of an extra dollar of non-government income

Table 3.3 Wages, government income support, and taxes, deciles

Family types:	*10* *$*	*20* *$*	*30* *$*	*40* *$*	*50* *$*	*60* *$*	*70* *$*
Single female with 1 child < 13 & 1 child 13–15							
Benefit	210	181	174	155	133	102	70
Tax	32	46	61	74	89	110	132
Additional net income	178	135	113	81	44	−8	−62
Net benefit as a per cent of F/T weekly earnings	49	31	24	16	8	−1	−10
Married couple, one earner (male) with 2 children <13 and 1 child 13–15							
Benefit	252	236	226	200	159	123	72
Tax	62	87	102	135	158	183	228
Additional net income	190	149	124	65	−1	−60	−156
Net benefit as a per cent of F/T weekly earnings	46	31	24	11	0	−8	−18

Note: F/T = Full-time.
Source: Gregory, Klug and Martin (1999).

Table 3.4 Effective marginal tax rates

	Income range decile boundaries		
Family types	*10–20*	*30–40*	*60–70*
Single female with 1 child under 13 and 1 child 13–15			
	$	$	$
Wage increase	62	38	66
Benefit reduction	29	19	33
Tax increase	14	13	22
Net income increase	19	6	11
Marginal effective tax rate (%)	69	84	84
Married couple, one earner (male) with 2 children under 13 and 1 child 13–15			
	$	$	$
Wage increase	66	72	103
Benefit reduction	16	36	51
Tax increase	24	33	46
Net income increase	26	3	6
Marginal effective tax rate (%)	61	96	94

Source: Gregory, Klug and Martin (1999).

that is lost either to tax increases or benefit withdrawal – can be extremely high (Table 3.4). For example, the effective marginal tax rate for a female single wage earner with two dependent children is 69 per cent over the income range from the 10th to the 20th percentile of the female weekly earnings distribution and 84 per cent over the income range from the 30th to the 40th percentile. The effective marginal tax rates for a married couple family, with one income earner and two dependent children is 61 per cent from the 10th to the 20th percentile of male weekly earnings and 96 per cent from the 30th to the 40th percentile.

These marginal effective tax rates matter a great deal for individuals during the normal operation of the labour market as through time employment income of some workers rises and that of others falls. They have a special significance when the overall wage distribution changes. This is illustrated in Table 3.5 by assuming that the Australian wage distribution is replaced by that of the US and Australian welfare and tax systems remain unchanged. Table 3.5 lists the 1997 average full-time earnings of men and women at the 10th percentile for Australia and the US. Full-time weekly earnings representing the US wage structure

Table 3.5 Wages, welfare payments, and taxation, Australia and the US: 10th percentile, 1997

	Australian pay structure Australian welfare system			*US pay structure Australian welfare system*		
	F/T weekly earnings A$	*Gross income $*	*Net income $*	*F/T weekly earnings $*	*Gross income $*	*Net income $*
Male	414	414	345	297	297	257
Female	367	367	312	233	297	273
Family types:						
Single with children, female						
1 Child < 13	367	505	474	233	438	421
1 Child < 13, 1Child 13–15	367	577	545	233	510	492
Married couple, no children						
One earner, Male	414	478	434	297	443	408
One earner, Female	367	464	426	233	424	401
With children, one earner						
Male with 1 child < 13	414	542	480	297	504	478
Female with 1 child < 13	367	525	475	233	485	461
Male, with 2 children < 13, 1 child 13–15	414	666	604	297	628	592

Source: Gregory, Klug and Martin (1999).

are expressed in Australian dollars by multiplying the median Australian earnings by the 10/50 US decile ratio.

For a single adult male placed at the 10th percentile of the Australian male pay distribution, the fall in weekly earnings accompanying a move to the US wage distribution is large, 28 per cent or A$117. Single adult males at this income level cannot access government income support and the only offset to the wage fall is lower taxation. After taxes, the net wage is reduced 26 per cent or A$88. For a single female, a movement to the US wage distribution would involve a 36 per cent reduction in the gross wage. Low-paid women fare particularly badly in the US. This wage is so low that welfare payments could be accessed even though the female is employed. After tax adjustments, her net income reduction is only 11 per cent.

The most interesting results occur for families with dependents. Government income support places a large wedge between wage and income changes and is very significant as the wage distribution changes. The income fall associated with a A$117 gross weekly earnings change for men and a A$174 fall for women varies between A$12 and A$53 for the families listed. In both cases more than half of the wage fall is offset by government subsidies.

These interactions between wages, welfare payments and income taxes have a number of important implications:

- As long as the current Australian welfare and tax system remain in place, a family with dependent children can be largely insulated from relative wage changes over most of the wage distribution. Hence, for those employed, the income effects of a widening earnings distribution below the median wage are predominantly of concern for single people, those without dependents and those with sufficient assets not to qualify for welfare benefits.
- As the wage falls the labour cost to the employer is reduced, irrespective of family type, and the demand for labour may increase. The Australian welfare system ensures that relative wage changes are accompanied by *de facto* wage subsidies to a wide range of employees with dependents. Many low-paid workers with dependents therefore could be largely indifferent to wage falls and there may be no supply response because the wage fall is offset by automatic increases in government income support and decreases in taxation.
- For a significant fraction of the labour force – those with dependent children – a change in relative wages effectively alters the proportion of their income derived from government. For them, possible policy changes to the welfare and tax system may be more important than wage dispersion changes or changes in labour market institutions.
- The rapid growth of welfare expenditure in Australia has often been seen as a response to the higher levels of unemployment and the increase in those who receive sole parent and disability pensions, which can act as substitutes for unemployment benefits. The development of '*de facto*' wage subsidies for the employed with dependents means that the growth of welfare expenditure is now directly linked to the fall in low wages and to employment growth at low wages.
- Even if the labour market policy of lower wages for the low paid increases employment and decreases unemployment, and thereby

saves expenditure on unemployment benefits, there will be an offset to this source of expenditure reduction from two sources. First, some of the unemployment benefit savings will be replaced by a wage subsidy for the newly employed at low wages. Second, there will be increased expenditure on wage subsidies for those previously employed but now subject to wage falls. The wage subsidy effect is likely to dominate the unemployment benefit savings because for those with dependent children the wage subsidy applies to all employment at low wages, subject to a wage fall, whereas the savings of unemployment benefits only applies to the increase in employment.

This welfare system is increasingly being seen as incompatible with the labour market reform process for three reasons. First, as wage inequality increases the system is becoming very demanding of the government budget. Each widening of the wage distribution that affects families is associated with further claims on the government budget. Second, there is increasing concern that there may be large efficiency losses associated with insignificant income gains for moving up the pay distribution and insignificant income losses from moving down the wage distribution. Employees with dependent children may see little gain from accepting a better paid job. Third, the system places very high tax rates on second income earners with children because the income tests associated with the welfare system are largely based on family income. Thus, Beer has shown that:

> A low income family with three children is financially *worse off* if the mother works between 10 and 24 hours per week than if she works just 9 hours per week. By increasing her hours worked from 5 to 35 hours per week the family benefits by just $12 per week. For the same family with only one child, the increase is around $85 per week. (Beer (1997), emphasis in the original p. 30)

4.2 The replacement ratio

The high marginal effective tax rate generated by the interaction of the welfare and tax system can also impinge on the change in the replacement ratio when low wages fall. If a single male loses a job at the 10th percentile of the male distribution of full-time weekly earnings, unemployment benefits may replace 57 per cent of the after-tax income loss (Table 3.6). For a married couple family with a male earner, dependent spouse and two dependent children welfare payments will replace 82 per cent of after-tax income.

Table 3.6 Replacement ratios

Family types	*Percentiles*		
	10th %	*20th %*	*40th %*
Single male			
Australia	57	51	42
USA	77	61	45
Single female			
Australia	63	56	49
USA	72	67	56
Single female with 1 child under 13 and 1 child 13–15			
Australia	64	62	59
USA	71	67	62
Married couple, one earner (male) with 2 children under 13 and 1 child 13–15			
Australia	82	79	76
USA	84	83	77

Source: Gregory, Klug and Martin (1999).

What would happen to the replacement ratio if the current Australian welfare system was combined with the US wage structure? For all groups replacement ratios increase but once again family structure matters. For Australian single men moving from employment at the 10th percentile to unemployment benefits the replacement ratio increases from 57 per cent under the Australian wage structure to 77 per cent under the US wage structure because income from employment falls. For married couples with dependent children the change is of the order of two per cent (82 to 84 per cent). The move to a US wage structure involves little income change from employment because the large wage falls are almost fully offset by increased government welfare payments and reduced tax liabilities. For these families the relationship between taxation, welfare payments, and falling wages generates considerable demands on the government budget rather than a reduction in employment income and possible labour supply responses.

The major debate in the US associated with falls in low wages is primarily a demand side focus. What is the increase in employment generated by a fall in low wages? Are the employment effects large? The same debate is important in Australia because if the labour market deregulation policy is to be effective, lower wages must generate more jobs. Hopefully the positive employment response will be larger than the negative wage effect so that the income of the low paid group increases.

But the interaction of the welfare and tax system may suggest that supply side effects may be more important and a special feature of the Australian labour market. The traditional supply side analysis, which suggests that a welfare system with access to income support for unlimited duration provides a floor below which minimum wages cannot fall, may apply in Australia only to those without dependents. For this group, replacement rates increase when wages fall. For those with dependent children, replacement ratios are relatively insensitive to wage changes. As low wages fall, income associated with employment changes marginally. At the margin the source of income shifts from the labour market to the government budget.

5 Australian labour market reform compared with NZ and UK outcomes

To conclude, we glance briefly at labour market outcomes after the NZ and UK labour market deregulations and place them against Australian and US experiences. A complete assessment of reform outcomes is a complex and long process and in this section we can focus briefly only on employment growth, real wage and wage relativity changes by presenting and describing the basic data. Although this is a simple approach it does lead to a number of strong presumptions as to the short-run relationships between labour market outcomes and reforms.[6]

First, with respect to average real wages there is a diversity of experiences with real wages increasing considerably in the UK after the reforms but not increasing at all in NZ, and increasing in Australia only over the last few years (Figure 3.4). The UK experience presents a significant puzzle in that reforms designed to weaken unions and prevent real wage increases appear to have been associated with a large acceleration of real wage growth.

Second, Australia, UK and NZ have shared an increase in wage inequality but the extent of the changes has differed (Table 3.1). The increase in UK wage inequality during the 1980s exceeds that of the US and appears to be the largest increase among OECD countries (OECD (1993)). In NZ the change in wage relativities since the 1991 reforms have been moderate (Dixon (1998)). In Australia, wage falls at the bottom of the wage distribution, relative to the median, have been similar to the US but changes have occurred at much the same pace before and during the reform process.

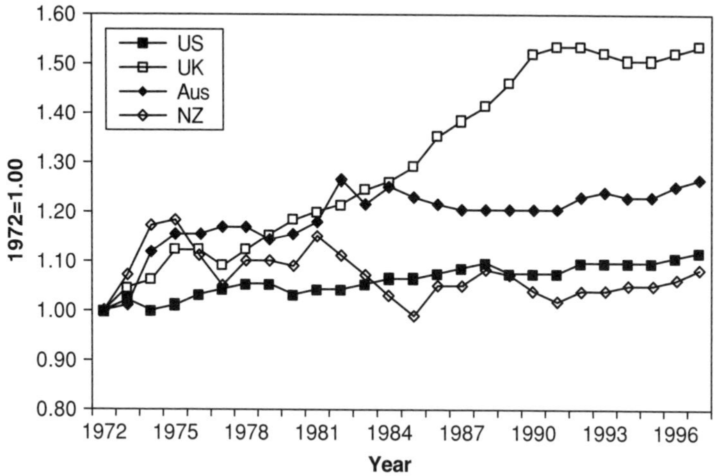

Figure 3.4 Real total compensation per employee, 1972–97
Source: *OECD, Economic Outlook.*

Third, UK, NZ and Australian labour market deregulation, and the mixed pattern of average real and relative wage changes, has not delivered the hoped for employment increases (Figure 3.2). There is a close grouping of the employment series of the four countries over the 1960–75 period, indicating that these economies evolved in a similar way. Then, after 1975, there is an increase in employment variance from year to year in the UK, NZ and Australia but by 1998 the employment–population ratio of each country is within 5 percentage points of the 1960 level. Very little has changed over the last 40 years. The different US experience is very noticeable. The employment–population ratio increases almost 20 percentage points relative to the 1960 level. After the US, the country with the strongest employment growth is Australia with an employment outcome almost 10 percentage points above that of the UK and NZ. Australia has been subject to least labour market reform.

Finally, during the initial years following reform the UK and NZ lost considerable employment which has not been clawed back. Of course, some of the employment loss came about because of the way these countries chose to fight inflation – with the adoption of tight monetary policy and overvalued exchange rates – rather than adopting an income accord process as in Australia. In NZ, the employment loss occurred immediately before the Employment Contract Act which was introduced in the depths of the recession.

It should be stressed that this is a very cursory look at the data, and employment and wage outcomes also depend on other factors apart from labour market reform. Nevertheless, advocates of labour market reform often seem to imply that reform itself will be sufficient to produce desirable outcomes. The data clearly do not indicate this. None of the reform countries have generated a significant increase in employment growth rates.

The aggregate labour markets of NZ and Australia have not gained large returns at this point. In NZ if real wage and employment changes are combined then it is clear that labour has fallen behind; the employment–population ratio has fallen and real wages have remained constant. In Australia, labour seems to have moved slightly ahead; there have been small and marginal increases in the employment–population ratio and some real wage growth over the 1990s. UK labour seems to have fared marginally better with large real wage increases not completely offset by significant employment declines. It is only in the US that labour income has increased considerably with large employment gains and small real wage increases. Labour market reforms may have been worthwhile in the reform countries but the aggregate employment data seem to indicate that any positive gain is small unless it could be argued that in the absence of reforms the post-1975 outcomes would have been significantly worse.

6 Concluding remarks

Long periods of low employment growth in Australia, and increasing wage inequality and strong employment growth in the US, are slowly and fundamentally changing the way Australian governments perceive the objectives of labour market policy and the role of labour market institutions.

One change is that the century-long tradition of using labour market institutions and labour market policy to achieve a more equitable income distribution is gradually being abandoned in the belief that greater wage inequality will create more employment and that the employment gains will sufficiently offset the wage falls of the low-paid to make the policy worthwhile. To date, however, a significant move away from centralised wage fixing, and a widening of wage relativities, has not created an employment dividend. Average real wages and labour productivity have begun to increase, as they have in the US, but on average over the last few years employment growth is just matching population growth.

Another important change has been to gradually alter the welfare system so that '*de facto*' wage subsidies are playing a much greater role for low-paid workers with dependent children. The large increase in wage subsidies has largely offset the increase in wage inequality for this group but it is unlikely that this process can be maintained if wage inequality continues to increase. First, the subsidies are generating considerable and growing demands on the government budget. Second, together with the tax system the subsidies have generated high marginal tax rates and increasingly it is being supposed that these have bad effects on work incentives. Third, the inability of policy to generate sufficient employment growth has generated some frustration. It has meant that the policy focus is shifting again and this time it is moving towards reform of the welfare system to increase work incentives. In a world where wage inequality is increasing this must inevitably increase economic hardship among disadvantaged groups, at least in the short run.

There has been some recognition that replacement ratios are increasing for the low-paid without dependents as low wages fall and unemployment benefits are indexed on average wage changes. Government has responded by tightening eligibility tests for receipt of benefits. As the labour market policy fails to generate sufficient job growth, it is probable that the Australian government will take the next step and introduce unemployment benefits of fixed duration and reduce the basic payment. When this occurs the effect of the growing wage inequality on income inequality will increase.

One concluding remark. A chapter which consists primarily of describing past labour market changes, and conjectures on their effects on the evolution of labour market policy, runs the risk that the future may be very different. Is it likely these economies are about to return to pre-1975 employment and real wage growth rates and a narrowing of wage disparities? There is no evidence that post-1975 trends towards widening wage relativities has ceased in Australia, nor is there any evidence that employment has moved to a new growth path. There is considerable evidence, however, that labour productivity growth may have returned to pre-1975 levels but this productivity growth has been diverted to average real wage increases rather than employment growth. Australian labour market reforms have not replicated US labour market outcomes where evolving technical change in the post-1975 period has been associated with above average employment growth and below average real wage increases. The most recent data suggest that a UK outcome is more likely to flow from the current round of Australian reforms with increases in average real wages, a further significant increase in wage dispersion, and no significant growth in the employment–population ratio.

Notes

1 During the 1950s and 1960s there seemed to be no adverse efficiency effects of Australian labour market institutions unless it could be argued that they prevented 'income catch up' to the US.

2 It was not believed that wages could be increased to any level without regard to productivity. There was always some concern as to the trade off between average real wages and employment levels, and between average wage increases and inflation, but in general there was little concern with adverse effects of wage compression and relative wage rigidity.

3 There were three ways a neoclassical economist might rationalise the coexistence of high Australian employment levels, low unemployment, and rigid relative wages. One way was to argue that by chance the relationship between shifts in demand and supply always offset each other and the pattern of wage relativity was the same as that which would be produced by a free market.

It might also be argued that although relative wages were fixed in terms of occupations and skills, worker quality was an important dimension of adjustment that economists had underemphasised and changing worker quality effected labour market equilibriums.

Finally, it was always possible to deny the facts. Good data on market wages and measures of excess demand and supply for different types of labour are not easy to find. Almost all wage data referred to awards which are the extensive set of legally enforced minimum wages for each occupation and skill level. Hence it could be argued, although not in my view credibly, that there was indeed considerable wage flexibility which was not evident in award data.

With respect to the lack of a visible employment effect of compression this might be explained by the fact that those with less formal education or labour market experience were just more efficient than their US counterparts because the Australian education system was better, or demand for the less skilled, relative to supply, was greater than in the US.

4 There is some controversy as to the nature of real wage growth in the US. The debate centres on both the wage series and the price deflator. OECD data, real compensation for employees, which are used in Figure 3.1, show a slight real wage increase. The Bureau of Labour Statistics series, average weekly earnings production and non-supervisory workers on private non-farm payrolls deflated by CPI, indicates a 17 per cent fall.

5 Income support is paid without time limit and without an insurance element. Payments are based on income and asset tests. There are standard base rate payments which vary according to the marital status and age of the unemployed person. The base rate of payment is around 25 per cent of full-time average weekly earnings but there are additional income payments which include rent assistance, subsidized pharmaceuticals and numerous programmes providing income provision for children. The base rate and additional income payments are withdrawn as non-social security income increases. These withdrawal rates ensure that if the employed are low paid and responsible for dependents they receive some income support from government.

6 For a further discussion see Gregory (2000).

References

Beer, G. (1997) 'Is It Worth Working? The Financial Impact of Increased Hours of Work by Married Mothers with Young Children' (paper presented at the 26th Annual Conference of Economists, University of Tasmania, 28 September–1 October).

Dixon, S. (1998) 'Growth in the Dispersion of Earnings: 1984–97', *Labour Market Bulletin*, vols 1 and 2, pp. 71–107.

Gregory, R. G. (2000) 'The Impact of Labour-Market and Economic Reforms in the UK, NZ and the US', in S. Bell (ed.), *The Unemployment Crisis in Australia* (Melbourne: Cambridge University Press), pp. 105–25.

Gregory, R. G., E. Klug and Y. Martin (1999) 'Labour Market Deregulation, Relative Wages and the Social Security System', in S. Richardson (ed.), *Reshaping the Labour Market: Regulation, Efficiency and Equality in Australia* (Melbourne: Cambridge University Press), pp. 200–22.

Maloney, T. (1997) 'Has New Zealand's Employment Contracts Act Increased Employment and Reduced Wages?', *Australian Economic Papers*, vol. 36, no. 69 (December), pp. 243–64.

Martin, Y. M. (1999) 'The Economic Survival of Indigenous Mothers in a Changing Labour Market' (PhD Dissertation), ANU (July).

OECD (1993) 'Earnings Inequality: Changes in the 1980s', *OECD Employment Outlook* (July), pp. 157–84.

Schmitt, J. (1995) 'The Changing Structure of Male Earnings in Britain, 1974–1988', in R. Freeman and L. Katz (eds), *Differences and Changes in Wages Structures* (Chicago: University of Chicago Press).

Silverstone, B., A. Bollard and R. Lattimore (eds) (1996) *A Study of Economic Reform: The Case of New Zealand* (Amsterdam: North-Holland).

4

Wage Indexation and the Evolution of Returns to Education in Italy, 1978–92

Marco Manacorda[1]
Centre for Economic Performance, London School of Economics and Department of Economics, Queen Mary College, University of London, UK

1 Introduction

In this chapter I study the effect of a specific institution – the Scala Mobile (SM) – on changes in returns to education in Italy between the late 1970s and the early 1990s, using micro data from the Bank of Italy's Survey of Households' Income and Wealth.

A feature that makes this institutional arrangement almost unique is that it affected – although with a different degree on intensity – the whole distribution of wages. Broadly speaking, the Scala Mobile was an indexation mechanism granting the *same* absolute wage increase to *all employees* as prices rose. In principle, by awarding the same wage increase to both low- and high-wage workers the Scala Mobile had the potential to compress wage differentials.

Over time, the equalizing effect of this indexation mechanism declined and by the end of the period of observation it was virtually zero. This provides a unique experiment to test whether this institution had any effect on the structure of wages. One can do so by looking at changes in returns to education over time since – for this institution to have an effect – one might expect returns to education to compress more at the beginning than at the end of the period. Indeed, the data show that between 1978 and 1992, returns to education first decreased and then increased in Italy, so that by the early 1990s their level was approximately equal to the level in the late 1970s. This possibly suggests that in the absence of this institution returns to education would have increased over the entire period of observation.

One difficulty with concluding that the earlier compression in the returns to education was due to the effect of the Scala Mobile is that one might argue that this institution had no effect on the structure of wages and, in the absence of it, wage differentials would have evolved as they in fact did. This would be the case if the latent structure of returns to education 'happened' to move as predicted by the Scala Mobile, and the latter just predated the former. One way to address this criticism is to identify a source of variation in the Scala Mobile that is exogenous to changes in the latent structure of wages. The Scala Mobile, however, affected all employees and in this sense it was intrinsically a 'macroeconomic' institution. So, one does not have a natural control group to identify a counterfactual distribution of wages. In order to distinguish the effect of this institution from any other macroeconomic factor, I assume – and later I provide some corroborating evidence – that the gender–earnings gap would have changed at a constant rate over the whole period of observation had the indexation mechanism not been at work. This is equivalent to attributing any deviation around this trend to the Scala Mobile. Since the Scala Mobile potentially compressed the gender–earnings gap, for this to be true one would expect this gap not to change uniformly across periods but to fall more when the Scala Mobile was stronger. That is precisely what I find in the data and I exploit this feature of the data to identify separately the effect of the Scala Mobile from other sources of wage changes. Based on this assumption, I show that, if the Scala Mobile had not been curbed, returns to education would have decreased between 1978 and 1992.

This basic conclusion mimics the results of my previous paper (Manacorda (2000)) where I look at changes in each percentile of the unconditional distribution of earnings, separately for men and women. However, this framework examines changes in the wage structure 'between' groups (by education and age) rather than within groups. It is known that changes in the wage structure between and within groups in the US are somewhat distinct economic phenomena – see for example Katz and Autor (1999). Broadly speaking, the former shows a downward trend in the 1970s and an upward trend in the 1980s, while the latter appears to have risen monotonically over both decades. One would like to know whether the same happened in Italy and – if this is not the case – how one can explain these different trends. Erickson and Ichino (1995) examine explicitly the evolution of earnings differentials between education and age groups in Italy and the US until the late 1980s and they find different trends, with returns to education declining in Italy between the late 1970s and the late 1980s. They conclude that the trends in the two countries differ because of a combination of market forces, institutions, and changes in inflation. However one does not know how much weight to attach to these different explanations and this chapter is an attempt to answer this question.

2 Changes in the earnings structure 1978–92

2.1 The data

The data I use are the individual records of the Bank of Italy Survey of Households' Income and Wealth (SHIW), for the period 1977–93. The survey was run on a yearly basis until 1987 (with the exception of 1985) and subsequently every other year. Since I do not have repeated observations over the same individuals (the survey comes in the form of repeated cross-sections) I look at changes by cells defined over four categories of education (5th grade or below, 8th grade, 13th grade and college or above), four age groups (21–30, 31–40, 41–50, 51–65) and gender. Since some of the cells tend to be relatively small, and the associated estimates rather imprecise, I take average log earnings for each cell over three-year intervals centred on the following years: 1978, 1981, 1985, 1988 and 1992.[2] For brevity 1978 now means the average value between 1977 and 1979 and similarly for the other years. My basic observations are then the 160 cells defined by the interaction of education (4), sex (2) age (4) and time (5).

Yearly labour income, which is the earnings variable used in this study, is defined net of taxes and social security contributions and inclusive of 13th month wages, bonuses and overtime payments. I will refer to this indifferently as 'earnings' or 'wage' but this is really annual take-home pay. The data are weighted by the sampling weights. Sampling weights for each cell are given by the sum of the weights for the individuals in each cell.

The sample is restricted to full-year employees, men and women, aged 21–65. Overall, I have 40,507 observations.[3] The sample size increases from 4,442 in 1978 to 10,824 in 1992 and the average cell size increases from 138 in 1978 to 338 in 1992. College workers constitute a relatively small share of the sample. Their average cell size within each age–gender group increases from 36 in 1978 to 137 in 1992 and their relative weight from 7 to 10 per cent. Workers in the intermediate two groups account for almost 60 per cent of the total observations. As expected there is a trend of increased educational attainment, with those with 13th grade accounting for 25 per cent of the total sample in 1978 and 39 per cent 14 years later, and those with 5th grade reducing their relative weight from 39 to 17 per cent.

2.2 Descriptive evidence

In Table 4.1 I report log earnings relative to the mean by education, gender and age, and interactions of these at each point in time. These data are obtained aggregating over the 160 cell averages with a fixed weighting scheme, where the weights are given by the average relative weight of each cell over the whole period of observation. In this way one purges variations in the structure of earnings from any effect due to compositional changes. Alongside I also report annualized log changes over each period.

Table 4.1 illustrates that while men at the top of the distribution gain substantially, with the college premium increasing by about 9 percentage points over the whole period, those at the bottom do not seem to experience substantial changes in their relative earnings. Returns to education change dramatically for women who start from a relatively more dispersed earnings distribution and lower levels of earnings at any level of education. The earnings differential between the two bottom groups (8th–5th) falls by 14 percentage points between 1978 and 1988 from 19 to 5 per cent, but the college premium increases over the same period by 4 percentage points.

The unconditional male–female earnings gap falls between the late 1970s and the late 1980s with a reduction of 6 percentage points (from 23 to 17 per cent) but in the early 1990s opens up again with an increase of 2 percentage points.

Age differentials stay basically unchanged until the late 1980s when they show some tendency to decompress. For example, the difference in earnings between those in their 30s and those in their 20s falls from 14 to 10 per cent between 1978 to 1988 then to increase by 5 percentage points in the last four years.

The remainder of Table 4.1 shows that young college graduates gain all over the period of observation (with an increase of 11 percentage points in the college premium from 1977 to 1992 for those in their 20s and a rise of 9 percentage points for those in their 30s) while older and poorly educated workers benefit from the compression in the 1970s and 1980s and lose afterwards. The differential between 8th and 5th grade workers in their 50s falls by approximately 7 percentage points in the first 10 years to increase again in the last years by about 3 percentage points.

Table 4.1 Changes in the structure of relative earnings, 1978–92

	Log levels					*Annualized log changes (× 100)*			
	1978	*1981*	*1985*	*1988*	*1992*	*1978–81*	*1981–85*	*1985–88*	*1988–92*
I Education									
College	0.13	0.14	0.14	0.17	0.20	0.38	−0.11	0.96	0.68
13th	0.08	0.07	0.07	0.06	0.07	−0.29	−0.19	−0.32	0.32
8th	−0.03	−0.02	−0.04	−0.03	−0.06	0.25	−0.35	0.12	−0.66
5th	−0.12	−0.12	−0.09	−0.10	−0.09	−0.06	0.73	−0.08	0.16
II Gender									
Men	0.08	0.07	0.07	0.06	0.07	−0.41	0.03	−0.36	0.21
Women	−0.15	−0.12	−0.13	−0.11	−0.12	0.76	−0.07	0.67	−0.39
III Age									
21–30	−0.11	−0.11	−0.12	−0.09	−0.13	0.07	−0.18	0.85	−1.08
31–40	0.03	0.03	0.03	0.01	0.02	−0.02	−0.08	−0.59	0.16
41–50	0.06	0.05	0.06	0.05	0.08	−0.19	0.05	−0.19	0.69
51–56	0.03	0.04	0.05	0.05	0.06	0.21	0.34	−0.01	0.33
IV Education and gender									
Men									
College	0.21	0.24	0.23	0.26	0.27	1.07	−0.31	0.99	0.31
13th	0.19	0.17	0.16	0.15	0.16	−0.80	−0.28	−0.10	0.11
8th	0.05	0.04	0.04	0.03	0.02	−0.17	−0.07	−0.38	−0.15
5th	−0.03	−0.05	−0.03	−0.05	−0.03	−0.65	0.56	−0.92	0.70
Women									
College	0.05	0.04	0.04	0.07	0.11	−0.35	0.11	0.93	1.06
13th	−0.06	−0.05	−0.05	−0.07	−0.04	0.37	−0.07	−0.60	0.61
8th	−0.21	−0.17	−0.21	−0.17	−0.24	1.25	−1.01	1.32	−1.87
5th	−0.40	−0.35	−0.30	−0.23	−0.29	1.72	1.24	2.45	−1.46

V Education and age									
Age: 21–30									
College	−0.01	0.04	0.09	0.13	0.07	1.87	1.10	1.43	−1.49
13th	−0.05	−0.07	−0.06	−0.06	−0.08	−0.61	0.06	−0.01	−0.33
8th	−0.17	−0.15	−0.17	−0.13	−0.21	0.72	−0.57	1.15	−1.98
5th	−0.23	−0.25	−0.27	−0.17	−0.18	−0.66	−0.50	3.39	−0.39
Age: 31–40									
College	0.11	0.11	0.12	0.15	0.17	0.06	0.18	1.12	0.42
13th	0.11	0.11	0.09	0.06	0.08	0.05	−0.48	−0.94	0.35
8th	0.00	0.00	−0.01	−0.03	−0.04	0.16	−0.37	−0.42	−0.46
5th	−0.12	−0.14	−0.10	−0.14	−0.11	−0.53	1.06	−1.42	0.73
Age: 41–50									
College	0.11	0.11	0.12	0.15	0.17	−0.40	−1.14	1.07	1.70
13th	0.11	0.11	0.09	0.06	0.08	−0.47	−0.10	−0.35	0.73
8th	0.00	0.00	−0.01	−0.03	−0.04	−0.10	−0.26	−1.17	0.82
5th	−0.12	−0.14	−0.10	−0.14	−0.11	0.00	0.75	0.41	0.28
Age: 51–65									
College	0.22	0.21	0.16	0.19	0.26	1.09	−0.44	−0.40	2.26
13th	0.20	0.19	0.18	0.17	0.20	0.02	−0.32	0.50	1.52
8th	0.08	0.08	0.07	0.03	0.07	−0.17	0.15	1.15	−0.35
5th	−0.11	−0.11	−0.08	−0.07	−0.06	0.36	0.86	−0.76	−0.19

Notes: Table 4.1 reports the average log earnings by cell at five points in time: 1978, 1981, 1985, 1988, and 1992, and the annualized proportional change (×100) over each time interval. Wages are standardized relative to the average level of earnings at each point in time. Aggregation across elementary cells is performed using a fixed weighting scheme, with weights given by the average weight of each cell over time.
Source: SHIW individual records.

Overall, it appears that the distribution compresses from the bottom, favouring in particular women and less educated workers. The compression seems to be stronger for those groups who start with a more dispersed initial distribution of earnings: these are again women and older workers. At the top some decompression is going on. Interestingly, while the compression from the bottom seems to come to a halt in the late 1980s, the trend at the top seems to be unaltered. If anything one would suspect that something changed for low skilled workers. I will argue below that all these three features (higher increases for those in the bottom tail of the earnings distribution, faster compression within groups with more dispersed earnings and timing of the change) are consistent with the effect of the Scala Mobile on the cross-sectional distribution of wage changes and with changes in its 'toughness' over time. At the top, I show in Section 3 that the Scala Mobile had a relatively weak effect. One way to interpret the data then is that, if the compression at the bottom came from the indexation, in the absence of indexation the distribution of earnings would have widened at the bottom too.

The pattern I have described is reflected in the overall evolution of earnings inequality. In Table 4.2 I decompose changes in inequality, as measured by the variance of the logarithm of earnings, into a between groups component, defined by the interaction of age and education, and a component due to variation within these groups. To do this I regress the logarithm of earnings in each year on a linear term in years of completed education and a quadratic term in age. Table 4.2 tells a simple story: inequality first decreases and then increases with a turning point in the late 1980s. Whatever dimension one looks at (total, within or between), this holds true. Age and education (and gender) explain between one-fourth to one-fifth of the total variability of earnings and, consistently with Table 4.1, inequality falls dramatically for women and much less for men. In 1988 the two distributions display a remarkably similar level of dispersion. Interestingly, changes in between and within inequality show similar trends suggesting that these are driven by similar forces.

In order to summarize the salient features of changes in the earnings distribution, I postulate that changes by cell can be expressed as linear function of years of completed education, a quadratic term in age, an intercept for female workers, plus a common macroeconomic term. I also assume that there is an additive error term that picks up measurement error as well as any other idiosyncrasy in earnings.[4] Finally, I assume that the marginal distribution of changes in earnings is characterized by changing returns to education, age and gender:

Table 4.2 Changes in earnings inequality, 1978–92

	Variance log earnings					*Annualized changes in variance log earnings (×100)*			
	1978	*1981*	*1985*	*1988*	*1992*	*1978–81*	*1981–85*	*1985–88*	*1988–92*
I Men and Women									
Total	0.115	0.097	0.088	0.077	0.097	–0.60	–0.23	–0.37	0.50
Between	0.013	0.014	0.012	0.011	0.017	0.03	–0.05	–0.03	0.15
	(0.115)	(0.149)	(0.139)	(0.138)	(0.180)				
Within	0.102	0.082	0.075	0.066	0.08	–0.67	–0.18	–0.30	0.35
	(0.885)	(0.851)	(0.861)	(0.862)	(0.820)				
II Men									
Total	0.091	0.082	0.073	0.072	0.084	–0.30	–0.23	–0.03	0.30
Between	0.013	0.015	0.014	0.014	0.019	0.07	–0.03	0.00	0.13
	(0.145)	(0.185)	(0.185)	(0.196)	(0.226)				
Within	0.078	0.067	0.06	0.058	0.065	–0.37	–0.18	–0.07	0.18
	(0.855)	(0.815)	(0.815)	(0.804)	(0.774)				
III Women									
Total	0.127	0.101	0.09	0.071	0.102	–0.87	–0.28	–0.63	0.78
Between	0.022	0.017	0.016	0.01	0.023	–0.17	–0.03	–0.20	0.33
	(0.174)	(0.172)	(0.178)	(0.146)	(0.225)				
Within	0.105	0.084	0.074	0.061	0.079	–0.70	–0.25	–0.43	0.45
	(0.826)	(0.828)	(0.822)	(0.854)	(0.775)				

Notes: Table 4.2 reports the decomposition of the total variance of log earnings into the portion explained by a linear term in education and a quadratic term in age (between) and the residual part (within), for men and women together and separately. In brackets I report the proportion relative to the total.
Source: SHIW individual records.

$$\Delta w_{ct} = \gamma_{0t} + \gamma_{1t} \text{ education} + \gamma_{2t} \text{ age} + \gamma_{3t} \text{ age}^2 + \gamma_{4t} \text{ sex} + u_{ct} \quad (1)$$

where w is log earnings and the subscript '*c*' refers to cell means, where the cells are defined by the interaction of age, sex, and gender.[5]

In column (1) of Table 4.3 I report the estimation results for the marginal distribution of changes in earnings ((1)). Education is a linear term that represents the minimum numbers of years necessary to achieve any formal level of education while age is given by the midpoint in each interval.[6] For brevity I only report the coefficients on education and sex. I allow the coefficient on the education variable (as well as on age and sex) to change unrestricted from period to period.

The dependent variable is given by the annualized earnings change over each time interval (1978–81, 1981–85, 1985–88, 1988–92), expressed in percentage points. Estimation is performed on the 128 cell differences using generalized least squares (GLS) with weights given by the inverse sampling variance of the dependent variable. Although the estimates show some convexity in changes to returns to education, they are rather imprecise. To achieve more precision, I impose some parametric restrictions on the evolution of changes in returns to education. In column (2) I restrict changes in returns to education to vary along a quadratic trend (which takes the value 0 in the first period, 1 in the second, etc.). In column (3) I use the interaction of education with a linear trend and in column (4) I impose no variation in changes in returns to education over the different periods. For each of these specifications, I report a goodness-of-fit test that gives an indication as to whether the model fits the data as well as the unrestricted specification of column (1).

As can be seen from Table 4.3, specifications (2) and (3) do as well as the model in column (1). But as we restrict changes in returns to education to be constant, we have a significant loss of fit. If one takes the most parsimonious model of column (3), one can conclude that *changes* in returns to education show some positive trend, which is to say that returns to education (*in levels*) accelerate over time. While in the first period of observation, differentials *fall* by approximately 0.26 percentage points (-0.087×3), their decline tends gradually to slow down. Between 1981 and 1985 they narrow by around 0.1 percentage points ($(-0.087 + 0.062) \times 4$) and they start then to *increase*, with a rise of 0.1 percentage points in the second half of the 1980s ($(-0.087 + 0.062 \times 2) \times 3$) and an increase of almost 0.4 percentage points in the last period ($(-0.087 + 0.062 \times 3) \times 4$). The estimates suggest that the differential between 13th grade and 8th grade falls by approximately

Table 4.3 Changes in the structure of earnings
Dependent variable: annualized proportional changes in earnings by cell (×100)

	Specification							
	(1)		*(2)*		*(3)*		*(4)*	
Years of education	–0.008	(0.079)	–0.018	(0.074)	–0.087	(0.052)	0.037	(0.024)
*81–85	–0.047	(0.092)						
*85–88	0.020	(0.093)						
*88–92	0.123	(0.087)						
*trend			–0.063	(0.097)	0.062	(0.023)		
*trend^2			0.036	(0.027)				
Female	1.335	(0.674)	1.345	(0.670)	1.419	(0.670)	1.286	(0.687)
*81–85	–1.342	(0.783)	–1.364	(0.777)	–1.460	(0.776)	–1.396	(0.797)
*85–88	–0.409	(0.791)	–0.404	(0.787)	–0.529	(0.784)	–0.395	(0.804)
*88–92	–1.776	(0.734)	–1.789	(0.730)	–1.838	(0.732)	–1.614	(0.747)
Adj. R^2	0.944		0.944		0.944		0.941	
Chi^2			0.29	(0.59)	4.51	(0.10)	22.00	(0.00)
d.f.			1		2		3	

Notes: Table 4.3 reports the results of a regression of annualized proportional earnings changes by cell defined by sex, four age groups (21–30, 31–45, 41–50, 51–65), four education groups (5th grade, 8th grade, 13th grade, 18th grade) and four time intervals (1978–81, 1981–85, 1985–88, 1988–92) on a linear term in education (years of completed education), four period dummies, a quadratic term in age and a sex dummy ((1)). All specifications include the interaction between age and time dummies. 'Trend' is a linear trend equal to 0 in the first period, 1 in the second period, etc.
'Female' is a dummy variable for female workers.
Control group: Men, 21–30, 5th grade, in 1978–81.
Number of observations: 128.
Estimates obtained with GLS with weights given by the inverse sampling variance of the dependent variable.
Standard errors in parenthesis.
Chi^2 is a test for the goodness of fit relative to the model in column (1). Under the null that the two models fit equally well the data, the statistic is distributed as a Chi^2 whose number of degrees of freedom is reported in the last row. The *P*-value is reported in parenthesis.
Source: SHIW individual records.

2 percentage points between 1978 and 1985 and subsequently rises by 3 percentage points.

To visualize the trend, in Figure 4.1 I depict the evolution of the return to one extra year of education obtained by cumulating the changes in returns to education as predicted from specification (3) in Table 4.3. The series is standardized to the level in 1977, as estimated in a separate cross-sectional regression.

Interestingly, the male–female earnings gap also falls during the period of analysis. Most of the decline takes place between 1978 and 1981, with a fall of more than 5 percentage points in three years (1.419×3). The gender gap narrows, although at a slower pace, in the subsequent periods, and in the last period it reverts to its trend as it increases by almost 2 percentage points in four years ($(1.419-1.838) \times 4$). In the rest of the chapter I attribute the differential evolution of the gender gap over different time intervals to the effect of the Scala Mobile. In Section 3 I show how the Scala Mobile was potentially able to produce this pattern and I provide some evidence that indeed it was the Scala Mobile – and not other forces – that shaped variations around this trend.

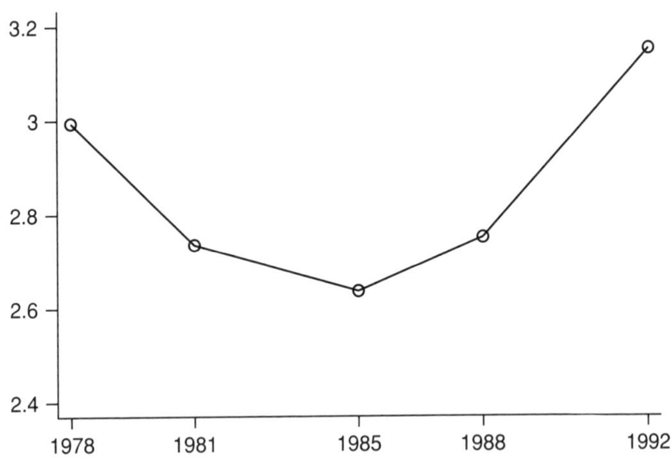

Figure 4.1 Changes in the average return to one extra year of education, 1978–92
Notes: Figure 4.1 reports the estimated return to one extra year of education, conditional on gender, age, and a common macroeconomic effect. The values are expressed in percentage points. The series is obtained based on the results of specification (3) in Table 4.3. See text for details.
Source: SHIW individual records.

3 The effect of the Scala Mobile on the earnings structure

3.1 Institutional features

The Scala Mobile (hereafter SM) was an indexation mechanism meant to ensure a partial automatic coverage of wages in face of past inflation.[7] Similar to many North American cost-of-living (COLA) agreements allowance (see Card (1983)), in its original formulation the escalator implied the *same* quarterly absolute increase in nominal wages (SM point) for all employees for any percentage point increase in the consumer price index. If we denote nominal wages, by W the Scala Mobile point, by α the level of prices by p, some base period for computing price changes by 0, the contingent increase in wages from time $t-1$ to time t for individual i, denoted by ΔSM_{it}, is:

$$\Delta SM_{it} = \alpha_t(\Delta P_t/P_0) \tag{2}$$

If by lower case letters we denote logarithms, the proportional change in wages due to the SM is:

$$\Delta sm_{it} = \Delta SM_{it}/W_{it-1} \approx (\alpha_t P_{t-1}/P_0)(1/W_{it-1})\Delta p_t \tag{3}$$

Note that while absolute contingent increases in (2) do not depend on individual variables (indexed by i), proportional changes (3) do, since they are inversely related to the individual's initial wage.

The proportional increase in wages for individual i is directly related to the inflation rate (Δp) and to the SM point (α) relative to the real starting wage (W/P). The relative wage of two individuals i and j ($W_i > W_j$) then changes with the SM as follows:

$$\Delta sm_{it} - \Delta sm_{jt} \approx (P_{t-1}\alpha_t/P_0)/(1/W_{it-1} - 1/W_{jt-1})\Delta p_t < 0 \tag{4}$$

So, for each pair of wage observations, the potential equalizing effect of the SM varies directly with inflation and the value of the SM point, and with some measure of distance between these two wages. One might wonder how differentials would have evolved if inflation had been unchanged but only the SM point (α) varied over time. That is equivalent to computing (4) where the Δp_t is fixed at some reference period, say period 1:

$$\Delta sm_{it} - \Delta sm_{jt|\Delta p} = (P_{t-1}\alpha_t/P_0)/(1/W_{it-1} - 1/W_{jt-1})\Delta p_1 \tag{5}$$

Analogously, one can experiment with a counterfactual obtained by varying only the inflation rate but letting the SM point be constant gives:

$$\Delta sm_{it} - \Delta sm_{jt|\alpha} = \alpha_1 (1/W_{it-1} - 1/W_{jt-1}) \Delta p_t \tag{6}$$

To get a better idea of how the SM worked, in Table 4.4 I report an illustration based on data for the first quarter of 1978. I take two individuals, one with a high level of earnings and one with a low level of earnings (corresponding approximately to the top and bottom deciles of the distribution of earnings in December 1977).

Their initial earnings in thousand lire are, respectively, 461 (W_{it-1}) and 192 (W_{jt-1}) and the ratio between their earnings is 2,400 (W_{it-1}/W_{jt-1}). The price index (P_t/P_0) with base ($t = 0$) January 1977 = 100 is 162. In three months this rises by 5 points to 167 ($\Delta P_t/P_0$). This triggers an increase of 12,000 lire for both workers (ΔSM_{it}), obtained as the product of the SM point ($\alpha = 2,400$) and the price rise. The differential then falls to 2.32 and the proportional reduction is approximately 3 per cent (2.32/2.40 – 1). A similar number can be obtained by using (4) directly ($2,400 \times 162/100 \times (1/461 - 1/192) \times 3$).

Table 4.4 The Scala Mobile at work: an illustration

	Initial earnings (a)	*Price index (b)*	*Change in prices (c) = Δ(b)*	*SM point (d)*	*Contingent increase (e) = (c)∗)d)*	*Final earnings (f)= (a) + (e)*
High wage	461	162				
		167	5	2.4	12	473
Low wage	192	162				
		167	5	2.4	12	204
High/low	2.40					2.34

Notes: Table 4.4 shows the salient feature of the functioning of the Scala Mobile. Data refer to the first quarter 1978 and earnings are expressed in thousands of lire. In column (a) I report the level of earnings at the end of 1977 for two individuals respectively in the top and bottom decile of the earnings distribution. Columns (b) and (c) report, respectively, the value of the price index (January 1977 = 100) in January 1978 and three months later, and the associated increase. Column (e) reports the nominal increase in earnings accruing to each individual obtained as the product of the price increase (c) and the value of the SM point (d) which at the time was set equal to 2,389. In column (f) I report the value of earnings in April 1978 under the assumption that there is no other source of increase. This is simply the sum of the initial level of earnings (a) and the escalated increase (e). Because of the SM, the ratio between the high and the low wage falls from 2.40 to 2.34.

Source: SHIW individual records and ISTAT, *Annuario Statistico Italiano* (various issues).

3.2 The evolution of the SM: econometric evidence

In this section I integrate data on earnings with information on contingent payments based on the institutional parameters of the model (the SM point and the series of changes in prices) as published in ISTAT, *Annuario Statistico Italiano* (various issues). I estimate contingent payments for each individual in the sample and then I average across individuals in each cell by pooling observations across contiguous years, as in Section 2.[8] The annualized inflation rate declines from approximately 14 per cent in the late 1970s–early 1980s, to around 6 per cent in the late 1980s–early 1990s. This also contributed to the decline in the potential equalizing effect of the SM (see (4)).

In order to document changes in the toughness of the SM, I abstract from changes in inflation and compute variations over time in contingent wage changes owing to variations in the SM point (see (5)). In Figure 4.2 on the horizontal axis I report the average level of earnings by cell at

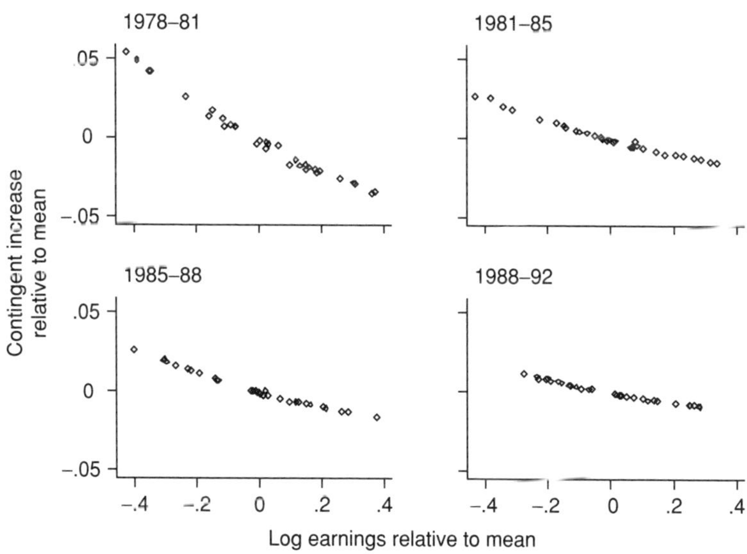

Figure 4.2 The decline in the Scala Mobile toughness, 1978–92
Notes: Figure 4.2 reports on the horizontal axis the average level of initial earnings and on the vertical axis the average annualized contingent earnings changes as implied by the Scala Mobile in each period for the 32 cells defined by age, sex, and education. Data are obtained at a fixed inflation rate (see text for details).
Source: SHIW individual records and ISTAT, *Annuario Statistico Italiano* (various issues).

the beginning of each period (1978–81, 1981–85, 1985–88 and 1988–92) and on the vertical axis the proportional contingent increase as implied by the SM, *at a fixed inflation rate*. Changes are expressed as a deviation from the change at the mean log level of earnings.[9]

As the curve becomes flatter, the potential equalizing effect of the SM declines. Between 1978 and 1981 the SM implies a reduction of 1.1 percentage points a year in the differential between two individuals whose earnings are initially 10 per cent apart. By the end of the period this falls to less than 0.4 percentage points.

Two reasons contributed to the decline. First, under the pressure of rank and file workers and the association of entrepreneurs, the government in 1983 reduced the value of the SM point by approximately 15 per cent relative to its 1977 level. Second, in 1986, the system was made semi-proportional (approximately by granting a 100 per cent coverage of a given minimum wage, plus a 25 per cent coverage of the difference between the actual wage and the minimum wage). This further dampened the equalizing effect of the SM.

The graph shows some slight convexity: for any proportional difference in relative wages, the potential equalizing effect of the SM declines as we move to the top of the wage distribution (see (4)). For any given difference in wages, one would expect the SM to have a relatively strong effect at the bottom of the distribution, namely among women and low educated workers, which is essentially what we found in the data in Section 2. Also, and most important, the SM is likely to have a strong effect on inequality within those groups for whom initial inequality is higher – i.e. again, for women relative to men and for older workers relative to younger ones.

In order to assess the potential effect of the SM on returns on education, I assume that Δsm_{ct}, the average proportional contingent change for cell c between time $t-1$ and time t, can be represented as an additive function of years of completed education, a quadratic term in age, and a gender dummy. Again, I assume that returns to each of these observable characteristics vary over time and I allow for a common macroeconomic shock:

$$\Delta sm_{ct} = \theta_{0t} + \theta_{1t}\text{education} + \theta_{2t}\,\text{age} + \theta_{3t}\,\text{age}^2 + \theta_{4t}\text{sex} + e_{ct} \quad (7)$$

In Table 4.5 I estimate (7) using GLS. I reproduce the same structure as in Table 4.3 where I allow for changes in returns to 1 extra-year of education to vary unrestricted from period to period and then I impose some parametric restrictions and test for them. Specification (2) does

Table 4.5 Changes in the Scala Mobile

Dependent variable: annualized proportional contingent changes in earnings by cell (× 100)

	Specification							
	(1)		*(2)*		*(3)*		*(4)*	
years of education	−0.332	(0.027)	−0.317	(0.024)	−0.213	(0.017)	−0.057	(0.006)
*81–85	0.196	(0.031)						
*85–88	0.271	(0.028)						
*88–92	0.296	(0.027)						
*trend			0.205	(0.026)	0.061	(0.006)		
*trend^2			−0.037	(0.007)				
Female	2.915	(0.226)	2.900	(0.227)	2.793	(0.255)	2.630	(0.343)
*81–85	−1.827	(0.261)	−1.797	(0.260)	−1.687	(0.293)	−1.627	(0.394)
*85–88	−2.369	(0.239)	−2.360	(0.239)	−2.210	(0.269)	−2.089	(0.361)
*88–92	−2.636	(0.230)	−2.620	(0.231)	−2.523	(0.260)	−2.322	(0.348)
Adj. R^2	0.984		0.984		0.980		0.962	
Chi^2			1.33	(0.25)	29.47	(0.00)	132.76	(0.00)
d.f.			1	2	3			

Notes: Table 4.5 reports the results of the estimation of (7). See also notes to Table 4.3.

a relatively good job in accounting for the evolution of differentials by education conditional on age and sex. Contingent payments tend to compress earnings differentials by education and gender. Over time their equalizing effect falls, although at a declining rate. The implied change in earnings associated to one extra year of education owing to the SM is almost 1 percentage point between 1978 and 1981 (-0.317×3) and it declines to around 0.1 percentage points between 1988 and 1992 $((-0.317 + 0.205 \times 3 - 0.037 \times 3^2) \times 4)$. As anticipated in Section 2, the SM implied a strong equalizing effect on the male–female earnings gap. While at the beginning of the period of observation the SM implied a reduction in the gap of approximately 9 percentage points (2.900×3), in the last four years this was approximately 1 percentage point $((2.900 - 2.620) \times 4)$. This is broadly consistent with the observed evolution of the gender–earnings gap which, as we have seen in Table 4.3, first decreased and then increased. A way to interpret the data, then, is to assume that the gender gap was growing (or possibly constant) over time but that this trend was counteracted by the SM. As the SM declined, the gender gap increased as it would have done all over the period in the absence of the SM. This is substantially the identifying assumption I use in the next section (3.3), where I assume that the 'latent' gender–earnings gap was increasing along some linear trend and I attribute any deviation around this trend to the SM.[10]

3.3 The effect of the SM on the earnings structure: econometric specification and identification

To estimate ultimately the impact of the SM on the earnings structure, I assume that total changes in earnings are related to contingent changes through some linear function:

$$\Delta w_{ct} = \gamma_{0t} + \eta \Delta sm_{ct} + \gamma_{1t}\text{education} + \gamma_{2t}\text{age} + \gamma_{3t}\text{age}^2 + \gamma_4\text{sex} + d_{ct} \quad (8)$$

The model postulates a simple relationship between contingent and non-contingent changes: conditional on some function of age, education, sex, and time, the SM shifts the entire earnings distribution by assigning to each individual a proportional growth in earnings that is inversely related to the level of initial earnings. However, not the whole amount of contingent changes translates into total ones but only a portion η, which is my parameter of interest. If $\eta = 0$, the SM does not have any effect. For $\eta = 1$ contingent changes translates one-to-one into total changes. For values between 0 and 1 the SM is partly undone by other sources of changes so it tends to compress the distribution of earnings, although not as much as one might have expected from the simply descriptive evidence presented above.

Note that in (8) I rule out that, once I condition for the SM, changes in the gender–earnings gap can vary over time. As said, this is equivalent to assuming that I allow this gap to follow some trend but I attribute any deviation around this trend to the effect of the SM. This hypothesis is ultimately untestable with my data, the reason being that one does not have a control group of otherwise similar individuals to check how this gap would have changed in the absence of the SM. One way to gauge some indirect evidence on this, however, is to recall that the SM had a potentially smaller effect at the top of the distribution and a smaller effect the lower the dispersion of earnings within groups. For my identifying assumption to be true, one would then expect that for highly educated (and therefore high earning) workers, the gender gap follows some linear trend. Also, one would expect that the higher is the initial dispersion within a group, the higher is the compression.

Figure 4.3 reports the evolution of the gender–earnings gap for the four education groups. One can easily see that most of the compression in the gap comes from the bottom on the distribution, i.e. those with 5th grade. As we move up the distribution, the gap stays basically constant over time, with possibly some increase at the end. Also, one might notice that low educated workers start from a relatively higher gap (around 40 per cent) and over time this is brought in line with the gap of the other groups (around 20 per cent). Both these hypotheses speak in favour of my identifying assumption and suggest, if anything, that in the absence of the SM women would not have fared much better in the late 1980s than in the late 1970s.

3.4 Estimation results

In Table 4.6 I report the results of my estimation. I regress annualized changes in earnings by cell on annualized contingent increases, a linear term in education, a quadratic term in age, all interacted with year dummies. The model also includes a gender dummy, but *no interaction* between sex and year dummies. It is interesting to see that once I condition on latent changes in the earnings structure as picked up by the restrictive specification in (8), the Scala Mobile shows a strong effect of the distribution of earnings changes. It turns out that about 80 per cent of contingent changes translate into total ones. The point estimate is not very precise and suggests that one cannot reject a value of $\eta = 1$. In the remaining columns of Table 4.6 I report more restrictive

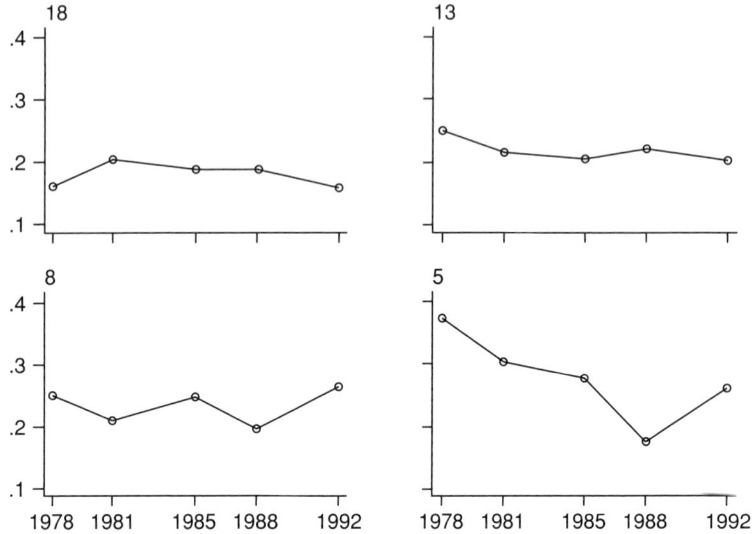

Figure 4.3 Changes in the gender–earnings gap, by education, 1978–92
Notes: Figure 4.3 reports the male–female log earnings differential by education (college graduates (18), those with 13th grade, 8th grade, and 5th grade, respectively). All series are obtained at fixed composition of observable characteristics. See notes to Table 4.1 for details.
Source: SHIW individual records.

specifications for the evolution of changes in returns to education. As in Table 4.5, a specification with a quadratic term in the linear trend is not rejected while more restrictive specifications do not to fit the model as well as in column (1). Column (2) tells a simple story: conditional on contingent increases, wage differentials by education grow over the period of observation, although at a declining rate. By the end of the period, returns accelerate again. The return to one extra year of education increases by around 0.7 percentage points between 1977 and 1981 (0.224×3), 0.3 percentage points between 1981 and 1985 ($((0.224 - 0.209 + 0.061) \times 4)$), 0.15 percentage points between 1985 and 1988 ($((0.224 - 0.209 \times 2 + 0.061 \times 2^2) \times 3)$) and finally by 0.6 percentage points in the last period ($((0.224 - 0.209 \times 3 + 0.061 \times 3^2) \times 4)$). Cumulating these changes gives a rise in latent returns to education of 1.7 percentage points over 14 years. This implies that returns to 8th grade relative to 5th grade would have increased over the period of observation by about 5 percentage points. Analogously, returns to

Table 4.6 The effect of the Scala Mobile on the structure of earnings
Dependent variable: annualized proportional changes in earnings by cell (× 100)

	Specification									
	(1)		*(2)*		*(3)*		*(4)*		*(5)*	
Scala Mobile	0.818	(0.203)	0.808	(0.203)	0.686	(0.199)	0.727	(0.173)	0.599	(0.261)
years of education	0.252	(0.097)	0.224	(0.092)	0.079	(0.067)	0.105	(0.028)	0.164	(0.103)
*81–85	−0.203	(0.095)								
*85–88	−0.172	(0.101)								
*88–92	−0.112	(0.098)								
*trend			−0.209	(0.101)					−0.175	(0.105)
*trend^2			0.061	(0.027)	0.011	(0.026)			0.055	(0.027)
Female	−0.490	(0.243)	−0.482	(0.243)	−0.390	(0.244)	−0.419	(0.233)	−0.320	(0.274)
Adj. R^2	0.947		0.947		0.945		0.946		0.948	
Chi^2			2.09	(0.15)	13.63	(0.00)	14.06	(0.00)	2.42	(0.12)
d.f.			1		2		3		1	
Exogeneity test									0.493	(0.389)
Estimation method	OLS		OLS		OLS		OLS		2SLS	

Notes: Table 4.6 reports the results of the estimation of (8). Two-stage least squares (2SLS) are obtained using the interaction of a sex dummy with time dummies as an instrument for the 'Scala Mobile'.
'Exogeneity test' is a test for the exogeneity of contingent earnings changes.
Under the null hypothesis that contingent earnings changes are exogenous, the statistic is distributed as a *t*-student.
P values in brackets.
See also notes to Table 4.3.

13th grade relative to 8th grade would have increased by about 8.5 percentage points in 14 years.

It is also interesting to notice that once I condition for the SM, the change in the gender gap is negative, albeit only marginally significant, suggesting that the reduction in the gender–earnings gap was exclusively the product of the SM. If anything the gender gap would have increased (women would have lost) by about 0.5 percentage points a year.

One of the problems with these estimates is that one might be spuriously attributing to the SM some effect which instead is due to 'market forces'. In other words, as long as some latent compression (decompression) of the earnings structure was going on for reasons other than the SM (and over and above the one picked up by my parametric specification for latent earnings changes), and to the extent that latent earnings changes are correlated with contingent payments, estimation of (8) with GLS will lead to biased estimates for the effect of the SM.

One way to get round this is to use instrumental variables. Under my maintained assumption that deviations around a linear trend in the gender–earnings gap depend only on the SM, one can use the interaction of the gender dummy and the year dummies in (8) as an instrument for the SM. That is what I do in column (5) of Table 4.6 where, for brevity, I only report the results for the same specification as in column (2), i.e. the one with a quadratic trend interacted with a linear term in education. It turns out that the point estimate declines from 0.808 to 0.599, suggesting some positive correlation between the omitted components of changes in the latent earnings distribution and contingent changes. Yet, the estimate is rather imprecise and one cannot distinguish statistically between the two columns. This is confirmed by the value of the exogeneity test at the bottom of the table. This suggests that one cannot reject equality of GLS and 2SLS estimates. Interestingly the 2SLS estimates push the coefficient associated to the gender dummy to zero, suggesting that the gender–earnings gap would have stayed constant if not for the SM.

Based on these results, I next estimate a counterfactual series of changes in returns to education. To do so, I simulate a series of changes in earnings that is obtained by attributing to each cell a contingent growth as the one implied by the SM. Since part of the observed decline in the equalizing effect of the SM is owing to changes in the inflation rate across periods, in constructing this counterfactual distribution I fix the SM point at its value in the first period (see (6)) but I use the actual inflation rate in each period. Also, because we know that not all the contingent changes translated into total ones, I use the estimated value for η from column (5) of Table 4.6 ($\eta = 0.599$) to compute this counterfactual distribution.

By cumulating changes over time, I reconstruct the overall evolution of returns to education. That is what I do in Figure 4.4 where I report the actual distribution of returns to education, as plotted in Figure 4.1, alongside their evolution had the SM being as 'strong' as in the first period of observation (i.e. if the SM point had not changed in real terms). This makes it very clear that had the SM not been curbed, the return to one extra year of education would have *decreased* by approximately 0.4 percentage points over 14 years, while on average this, if anything, increased. The difference between these two series is then the 'genuine' effect of the decline in the SM toughness.

Note that by the end of the period returns to education would have started to increase, even at fixed SM toughness. This happens because latent returns to education (the term in education and its interactions with time in (8)) increase over time while inflation decreases, so dampening the equalizing effect of the SM. I estimate that if latent inequality had not increased and the SM had not been curbed, between 1978 and 1992, returns to education would have decreased by approximately two percentage points, almost five times as much as my estimates in Figure 4.4.

4 Conclusion

In this chapter I have examined changes in returns to education in Italy from the late 1970s to the early 1990s. I have shown that the Scala Mobile tended to compress the structure of wages and, as it was curbed in the 1980s, earnings differentials started to become more unequal. This happened because, at the same time, there was an underlying tendency for the returns to education to increase that was previously offset by the Scala Mobile.

Freeman and Katz (1995) suggest a supply–demand–institution explanation for the different trends in earnings structures on the two sides of the Atlantic during the 1980s, and one would like to know what is the relative contribution of these different forces in explaining the trend in returns to education in Italy. It is known that most of the changes in the returns to education in the US can be explained in terms of changes in relative demand and supply of skills (Katz and Murphy (1992) and, more recently, Card and Lemieux (2000)). In this chapter, I argue that institutions played a non-negligible role in shaping the evolution of returns to education in Italy.

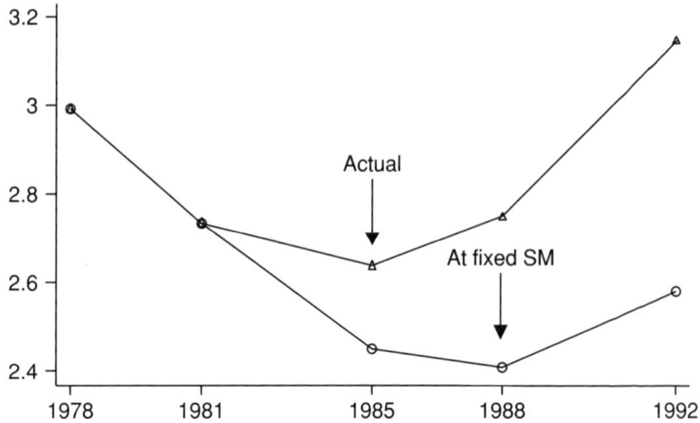

Figure 4.4 The effect of the decline in the Scala Mobile point on the return to one extra year of education, 1978–92

Notes: Figure 4.4 reports the estimated returns to one extra year of education, conditional on gender, age, and a common macroeconomic effect (the same as in Figure 4.1) and the estimated counterfactual distribution obtained by setting the SM point to its value in 1978. The series is estimated based on the estimates in column (5) of Table 4.6.

Source: SHIW individual records and ISTAT *Annuario Statistico Italiano* (various issues).

One additional finding of this chapter is that much of the compression of the gender–earnings gap which occurred in the late 1970s and early 1980s can also be traced down to the effect of the indexation mechanism. My most conservative estimates show that, in the absence of this mechanism, women in the Italian labour market would have not fared much better in the late 1980s than in the late 1970s.

Notes

1 I am indebted to David Card for his generous help. I also benefited from discussions with Richard Blundell, Alan Manning and, especially, Richard Freeman.

2 I take data only for the first and last year of each time interval to calculate averages (so, respectively: 1977 and 1979; 1980 and 1983; 1984 and 1986; 1987 and 1989; 1991 and 1993). To calculate average values by cell I regress individual earnings over a full set of cell dummies and a set of year dummies within each period. The coefficient on each cell dummy is the estimated average log earnings by cell.

3 I start with 50,908 observations from 10 repeated cross-sections. Of these, I drop 6,638 observations for workers who have worked only part of the year, 1,729 observations for workers aged less than 20 years or over 65, 109 observations for workers with missing education, and two observations for workers

with no reported sex. I drop top executives (1,186 individuals) for which I do not have direct information on the parameters of the indexation mechanism and finally 737 observations for those with earnings below the first percentile or above the top one.

4 Since the aggregation process induces some heteroscedasticity in earnings changes by cell, I take this into account estimating the standard errors.

5 Note that (1) allows for group fixed effects in the specification for levels.

6 The education variable takes the values: 5, 8, 13, 18. The age variable takes the values: 25, 35, 45, 57.5.

7 In this section I describe the salient features of the Scala Mobile. The interested reader can refer to Erickson and Ichino (1995) and Manacorda (2000) (and references therein) for more details on this institution.

8 See Manacorda (2000) for the exact procedure used in this paper to impute SM payments to individuals in the SHIW sample.

9 I have regressed contingent changes by cell in the first period (1978–81) on a third-order polynomial in the level of initial earnings. I have then used the estimated coefficients and the value of current inflation relative to the inflation rate in the first period to make predictions in any other period.

10 This is different from the assumption used in Manacorda (2000). There the identifying assumption is that, within each time period, the gender–earnings gap would have reduced at the same rate across the skills distribution, if not for the Scala Mobile.

References

Card, D. (1983) 'Cost-of-Living Escalators in Major Union Contracts', *Industrial and Labour Relations Review*, vol. 37, pp. 34–48.

Card, D. and T. Lemieux (2000) 'Can Falling Supply Explain the Rising Return to College for Younger Men? A Cohort-Based Analysis,' Center for Labor Economics Working Paper, no. 13 (March) University of California at Berkeley.

Erickson, C. and A. Ichino (1995) 'Wage Differentials in Italy: Market Forces, Institutions, and Inflation', in R. Freeman and L. Katz (eds), *Differences and Changes in the Wage Structure*, NBER Comparative Labor Markets Series (Chicago and London: University of Chicago Press), p. 265–305.

Freeman R. and L. Katz (1995) *Differences and changes in the Wage Structure*, NBER Comparative Labor Markets Series (Chicago and London: University of Chicago Press).

ISTAT, *Annuario Statistico Italiano*, Rome.

Katz, L. and D. Autor (1999) 'Changes in the Wage Structure and Earnings Inequality', in O. Ashenfelter and D. Card (eds), *Handbook of Labor Economics* (Amsterdam: North-Holland), pp. 1463–555.

Katz, L. and K. Murphy (1992) 'Changes in Relative Wages, 1963–1987: Supply and Demand Factors', *Quarterly Journal of Economics*, vol. 107, pp. 35–78.

Manacorda, M. (2000) 'The Fall and Rise of Earnings Inequality in Italy: A Semiparametric Analysis of the Role of Institutional and Market Forces', Center for Labor Economics, University of California at Berkeley (March), mimeo.

Part II
Less Advanced Countries

5

Markets, Human Capital and Inequality: Evidence from Rural China*

Dwayne Benjamin
University of Toronto, Canada
Loren Brandt
University of Toronto, Canada
Paul Glewwe
University of Minnesota, USA

and

Guo Li
World Bank, Washington DC, USA

1 Introduction

Beginning in the 1980s, almost all of the socialist countries replaced their planned economies with economic systems that relied heavily on market forces to determine the production and allocation of goods and services. This transformation has affected the lives of nearly two billion people. Historically, the two main arguments in favour of planned economies were that they are more productive in the long run (because they avoided the inherent instability of market forces, and were able to mobilize more resources for investment than a decentralized system), and that they provide a more equitable distribution of income. The experience of both socialist and market economies in the twentieth century decisively rejects the first argument; it would be hard to find observers of almost any persuasion who claim that planned economies are more productive or more efficient than market economies. Yet the second argument may well be valid; planned economies may indeed be more equitable than market economies. This raises the possibility that some societies may wish to retain at least some of the policies of planned economies, despite their inefficiencies, to maintain a more equitable distribution of income. Consequently, for countries that abandoned

* We thank Richard Freeman and conference participants for comments. Benjamin and Brandt thank the SSHRC for financial support.

planning in favour of the market an important policy issue is the extent to which this policy shift has increased inequality.

This chapter examines inequality in China, the first socialist economy to begin the transformation from a planned to a market economy, using data collected in rural areas of Northeast China in 1995. As explained below, official statistics from China show a substantial increase in inequality in rural areas since the introduction of the market economy, yet there is very little evidence on the causes of this increased inequality and the mechanisms through which it increased. This chapter uses an unusually rich data set to examine these deeper questions.

We begin by reviewing a number of conceptual issues linking the transition from planned to market-based determination of incomes to inequality. In this discussion we highlight the potentially crucial roles that human capital, such as formal education, and market institutions might play in affecting the degree of inequality associated with transition. After providing a brief review of the existing literature on inequality in China, we turn to our own empirical explorations. Rather than trying to summarize the sources of inequality in a country as vast as China, we focus on households in six counties in Liaoning and Hebei. What we sacrifice in breadth of sample is more than made up for in the detailed household-level information.

We confirm some of the findings of the existing literature, namely that non-agricultural income has been the driving force in increases in inequality, and that the educated have been most able to take advantage of economic transition. However, we also show that the existing literature has underemphasized a number of important points. First, most of the inequality we observe is within villages, not driven by differences in income levels across locations. This is especially true of the role of non-agricultural income. Second, the role of human capital is paramount in determining the evolution of inequality, especially in the way it interacts with unevenly developed local market opportunities that characterize economic transition. Third, differences in capital accumulation (savings) across households will contribute even more to inequality in the future. Finally, on a practical note, several important data, measurement, and econometric issues associated with evaluating inequality have been ignored, which underlines the importance of survey design and data collection in future research on inequality in transition economies. Measuring the consequences of economic transition requires household surveys that can keep up with the changing nature of household economic activity. This point has been made before by Ravallion and Chen (1996), and our results confirm their insight.

2 Economic transition and inequality

2.1 Institutional background: transition and China's rural reform

The reform of China's rural sector dates from the late 1970s. The key to the reforms was implementation of the Household Responsibility System (HRS), which marked the re-introduction of family farming to China's agricultural sector after nearly 25 years of collectivized agriculture. Under HRS, households received land-use rights and residual income rights, in return for meeting tax and obligatory sales quotas to the state. The land-use rights were typically distributed to households on an egalitarian basis, using allocation rules based on household size and demographic composition. Ownership, however, remained vested in the village, or former collective, with a majority of villages electing to redistribute use rights to existing and newly formed households every 4–6 years.[1] By 1982, 98 per cent of Chinese rural households were producing under HRS.[2]

Simultaneously, price and marketing reforms were carried out that heralded a long-run decline in government planning of procurement and sales in the farm sector, and permitted new entry in both input and output markets.[3] By the early 1990s, procurement of agricultural products by the state commercial system had fallen to less than a third of total farm sales, down from over 70 per cent in the late 1970s. Restrictions on household sideline activities in agriculture were also relaxed. Combined, these reforms increased the returns to a household's labour in the farm sector, and in the process sparked an enormous boom in agriculture growth. Between 1978 and 1984, agricultural output grew 7.7 per cent per year, or two and a half times the rate between 1952 and 1978.[4]

According to Ho (1994), the incentive effects of HRS had an unintended consequence of making between 25 and 30 per cent of the rural labour force redundant in farming. The policy imperative of finding ways to absorb this surplus labour, fiscal decentralization, and a relaxation of restrictions on entry into industry spurred the development and growth of local enterprise under local government initiative.[5] Between 1980 and 1995, output in township and village enterprises (TVEs) grew at an annual rate of nearly 18 per cent, or nearly twice that in the state sector, while employment increased over the same period from 30 million to 128.6 million.[6] By 1995, output by these firms constituted a quarter of total industrial output. Beginning in the mid-1990s, many of these firms were privatized, and the growth of privately owned enterprises in China's rural sector accelerated under a less discriminatory regime.

Finally, long-standing restrictions on mobility and migration from rural-to-urban and rural-to-rural areas were gradually relaxed beginning in the mid-1980s.[7] Estimates differ, but one commonly cited estimate (Zhao (1999)) puts the number of migrants in China's urban areas at over 50 million. Much of this migration appears to be temporary, with a high percentage of the migrants ultimately returning to the countryside. Through their effect on wage earnings and remittances, these trends have potentially important implications for household behaviour and the distribution of income.

In summary, the reforms of the 1980s and 1990s yielded two main changes in the way that households earn a living. First, the market – however imperfectly developed – replaced egalitarian-motivated, administrative 'assignment' of income to households. Second, the reforms contributed to rapid increases in agricultural productivity, and the emergence of non-agricultural sources of income: economic development, in short. As we proceed, we will try to separate the impact of these two features of economic transition on income inequality, conceptually if not empirically.

2.2 Transition and inequality

Even if every Chinese family got richer after the reforms, it is difficult to imagine inequality falling with a move to market-based income determination. In fact, official statistics show that income inequality in rural China increased significantly the last decade and a half (Benjamin and Brandt (1997, 1999)). Results based on China's (annual) Rural Household Survey, show that the Gini coefficient increased from 0.21 in 1978 to 0.32 in 1994.[8] Khan and Riskin (1998) report results based on data collected in a nationally representative survey for 1988 and 1995, using standard international definitions for household income. They suggest even higher levels of inequality, but confirm the rising trend: the Gini coefficient increased from 0.34 in 1988 to 0.42 in 1995.

So inequality went up, but this tells us very little about why inequality rose, and leaves important questions unanswered. For example, is the increase transitory or permanent? Are the 'losers' in transition likely to fall further behind as the economy grows and becomes more market-oriented? How much of the inequality is the consequence of markets *per se*, as opposed to a product of the accompanying growth and economic development? How much of the inequality is owing to 'market'-based policies, and how much is owing to remaining vestiges of socialist organization? How important are regional or sectoral aspects of the income distribution? Are there any obvious government policies that can lessen some of the diverging trends? Is the rising inequality – regional or otherwise – a threat to the political sustainability of reforms?

Clearly, we cannot address all of these questions. Nevertheless, it is worth spending a short time tracing the economic avenues by which transition can increase inequality. We do this with a simple model that helps identify the key relationships that we want to explore in addressing these questions.

Imagine an economy with two villages A and B, with N_A and N_B people. The distribution of income can be described by:

$$F(y_{1A},\ y_{2A},\ \ldots,\ y_{N_A A},\ y_{1B},\ y_{2B},\ \ldots,\ y_{N_B B}) \equiv F(y) \qquad (1)$$

where y_{hv} is household h's income in village v, and y denotes the vector of everyone's income. In the most general framework, household income will depend on household endowments, x, and local economic conditions, including institutions, I, that determine how endowments convert to income:

$$y_{hv} = g(x; I_v) \qquad (2)$$

The function $g(\bullet)$ summarizes the mapping between endowments, village conditions, and household income. Perhaps the simplest form this function can take is that under a perfect markets model:

$$y_{hv} = w_v^{M'} x \qquad (3)$$

where endowments of villagers are valued at common village market prices, w_v^M, and households earn the full value of their endowments. We can take this model one step further by having factor prices equal across the two villages, in which case income inequality is driven entirely by the inequality of factor endowments. In this framework we can also calculate how much of the total inequality is due to differences in endowments between the villages.[9]

We can think of economic transition as a movement from a function $g(x; I_v)$ with planned-economy (and collectivist) institutions, I_v^C, to a perfect markets-based set of institutions, I_v^M.[10] While no simple model is likely to hold during the transition period, we can imagine the changes in inequality that result from the movement from a collectivist economy with one set of prices, to a market economy with another set of prices.

For simplicity, we begin by ignoring any changes in 'endowments' that result from transition.[11] In a rural economy (under collectivization), the key factors of production are: land, labour, human capital (education), physical capital, political connections, and good luck. Under collectivization, land was collectively owned, and implicitly equally distributed.

This is also true under the current transition, where land use-rights are distributed to households on an essentially constant *per capita* basis. *Per capita* labour is similarly distributed, then as now; the distribution of human capital is less clear. Physical capital, being collectively owned, was more equally distributed under collectivization. Political connections were not equally distributed, nor was good luck (fortune).

Under collectivization, household incomes were determined at the brigade (and team) level. Factor prices (work points) were set so that returns were relatively constant across agricultural tasks. Similarly, household incomes were adjusted on the basis of the number of dependents ('to each according to his needs'). The returns to human capital were further depressed by restricting the ability of households to engage in non-agricultural activities, where returns to education are typically highest. A simple representation of this institutional setting is: $y_{hv} = g(x; I_v^C) = w_v^c x + \gamma' z$, where w_v^C is the vector of endowment prices under collectivization, γ is the return to non-productive characteristics, and z (needs).

Thus, we expect a highly egalitarian distribution of village income, with village-level income inequality deriving only perhaps from differences in household misfortune, such as the illness of household members, or political connections (Morduch and Sicular (1999)). Under this institutional framework, it thus seems reasonable to view the primary source of inequality in the rural economy as deriving from across-village differences in endowments.

How might the distribution of income change with a movement to market pricing of endowments?[12] Since land is still (fairly) equitably distributed under the HRS, that will not likely be a source of changes in inequality. Similarly, the distribution of labour remains essentially equal among households. The main changes will occur in returns to human capital, returns to physical capital, and the return to household fortune. While they do not belong directly in a market economy, it is also likely that political connections will help determine relative success.

There are at least a couple of dimensions in which the returns to human capital might increase. First, under the HRS, better farmers can retain their surpluses, and so the implicit return to human capital in farming will rise. If this human capital is unequally distributed, we expect an increase in overall inequality. Of course, given the constraints on farm size, there are limits to how much inequality can be generated by differences in farming ability. Much more important, with reform restrictions on household engagement in non-agricultural activities were gradually relaxed. It is here where we expect the returns to skill to matter most. Skilled individuals can set up their own businesses, or work for others in non-agricultural pursuits, such as TVEs. To the extent that these opportunities are unequally distributed across households, because of inequality of human capital, connections, or good fortune, then we expect to see an increase in village inequality. With fixed distributions of endowments, this inequality will be reflected in changes in the factor prices. Applied to the entire rural economy, we expect to see an increase in inequality both between and within villages. Some villages, because of advantageous locations, might see greater non-agricultural development.

Of course, transition concerns the entire process of change, not the instantaneous movement to a new set of institutions. One prediction of a more gradual movement to a market-based, less agricultural economy is the emergence of a sector-based 'Kuznets curve'. Overall inequality will be higher, as some regions' average incomes rise through the taking advantage of the new non-agricultural opportunities. This might also be true within villages, as some households move into these more lucrative opportunities sooner than others. Only after a period of time, through the effect of migration, trade, or other factor mobility, will income differences between regions and across households be diminished.

The possibility of spatially uneven rural development, especially driven by the growth of TVEs is prominent in the literature.[13] Through the early 1990s, TVEs were the most rapidly growing segment of the industrial sector, and by 1997 absorbed more than 125 million workers.[14] Conventional wisdom, represented for example by Rozelle (1994), suggests that the growing concentration of these enterprises in richer parts of China led to widening interregional differences. Fiscal decentralization, restrictions on interregional factor mobility and protectionism tended to magnify these gaps.

There are a number of shortcomings to this work. First, some of the analysis, such as Howes and Hussain (1994), and Rozelle (1994), is carried out using *per capita* welfare measures at the aggregate level (e.g. the village, township, county, or provincial level). This has two effects. On the one hand, it effectively underestimates inequality because it ignores any differences arising from differences among households within these administrative units. In other words, it focuses solely on inter-local differences. At the same time, conclusions drawn from these data about the contribution of various factors, e.g. TVEs, to overall inequality are valid only insofar as most of the inequality is arising from differences in mean incomes between these units.

Still, the exercise can be informative about trends in inequality. We conduct this exercise ourselves in Figure 5.1. Here we calculate the country wide (rural) Gini coefficient, assuming that everyone in a province has the same income. This eliminates within province inequality by construction, so that all inequality is due to regional income differences. Figure 5.1 shows similar trends for inequality of both income and consumption. The Gini coefficient rises from around 0.10 in 1980 (at the beginning of the reforms) to 0.15 in 1997. This shows that Chinese inequality rose by 50 per cent because of widening regional disparities. However, if we take other measures of total rural inequality reported earlier as benchmarks, then at most one half (0.10/0.21 and 0.15/0.32) of national inequality can be attributed to income differences between provinces. This fraction is even smaller if we use benchmarks based on most other recent household surveys, where the current Gini coefficients are over 0.40. Thus, at least half, and probably more, of current inequality is owing to income differences among 'neighbouring' households.

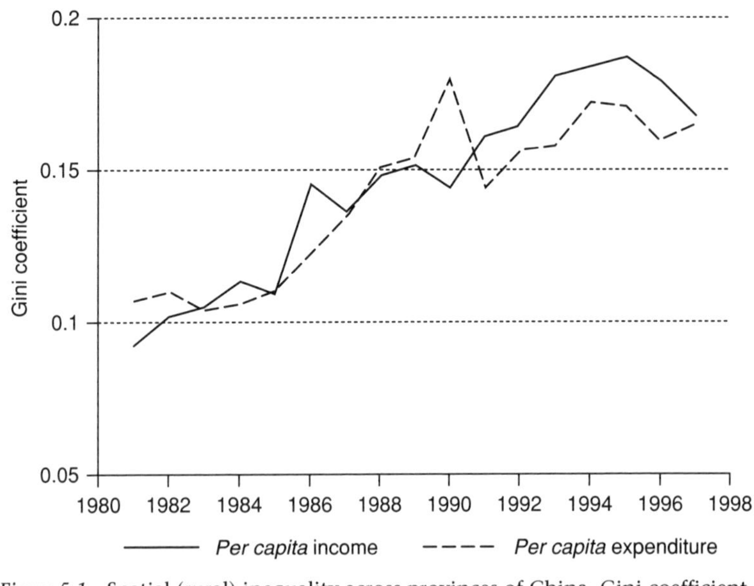

Figure 5.1 Spatial (rural) inequality across provinces of China, Gini coefficient, 1980–98

Notes: Figure 5.1 shows the simulated level of inequality (Gini coefficient), assuming that everyone in a province has the same living standards (*per capita* income or consumption).

Source: Author's calculations based on rural household survey data of the State Statistical Bureau. Provincial means are reported on an annual basis in *Zhongguo Tongji Nianjian* (Statistical Yearbook of China), various years.

Our back-of-the-envelope exercise yields similar results to more formal studies of spatial inequality. For example, Tsui (1991) confirms our estimates of the broad trends in provincial income inequality for the earliest part of our sample. Regarding the contribution of cross-province inequality to the total, Hussain, Lanjouw and Stern (1994) in a sample drawn from 10 provinces, find that only 15 per cent of inequality of household income was owing to provincial income differences. Cheng (1996) employs data from five provinces, and finds under 40 per cent of the inequality owing to cross-province income differences. Clearly, one expects that such results will be sensitive to the provinces examined, and the degree of measurement error in the household data. We pursue these questions later, with our own empirical explorations. The main point we make here is that uneven spatial economic development, owing to TVEs or other types of industrialization, only yields a half-story, at best, about links between transition and inequality. We must look at individual provinces and villages in order to appreciate more fully the impact of institutional change.

Other studies, e.g. Hare (1994), Kahn and Riskin (1998), Tsui (1998), used household-level data to explore the possible impact of uneven rural development on income inequality. These papers focus on the changing composition of rural household income (possibly owing to TVEs). While these studies do not separate the spatial and non-spatial dimensions, they verify the important contribution of income from non-agricultural sources to inequality. But, with the exception of Hare (1994), no attention is given to why income from alternative sources may differ at the household level. This is extremely important if certain kinds of income are more disequalizing that others, and for the design of policies that may help reduce inequality. Also, interpretation is difficult when income from alternative income sources is lumped together, e.g. income from off-farm wages is combined with that from family-run businesses. Insofar as these sources of income are less than perfectly correlated with each other, grouping them together may hide important aspects of emerging inequality and their links to household attributes and the external economic environment with which these households interact.

While it is simple to think of transition as a quick movement from collective to market-based factor prices, it is also misleading. Markets are likely to be imperfect for some time, so the function mapping endowments to incomes is likely much messier than suggested by the market clearing model. Instead of valuing household endowments at market factor prices, they will be valued at shadow prices:

$$y_{hv} = \bar{w}_{hv}{}'x \tag{4}$$

where $\bar{w}_{hv}$ is the vector of shadow factor prices. Shadow prices can depend on both village and individual household characteristics, and may be written as:

$$\bar{w}_{hv} = h(x, I^T, w, \varepsilon) \tag{5}$$

depending on the distribution of endowments, local institutions during transition, I^T, market prices, and other factors. Some aspects of transition might make inequality worse than the case in which the movement to a new market clearing outcome was instantaneous. Shadow prices might also be unequally distributed in a village, so that those with more endowments have their favourable position compounded by advantageous prices. This will especially be the case if there is quantity rationing in the various factor markets, so that those households with poor endowments cannot get 'full value' for their limited endowments of labour and land.

The most interesting possibility concerns the role of human capital. Not only might education be the key to accessing scarce non-agricultural opportunities, but it may play an independent role in helping households cope with dramatic economic change. Economic transition is almost certainly a process where information about income earning opportunities, and how best to take advantage of them, is highly imperfect. The more educated, either directly because of their education, or simply as a reflection of innate ability, may thrive in such an environment. This possibility was raised, most notably by Schultz (1975), but more recently by Rosenzweig (1995) in the context of development, and Orazem and Vodopivec (1995) in the context of transition. Indeed, given the nature of transition in China, the distinction between the pure effects of institutional transition and economic development is fuzzy, at best (Yang (1999)). Combined, we expect the distribution of human capital to interact with the extent of new economic opportunities in complicated ways that imply high returns to education, and increased inequality. On a related note, political connections can be viewed as a special kind of human capital, especially if there is political rationing of the economic opportunities themselves, or of the information about them (Morduch and Sicular (1999)).

At this point, we know very little about how returns to human capital in China's rural sector are evolving. Several recent studies, however, provide some preliminary estimates. First, in contrast to the pre-reform period, the return to education in agriculture during reform is positive (Tsui (1997)). Li and Zhang (1998), using household-level data for Sichuan for 1990, find a return of about 3 per cent to average years of schooling of family members in agriculture. Using the educational level of the household head, they find a similar return, with the return to education of those individuals schooled during the Cultural Revolution slightly lower. They do not find a significant return to schooling in the pre-reform period, consistent with the highly redistributive tendencies of the collective. Dennis Yang (1997) finds a similar return to education during the reform period, but argues that most of it is coming through its effect on the household's managerial capabilities as opposed to any effect it may have on household members' ability to perform routine tasks in agriculture. He finds a slightly lower return to schooling in off-farm wages.[15] An and Yang (1998) analysed the returns to schooling in total household operations and that to agriculture and non-agriculture activity separately. They find a much higher return to total household activity, and suggest that as much as half of the effect of human capital on earnings is coming through its effect on the allocative decisions households are making across sectors. While these results are suggestive, no linkages to inequality are explored.

Finally, the role of physical capital is likely to be very different in a transition economy than in either a purely collective or purely market-based one. Under collectivization, household accumulation of capital was severely restricted. With economic reforms, successful households can accumulate physical capital. With perfect capital markets, this will generate inequality on its own, to the extent that economic success is unequally distributed. However, if capital markets are imperfect, then the effect on inequality will be more severe. Unequal capital holdings might interact with unequal (or limited) access to capital, further compounding income inequality, especially to the extent that capital is a necessary input in the operation of non-agricultural (or even agricultural) businesses. We expect, therefore, the accumulation of capital to combine with the distribution of other factors (especially education) to generate even more inequality of income from non-agricultural sources, and income inequality overall.

In summary, we can think of transition as the movement from administered to market-determined prices of factor endowments. In this way we can speculate on the likely consequences of transition on incomes and inequality. However, transition is more complicated than that. Imperfect development of factor markets is likely to combine with the changing distribution of endowments to worsen inequality.

3 The data

We use two sources of household level data. Our main data set is the 1995 North and Northeast China Living Standards Survey (NNCLSS). We also use the China Health and Nutrition Survey (CHNS) for comparison.

3.1 The NNCLSS: sampling frame

This survey was carried out by the authors and Chinese colleagues in 1995 and extends to 780 households in six counties, 18 townships, and 30 villages in Hebei and Liaoning provinces (North–Northeast China). The survey provides detailed household-level information on income, expenditure (disaggregated for farm and non-farm activity), labour supply, and farm management. The basic structure of the survey was based on the World Bank's Living Standards Measurement Survey, described in more detail by Glewwe and Grosh (1998).

The six counties were not selected randomly, but chosen to correspond to the site of an intensive household-level investigation carried out by Japanese investigators in 1936 and 1937. Five villages in each county were selected, one of which had been fully enumerated in the 1930s. The other four villages in the county – including one from the same township as the administrative capital of the survey; one located in the same township as the village surveyed in the 1930s; and two drawn from a third township – were selected to try to obtain as representative a cross-section in each county as possible. 130 households were surveyed in each county: 50 from the village surveyed in the 1930s, and 20 from each of the remaining four villages. Households were chosen randomly using the most recent village registry.

3.2 The CHNS: sampling frame

We also use data collected for rural households as part of the CHNS. While this survey is longitudinal, we make use only of the single cross-section for 1993 (from the survey carried out in 1994). A detailed description of these data (as well as the data itself) can be obtained at the website.[16] The CHNS data include the provinces of Liaoning, Shandong, Jiangsu, Henan, Hubei, Hunan, Guangxi, and Guizhou, and provide a more nationally representative survey than our 1995 data. Missing, however, are provinces from China's southeastern coast (Zhejiang, Fujian, and Guangdong). In each of the eight provinces, three rural villages in four counties, for a total of 96 villages were sampled. Total sample size (of rural households) is around 1,800, with approximately 20 households sampled per village.

In Figure 5.2 we present a map that shows the locations of the provinces sampled in the two surveys. Only Liaoning is sampled in both surveys. On the same map, we show the *per capita* rural income levels in 1994. Most of the provinces have income levels in the middle two categories: 900–100; and 1,100–1,400 Yuan per year. Liaoning is in the richest category. So, this sample will likely understate the degree of heterogeneity in China as a whole, as it excludes both the very poorest, as well as the richest provinces. That said, it is difficult to imagine coming to any conclusions, statistical or anecdotal, that could generalize across all of China. Our conclusions will never be intended as China-wide statements. That said, each of the sample provinces has a population greater than most developing countries!

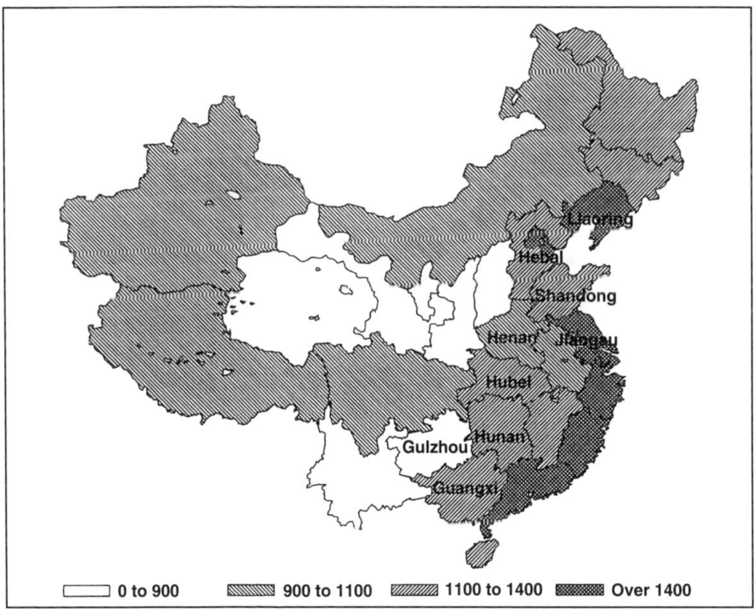

Figure 5.2 Sample provinces and rural *per capita* income, 1994
Notes: Map shows average provincial *per capita* income in 1994. Provinces sampled by CHNS and NCLSS are also labelled.
Source: Authors' calculations based on rural household survey data of the State Statistical Bureau. Provincial means are reported on an annual basis in *Zhongguo Tongji Nianjian* (Statistical Yearbook of China), various years.

4 Empirical results

4.1 Descriptive statistics

Table 5.1 provides descriptive statistics for the various sorts of income earned by households in our 1995 sample. For each source of income, we report unconditional means, including in our calculations any zeroes and negative values as well as the proportion of households with non-missing observations on each source of income. As a measure of income dispersion, we show the Gini coefficient, calculated only over the observations with positive values. The numbers are calculated using all 778 households with complete income and expenditure information, including several possibly 'big' outliers.

Average household, and household *per capita*, income in our sample are 13,071 and 3,510 RMB, respectively. These estimates are higher than those reported on the basis of the SSB's Rural Household Survey. Only 10 per cent of this difference can be attributed to the inclusion of the imputed value of capital services. Other reasons for these differences are probably driven by differences in survey methodology. Our LSMS-style survey is more comprehensive in its enumeration of income sources, and includes several built-in consistency checks with which to 'double-check' estimated income. Turning to consumption, average household expenditure is considerably lower than income, but still at a level that suggests that previous estimates of living standards have understated household incomes. At 1994 exchange rates, our estimate implies a *per capita*l income of US$400. Purchasing power parity (PPP) calculations suggest *per capita* income three times higher.[17] The difference between income and expenditure also implies significant household savings, a point to which we return later.

Farming is the most important economic activity for these households: it accounts for nearly half of total income, and all but 2 per cent of the households have positive farm income. In turn, nearly three-quarters of farm income comes from cropping income (mostly corn in Hebei, and rice and corn in Liaoning), with the remainder from sidelines such as vegetable gardens and greenhouses. Next important to farming, family-run businesses are the source of slightly more than 20 per cent of total household income.[18] Nearly a third of all households, or 247 households, are involved in a total of 274 non-agriculture businesses of some kind, with 10 per cent of the households involved in more than one enterprise. A third of the enterprises are in commerce, with 15 per cent in construction and transportation. On average, 2.2 individuals work in these enterprises, with the

Table 5.1 Sources and distribution of household income

Source of income	*Mean*[1]	*Percentage not zero*	*Gini coefficient*[2]
Men's wages	1,578	41	0.41
Women's wages	412	16	0.4
Farm income[4]	5714	98	0.48
Animal husbandry[5]	1506	77	0.75
Non-agricultural family[6] Enterprises	1837	30	0.64
Other income[7]	959	65	0.66
Imputed capital services (house + durables)	1065	100	0.39
Total income[3]	13,071	100	0.4
Total expenditure[3]	8378	100	0.28
***Per capita* income**	3510	100	0.39
***Per capita* expenditure**	2250	100	0.26

Notes: 1. Means are presented over the whole sample (778 households) in the first two columns.
2. The Gini coefficient is calculated only over those households with positive income from that particular source.
3. Total income is the sum of income from all sources including the imputed value of owner occupied housing and durables (imputed capital services). Similarly, total expenditure includes the value of imputed capital services.
4. Farm income includes crop income, plus income from agricultural sidelines (vegetables, fruit, wood, and greenhouses) and income from the sale of crop by-products.
5. Animal husbandry includes income from animal husbandry plus aqua-culture and agricultural businesses reported in the 'family-run business' section of the survey that are mostly poultry farms.
6. Non-agricultural family enterprises are family run businesses that are not directly 'agricultural'.
7. Other income includes rental income, remittances, transfer income, and interest income.

average enterprise having been in operation for almost five and a half years. Wage income is the source of about 15 per cent of total income, with three-quarters of that coming from male wages; 40 per cent of the households report income from this source.[19] The remainder of income comes from animal husbandry and an 'other' category, which includes such things as interest income, remittances, pension income, etc.

The Gini coefficient for household income for the entire sample is 0.40, and marginally lower for *per capita* household income. Our estimate is similar to that obtained by Khan and Riskin (1998) in a nationally representative survey that used comparable measures of income. Among the sources of income, income from wages and farm income are the most equitably distributed. The latter is largely a product of a fairly egalitarian distribution of land at the village level. The most unequally distributed items, on the other hand, are income from family-run business, animal husbandry, and our 'other' category. This suggests that we look to these items in our analysis of the factors underlying the increase in inequality.

Finally, household expenditure, a potentially superior estimate of long-run living standards, is considerably more equally distributed than income, with a Gini coefficient for household expenditure of 0.28. In Figure 5.3, we graph the kernel densities for these two measures, which reveals a much fatter upper tail for income. While some of this difference may be the usual product of measurement error in income relative to consumption, it may also reflect genuine differences between income and consumption, and potentially important savings behaviour.

4.2 Spatial dimensions of inequality

Following on the issues raised in our discussion of Figure 5.1, we now explore how much of the inequality in our sample is at the local level, as opposed to differences in average incomes across regions. For the pre-reform era, it is generally believed that most of the inequality was eliminated within localities, but not across regions.[20] With reforms, we might expect inequality to increase within villages, as collectivist institutions eroded. However, we might also expect inequality to increase

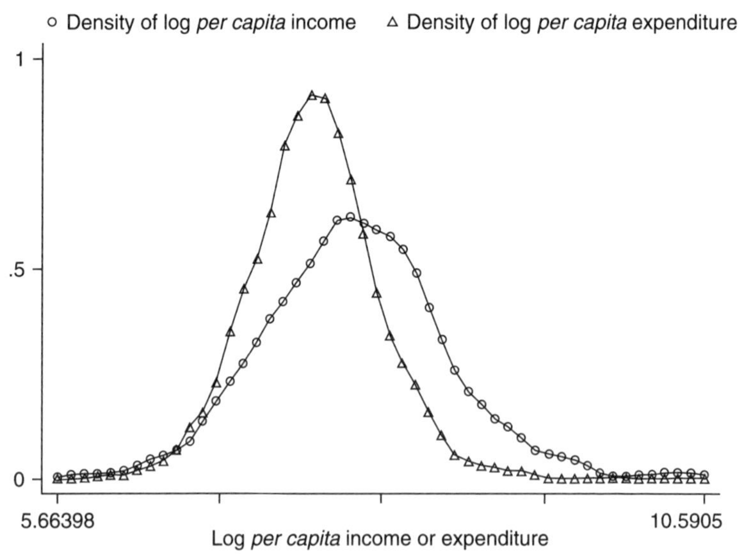

Figure 5.3 Kernel density estimates of log *per capita* income and expenditure

across regions as well, as some areas are in a better position to take advantage of non-agricultural and other opportunities arising as a product of market liberalization and reform. In the exercises below, we decompose inequality into that part due to differences between and within localities.

Table 5.2 reports decomposition estimates for a variety of measures of income and expenditure inequality, using a number of alternative definitions of 'location' (village, county and province). Expenditure data are not provided for the CHNS data, and so we report results for income only for that sample.[21] We take as our benchmark the Gini coefficient for income or expenditure. We also show the variance of logs and the Theil index. The decompositions are most easily done and explained using the variance of logs: the R^2 from a regression of log income on

Table 5.2 Proportion of income variation/inequality explained by location, 1993 and 1995

	TOTAL[3]	*Province*[4]	*County*[4]	*Village*[4]
	Per capita expenditure, 1995 Survey[1,5]			
Gini	0.261			
Variance of log(pcx)	0.219	0.09	0.167	0.249
Theil *L*	0.101	0.097	0.169	0.304
Theil *T*	0.128	0.077	0.13	0.248
	Per capita income, 1995 Survey[5]			
Gini	0.385			
Variance of log(pcy)	0.464	0.057	0.117	0.245
Theil *L*	0.238	0.098	0.167	0.329
Theil *T*	0.291	0.08	0.134	0.305
	Per capita income, CHNS 1993 Survey[2,6]			
Gini	0.495			
Variance of log(pcy)	1.175	0.036	0.151	0.267
Theil *L*	0.496	0.073	0.166	0.29
Theil *T*	0.469	0.076	0.173	0.303

Notes: 1. Sample size for the 1995 data is 773 for income, and 778 for expenditure. 2. Sample size for the 1993 CHNS is 1,653 (positive income observations). 3. TOTAL indicates the total sample inequality for each measure of inequality. 4. The remaining three columns show the proportion of each inequality index that is explained by differences in income across different geographic units (province, county, and village). 5. For the 1995 data, there are five villages in each of six countries (30 villages), split evenly between two provinces. 6. For the CHNS data, there are three villages in four counties in each of eight provinces (for a total of 32 counties and 96 villages).

location dummies provides an estimate of the percentage of the variation in log *per capita* income explained by location. The remainder represents the percentage arising from within location variation. We also report the decomposition for the Theil index, which has a similar interpretation, but is generally a preferred inequality index.

The results consistently show that most of the inequality is within, not between, whichever inequality index is chosen. This means that while differences in such factors as the level of rural industrial development, soil quality, nearness to urban centres, etc. affect mean incomes across localities, most of the inequality still comes from differences among households within these locations. For the NNCLSS, 25–30 per cent of the variation in both income and expenditure comes from between village differences, with even lower percentages arising from differences at the country or provincial level. The CHNS data suggest a similar spatial pattern, despite the fact that the CHNS sampling frame was chosen to maximize differences in economic development across villages. The basic insight to be gained from these decompositions is that understanding inequality in rural China requires understanding income determination within villages.

4.3 Inequality and sources of income

Which income sources generate the most inequality? We decompose income inequality by source using a straightforward method employed by Shorrocks (1982, 1983). With K sources of income, total income for household i is given by:

$$y_i = \sum_{k=1}^{K} y_{ik}$$

The vector of economy wide household incomes is given by $Y = Y_1 + Y_2 + \ldots + Y_k$, where Y and Y_k are vectors of total household income and income from source k for the whole economy. Average income is given by: $\bar{Y} = \bar{Y}_1 + \bar{Y}_2 + \ldots + \bar{Y}_k$. An increase in the mean income of source k by 1 penny leads to an increase in the mean of total income by one penny. A first order estimate of the proportional increase in mean total income is given by:

$$W_k = \frac{\mu_k}{\mu} \qquad (6)$$

where W_k is the share of income source k in total income, μ_k is mean income from source k, and μ is total mean income. So, a 1 per cent increase in income source k will increase average income by W_k per cent: the more important the income source is, the larger the increase in mean income will be.

To what extent does the same logic apply to measures of inequality? Does an increase in the dispersion of Y_k lead to an increase of inequality in direct proportion to its income share, W_k? Stated differently, under what conditions can we write an equality index, $I(Y)$, as:

$$I(Y) = \sum_{k=1}^{K} W_k I(Y_k) \tag{7}$$

This simple decomposition can be done only if each source of income is perfectly correlated with total income, i.e. if everyone is a 'clone' in terms of the structure of income, except in total income.[22] In such a case, an increase in the inequality of income source k will increase total income inequality in direct proportion to its share of total income.

However, to the extent that a particular type of income is earned by the rich, then an increase in inequality of this source of income is going to benefit the rich disproportionately, and so increase inequality in excess of its share of total income. On the other hand, an increase in inequality of income correlated with being poor will disproportionately benefit the poor, and so decrease inequality. Both the correlation of the source of income with total income, and its relative size will matter in any decomposition.

Shorrocks (1982) shows that, under reasonable conditions, a decomposition of total inequality can be calculated, so that the fraction of total inequality deriving from Y_k (for any inequality index) is:

$$S_k = \frac{\text{cov}(Y_k,\ Y)}{\text{var}(Y)} \tag{8}$$

How can we interpret S_k? First, we can compare S_k to zero. If S_k is negative, increases in the inequality of income source k will actually reduce inequality because of the income source earned by (and distributed to) the poor. Second, we can compare S_k to W_k. Since the rich tend to earn more income from all sources, increases in inequality of any income type increases overall income inequality. However, some sources may be relatively less disequalizing, and W_k is a useful benchmark. If S_k is greater than W_k, increases in the inequality of the distribution of Y_k can be viewed as disproportionately increasing income inequality.

4.3.1 Estimation issues

The parameter of interest is S_k, which can be estimated as the coefficient from a regression of y_{ik} on y_i:

$$y_{ik} = \alpha_k + \beta_k y_i + \varepsilon_{ik} \tag{9}$$

The error term is worth noticing. For starters, we only have a sample (not the population) and must recognize that there is sampling error. More seriously, the error term may contain less benign components. Measurement error is the most significant possibility. Assume that each source of income is measured as follows:

$$y^*_{ik} = y_{ik} + v_{ik} \tag{10}$$

where y^*_{ik} is the measured income, and y_{ik} (as before) is the true value. Then, because measured y_i is the sum of the various y_{ik}, there is a possibility of correlation between y_i and ε_{ik}. This generates two possible biases. First, the plim of $\hat{\beta}_k$ may exceed β_k, because of the positive correlation between the common measurement error in components in y_{ik} and y_i. For example, if a household overstates its non-farm income, this will spill over to the households total income. We will then overestimate the true association between non-farm income and total income. Second, we may instead get the usual attenuation bias of measurement error, in which case we will understate β_k.

This potential statistical problem can be addressed most easily by instrumental variable (IV) techniques. In our case we use *per capita* expenditure as an instrument for *per capita* income, because it is (mostly) measured independently of income.[23] Even if the instrument is imperfect, this exercise allows us to explore the possible sensitivity of our conclusions to measurement error. Intuitively, we have two separate indicators for a household's position in the income distribution, and thus an alternative way to estimate the correlation between the various income sources and total income.

For the NNCLSS, we calculate the decompositions over two samples: the full sample, and one with the richest household dropped (this household had income over 200,000). This household is rich because of high non-farm business income, so the decompositions are sensitive to inclusion of this household. The results are reported in Table 5.3. For each source of income, we report three columns of numbers: (1) The share of the source of income in total income (the benchmark W_k); (2) The raw correlation coefficient (i.e. the OLS coefficient from the regression of income of type *k* on total income); and (3) The 2SLS estimate of this coefficient (i.e. the measurement error corrected correlation).

Looking at the full sample ((1)–(3) columns), most income sources contribute to inequality in approximate proportion to their share of income. Women's wages have a small negative (equalizing) contribution, while men's wages contribute less to inequality than their share. Crop income contributes much less than its share to inequality. Restrictions on land ownership, and the administrative allocation of land, effectively place an upper bound on how much a household can earn from farming. In contrast, animal husbandry contributes more than its share, and non-farm family businesses contribute the most to inequality. These results suggest that it is income from these enterprises, not wages from TVEs, that is generating most of the inequality. The OLS and 2SLS coefficients do not differ significantly; however, the results are sensitive to the exclusion of the richest household. Dropping this household reduces the contribution of non-farm business income, but it does not change the overall story: in order to understand rural inequality we must understand non-agricultural income.

In the bottom panel of Table 5.3, we show comparable results using the CHNS. Even though the sampling frame is different, we find similar patterns to the NNCLSS. First, the income shares of each type are similar, even though the CHNS has some built-in gaps (such as the value of capital services). Crop income is the largest source of income, but contributes significantly less than its share to inequality. On the other hand, both animal husbandry and non-agricultural businesses contribute significantly more to inequality than their shares suggest. Our NNCLSS results do not seem to be an artifact of the sample.

In Table 5.4, we combine the previous two exercises, and explore how the contribution to inequality by income source varies over space. Our questions are: (1) How much of the contribution of non-agricultural income is driven by spatial differences in non-agricultural development? And (2) Does the contribution of non-agricultural income to inequality itself vary across villages? In columns (2) and (3), we show the coefficients that correspond to those reported in Table 5.3, except that we include village fixed effects. Here, we see that adding village fixed effects does not change the conclusions drawn from Table 5.3: differential incomes from non-agricultural sources contribute significantly more to within village inequality than is expected on the basis of their share in income. *F*-tests for village interaction terms show that the contribution of non-agricultural income to village inequality does vary across villages – perhaps owing to differences in local institutions.

Table 5.3 Decompositions of income inequality by source of income, 1993 and 1995

	Full 1995 sample			*1995 sample excluding highest income*[5]		
	Share[1] (*1*)	*OLS*[2] (*2*)	*2SLS*[3] (*3*)	*Share* (*4*)	*OLS* (*5*)	*2SLS* (*6*)
Source:						
Other income	0.073	0.061	0.090	0.072	0.047	0.080
Durables and housing	0.081	0.029	0.059	0.082	0.035	0.077
Men's wages	0.120	0.023	0.054	0.123	0.031	0.075
Women's wages	0.031	−0.001	0.015	0.032	0	0.020
Crop income	0.435	0.236	0.178	0.444	0.302	0.247
Non-ag businesses	0.141	0.433	0.478	0.125	0.312	0.333
Animal husbandry	0.119	0.219	0.125	0.122	0.273	0.168
	CHNS 1993 sample[6]					
	Mean[4]	*Share*	*OLS*			
Other income (*per capita*)	82	0.096	0.029			
Wage income (*per capita*)	206	0.240	0.147			
Crop income (*per capita*)	294	0.344	0.132			
Non-ag businesses (*per capita*)	187	0.219	0.379			
Animal husbandry (*per capita*)	51	0.059	0.287			
Total *per capita* income	856					

Notes: 1. The shares are the percentages of household income accounted for by each source of income. 2. OLS is the OLS estimate of the correlation between total *per capita* income and the *per capita* income of a given type. 3. 2SLS is the 2SLS estimate of this correlation, using total *per capita* expenditure (less capital services) as an instrument. This instrument is not available for the CHNS sample. 4. All means and correlations are reported weighted by the number of individuals in the household. 5. The income sources for the 1995 sample are described in Table 5.1. 6. For the CHNS, analogous income categories are created. Sample size in the CHNS is 1,653 (the number of households with positive income).

However, when the village interactions are estimated by 2SLS, we do not find statistically significant differences across villages. Perhaps the OLS result is owing to the higher fraction of measurement error at the village level, or alternatively, our results reflect the imprecision with which the instruments can predict differences in income between villagers.

4.4 Household income and consumption

We begin with an overview in Table 5.5 of the relationship between household endowments and total income and consumption. In the next section (4.5) we look in more detail at how these productive characteristics, such as land and human capital, affect the composition of income.

We specify the land variables as a combination of both the amount of land that the household has been allocated, and a dummy for whether or not the household has any land. It appears that land allocation is partially endogenous to the type of income earned. Rich households with sizable non-agricultural enterprises do not receive allocated land, or

Table 5.4 Decompositions of income inequality by source of income interactions with spatial inequality, 1993 and 1995[1,6]

		Full 1995 sample			
		Coefficients on PCY with village fixed effects		*F-Tests for different coefficients, by village*	
	Share[3] (1)	*OLS*[4] (2)	*2SLS*[5] (3)	*OLS* (4)	*2SLS* (5)
Source:					
Other income	0.073	0.064	0.101	4.71 (0.000)	1.22 (0.201)
Durables and housing	0.081	0.024	0.059	3.51 (0.000)	1.65 (0.018)
Men's wages	0.12	0.029	0.07	6.20 (0.000)	1.21 (0.204)
Women's wages	0.031	−0.001	0.013	0.72 (0.862)	1.02 (0.438)
Crop income	0.435	0.179	0.073	10.95 (0.000)	1.81 (0.006)
Non-ag businesses	0.141	0.468	0.56	10.09 (0.000)	1.28 (0.151)
Animal husbandry	0.119	0.237	0.122	5.69 (0.000)	0.38 (0.999)
		1995 sample excluding highest income[7]			
Other income	0.072	0.048	0.089	4.73 (0.000)	1.04 (0.416)
Durables and housing	0.082	0.029	0.08	2.75 (0.000)	0.91 (0.601)
Men's wages	0.123	0.038	0.099	5.49 (0.000)	1.04 (0.416)
Women's wages	0.032	−0.001	0.018	0.72 (0.869)	1.00 (0.470)
Crop income	0.444	0.249	0.149	7.93 (0.000)	1.33 (0.119)
Non-ag businesses	0.125	0.333	0.376	12.97 (0.000)	1.48 (0.051)
Animal husbandry	0.122	0.304	0.189	14.13 (0.000)	0.82 (0.074)

Notes: 1. All specifications are the same as in Table 5.3, except that village fixed effects have been added. 2. The *F*-tests (*p*-values in parentheses) are tests of the joint significance of the village × income interaction terms in a separate analysis of covariance specification. 3. The shares are the percentages of household income accounted for by each source of income. 4. OLS is the OLS estimate of the correlation between total *per capita* income and the *per capita* income of a given type (with village fixed effects). 5. 2SLS is the 2SLS estimate of this correlation, using total *per capita* expenditure (less capital services) and village interactions with this variable as instruments. 6. All means and correlations are reported weighted by the number of individuals in the household. 7. The income sources for the 1995 sample are described in Table 5.1.

Table 5.5 Determinants of household *per capita* income and consumption (standard errors in parentheses)[1,4]

	ln PCY		*ln PCX*	
	(I)	*(II)*[2]	*(III)*[2]	*(IV)*[2]
Average years of schooling of adults in the household	0.081	0.066	0.052 (0.008)	0.038 (0.008)
Number of members with technical training	0.171 (0.043)	0.109 (0.042)	0.135 (0.030)	0.103 (0.028)
Number of members with apprentice training	0.006 (0.045)	−0.016 (0.043)	0.040 (0.031)	0.016 (0.028)
Indicator for having allocated land	−1.389 (0.199)	−1.093 (0.218)	−0.547 (0.136)	−0.441 (0.145)
Log of allocated land	0.307 (0.032)	0.309 (0.036)	0.077 (0.022)	0.097 (0.024)
Share of land suffering adverse shock	−0.558 (0.143)	−0.613 (0.167)	−0.073 (0.098)	−0.208 (0.111)
Log household size	−0.510 (0.086)	−0.487 (0.085)	−0.370 (0.059)	−0.399 (0.057)
F-test for village fixed effects	n.a.	5.53 (0.000)	n.a.	7.23 (0.000)
F-test for village × education[3]	n.a.	1.51 (0.04)	n.a.	1.22 (0.20)
R^2	0.24	0.381	0.26	0.43

Notes: 1. The coefficients are from an OLS regression of ln PCY (*per capita* income) or ln PCX (*per capita* expenditure) on the variables shown in the table, plus controls for land quality and household age–sex structure (the coefficients of which are not shown). 2. In columns (II) and (IV), village fixed effects are added, with the *F*-test and *p*-value of the joint significance of the village fixed effects also reported. 3. In a separate specification, interaction effects between village and education (years of schooling) are added to the same village fixed effects-based specification. The *F*-tests for these interaction terms are reported in columns (II) and (IV). 4. The sample sizes are 773 for income, and 778 for expenditures. na – not available or applicable.

elect to return it, so the coefficient on whether a household has land is negative. However, once we account for this heterogeneity, it appears that an increase in land holdings increases *per capita* income. Unless land were distributed disproportionately to the poor, this implies that an increase in land inequality leads to higher inequality (conditional on all other sources of income remaining unchanged). While not an endowment variable *per se*, if a household suffers an adverse production shock (measured in terms of the reduction in output from a normal year), its income falls significantly, but expenditures do not. One interpretation of this pattern of coefficients is that households are able to smooth their consumption relatively more than their income in response to bad luck.

This suggests that the large gap between income and consumption may be related to savings (as opposed to only measurement error), and that these savings are used, at least partially, to smooth consumption.

Turning to the human capital variables, the coefficient on years of schooling implies a rate of return to schooling of around 6.6 per cent for income, and 3.8 per cent for expenditure.[24] Unless there is a complicated covariance of the measurement error in income and consumption with education, the difference between the income and expenditure coefficients may reflect a correlation between savings rates and education. Technical training also has a significant rate of return, for both income and consumption, but apprentice training is insignificant. In order to see whether the rate of return to schooling varies across villages, we estimated an ANOVA, controlling for the same set of variables as above. An *F*-test for the interaction terms between education and the village dummies is significant at the 5 per cent level. Later on, we explore in more detail how these differences across villages in the rate of return to human capital affect income inequality.

4.5 Household earnings activities

In Table 5.6 we explore the connections between education and the composition of income. Specifically, we report estimates of Probit equations for whether a household engages in animal husbandry, male wage labour, female wage labour, or non-agricultural farm businesses. The covariates are the same as in Table 5.5, including village fixed effects. The most important result is that education plays only a small role in determining what activities households engage in. Those households raising animals tend to be slightly less educated, while those working off the farm for wages, especially wage labour are slightly more educated, with average household education being highly related to female participation in wage labour. Most interestingly, schooling does not seem to matter in determining whether a household is operating non-agricultural business. Having family members with either technical or apprentice training, on the other hand, increases the likelihood of having male members working off the farm, or the family engaged in non-agricultural businesses.

Table 5.7 shows the estimated 'returns to schooling' for the various types of income. These regressions are estimated only over those households with positive earnings, so there may be selectivity biases on the various coefficients. Fixing this bias is impossible in the context of this chapter. However, we can speculate about its likely consequences. Regarding the education coefficient, if there is a positive rate of return to schooling for a given source of income, and households are positively selected into an activity, then the OLS coefficients will be biased downwards (towards zero). These biases might not be large, given the absence of strong education effects on most activity in Table 5.6, but we must note that the selection is not just into a specific activity, but also on whether a household has positive earnings (as opposed to losses) in that activity, which might be more strongly selected. For crop income and animal husbandry, we find only very small, but positive rates of return. Our estimates are consistent with those obtained in the previous literature. However, we estimate high rates of return in wage labour and non-agricultural income. Moreover, aggregating all types of non-crop income, we estimate a rate of return of about 10 per cent. This suggests that households have a rate of return to schooling, not just within each activity, but also in the construction of a portfolio of income types. The slightly higher return over all non-crop income might also reflect the

Table 5.6 Probits for household engagement in various activities (standard errors in parentheses)[1,3,4]

	Animal husbandry (1)	*Male wage labour (2)*	*Female wage labour (3)*	*Non-ag business (4)*
Mean probability:[2]	0.78	0.43	0.19	0.33
Average years of schooling of adults in the household	−0.072 (0.038)	0.076 (0.030)	0.151 (0.042)	−0.006 (0.031)
Number of members with technical training	0.150 (0.128)	0.241	−0.092	0.183 (0.106)
Number of members with apprentice training	0.032 (0.127)	0.182 (0.108)	0.017	0.299 (0.106)
Indicator for having allocated land	−0.348 (0.582)	0.838 (0.560)	1.760 (0.882)	0.17
Log of allocated land	0.129 (0.102)	−0.174 (0.094)	−0.104 (0.123)	−0.198
Share of land suffering adverse shock	0.043 (0.492)	0.059 (0.428)	0.063 (0.546)	−0.818
Log household size	0.312 (0.253)	0.564 (0.221)	2.189 (0.326)	0.534

Notes: 1. The coefficients are the estimated coefficients from Probit estimation of whether a household has income from a particular source. 2. The fraction of households engaged in each activity is in the mean probability row. 3. All equations include the same regressors as reported in Table 5.5, including village fixed effects. Some of the village effects predict an activity perfectly. 4. All estimation is conducted with sample weights equal to household size.

Table 5.7 Determinants of levels of household *per capita* income in various activities (standard errors in parentheses)[1,2]

	Crop income (1)	*Animal husbandry (2)*	*Male wage labour (3)*	*Female wage labour (4)*	*Non-ag business (5)*	*All Non-crop[3] (6)*
Average years of schooling of adults in the household	0.020 (0.013)	0.021 (0.045)	0.088 (0.026)	0.177 (0.062)	0.084 (0.061)	0.098 (0.026)
Number of members with technical training	−0.030 (0.046)	−0.080 (0.146)	0.178	0.204 (0.139)	0.133 (0.193)	0.237 (0.088)
Number of members with apprentice training	−0.055 (0.046)	−0.244 (0.163)	0.050 (0.086)	−0.032	−0.050 (0.179)	0.101 (0.091)
Indicator for having allocated land	−1.774 (0.257)	−1.952 (0.981)	0.794 (0.528)	2.660 (1.347)	−0.233	0.810 (0.489)
Log of allocated land	0.775 (0.039)	0.181 (0.145)	−0.211 (0.090)	−0.176 (0.187)	0.123	−0.208 (0.083)
Share of land suffering adverse shock	−0.942 (0.180)	−0.321 (0.651)	−0.168 (0.394)	−0.050 (0.771)	0.539 (0.926)	−0.073 (0.369)
Log household size	−0.903 (0.092)	−0.239 (0.329)	−0.489 (0.202)	−0.948 (0.424)	−0.746 (0.464)	0.155
Sample size	741	446	320	125	213	659
R^2	0.62	0.233	0.42	0.63	0.28	0.23

Notes: 1. The coefficients are estimated from regressions of log *per capita* income of each type on the same set of explanatory variables as described in Table 5.5 (including village fixed effects). 2. Regressions are weighted by household size. 3. 'All non-crop' is income from all income categories except crops and 'non-labour' income, i.e. the sum of animal husbandry, wage labour, and non-agricultural businesses.

fact that there is less selection bias in this equation, since fewer households are excluded. In summary, we find high rates of return to schooling in non-agricultural pursuits, though entrance into these activities is less related to education.

4.6 Savings and capital accumulation

In most empirical studies of inequality, measurement considerations dominate the choice between income and consumption (expenditures) as the measure of living standards. On these grounds, we usually prefer expenditures, since they tend to be better measured in developing countries. Furthermore, long run living standards are probably best reflected in consumption levels, as even accurately measured income may contain a significant transitory component. Our intention was to follow conventional practice, and draw most of our conclusions from the expenditure results. However, the divergence between income and consumption may reflect more than measurement error and transitory income shocks. As this is an economy in transition, households may not have settled into long run consumption patterns. In particular, high income households may be re-investing (saving) a considerable portion of their income, possibly in response to poorly developed external credit markets. In this case, we understate the differences in long-run living standards between households if we focus on consumption alone. Current income may be disproportionately related to future income (and consumption) through current savings. Essentially, savings is a mechanism by which 'luck' and economic success will be compounded in a transition economy, even more than that implied by equilibrium models, suggested (for example) by Deaton and Paxson (1994) for Taiwan. We explore this possibility in detail.

As we previously pointed out, there is a considerable gap between household income and expenditures. For any individual household, this is not surprising given the degree of measurement error in household surveys. While it is tempting to interpret the difference between income and consumption as savings, the difference ('savings') may be mostly noise. More surprising, however, is the extraordinary level of implied savings across the whole sample. Evaluated at the median, household income (excluding capital services) is 9,352 versus 6,449 in expenditures, implying household savings of 2,903–a savings rate of 31 per cent. Usually, reporting-error leads to higher levels of expenditure than income (which is under-reported), and negative 'savings.' We thus consider the possibility that some of this gap is genuine savings.

Our objective in this section is quite limited. We wish to evaluate whether, in fact, there appears to be savings 'signal' in the difference between income and consumption, and thus that savings rates may be genuinely high. We already saw indirect evidence of savings in Table 5.5, where we noted the differential response of income and consumption to an agricultural production shock. This was consistent with savings being used for consumption smoothing (self-insurance). With imperfect markets and diminished redistributive institutions, and presumably riskier income streams, it is plausible that households now engage in more precautionary savings.

Our main cross-check is to evaluate the relationship between contemporaneous savings and the estimated stock of household wealth, beginning with some 'back-of-the envelope' calculations. We construct estimates of the total investment by households in the accumulation of physical and financial assets. Financial assets consist of deposits in financial institutions, cash on hand, and net borrowing through formal and informal lending. We have year-end figures for each of these. We also have detailed data on durable goods expenditure, both that for household use, e.g. housing stock, and that used in agriculture and non-agriculture business activities. For these assets, we know the year purchased and the price paid. Almost all of this asset accumulation occurred in the 1980s and 1990s. In principal, total investment in asset accumulation should equal the sum of household savings over this period. These totals should not be confused with (but are related to) estimated net wealth, the current value of these assets. The difference between the two is depreciation and the effect of inflation on the value of these assets. Average total accumulated investment in productive and non-productive assets equals 25,856 yuan, and the median is 14 500, or almost 1.5 times estimated median income. Out of this total investment, forty percent represents the fixed investment in agriculture and non-agriculture activity. Given the significant increases in nominal incomes between 1980 and 1995, it takes savings levels on the order of 30% in order to generate the estimated level of wealth. Given the rapid development of family enterprises and imperfect or nonexistent capital markets, such levels of savings might be necessary.

A more formal exploration is presented in Table 8. Define the 'rate of savings,' r_s, as:

$$\ln\left(\frac{\text{income}}{\text{expenditures}}\right) = \ln(pcy) - \ln(pcx) \equiv r_s$$

In column (I), we show the results of regressing r_s on the same set of explanatory variables as Table 5.7. First note that the savings rate is positively related to the level of schooling. Perhaps more educated households have lower discount rates; perhaps they have better investment opportunities; or possibly they are better decision makers. Second, we confirm that adverse production shocks reduce savings.

In columns II and III, we link assets to income. While we expect the two variables are positively related, the more interesting question is whether the elasticity is greater than one. If so, it suggests that wealth increases more than proportionately with income, i.e., that wealth is highly 'disequalizing' or associated with high incomes. This suggests that not only is wealth unequally distributed (its Gini coefficient is 0.58), but that high income households have a disproportionate share of wealth. In column II we report OLS estimates, while in column III we report 2SLS estimates, where we try to correct for measurement in ln (pcy) using ln (pcx) as an instrument (like we did in tables 3 and 4). The OLS and 2SLS results are sufficiently different to lead to suspicion of measurement error bias. Focusing on the 2SLS results, the estimated elasticity is 1.5 and significantly higher than 1.0, suggesting that if these assets yield future income, it will accrue to higher income earners, and further increase inequality.

In columns IV–VI we try to see whether there is any significant relationship between the 'savings rate,' and accumulated wealth. In column (IV), we estimate the 'reduced form', observing that assets are highly related to the same variables as the 'savings rate,' most notably education and the production shock. In the next two columns, we estimate the 'structural' asset equation by OLS and 2SLS, instrumenting the savings rate for measurement error (since we know that the difference between income and expenditure will be mostly noise). We use the indicator of the degree of production shock, farm size, and whether there are young children or teenagers in the household as instruments for the savings rate. We thus assume that these instruments affect assets only through the savings rate. We use overidentification tests to confirm the internal consistency of the instruments, and also show that empirically there is no evidence of a correlation between the identifying instruments and the error term of the asset equation. The results in Column VI suggest that the rate of "savings" is significantly, positively related to the level of accumulated assets, with an elasticity of almost one, which suggests a proportional relationship between the savings rate and the level of wealth.

All of this evidence suggests that there is genuinely high savings by these households. This fact needs to be taken into account in any picture of inequality in the transition to a market economy. Given the significant rate of savings, especially by high income households, we might expect the level of inequality to be even higher in the future. Our results also suggest that the role of imperfectly developed capital markets may be greater than previously believed, not just for economic efficiency, but also for income inequality.

Table 5.8 Savings and Asset Accumulation (standard errors in parentheses)

	I	*II*	*III*	*IV*	*V*	*VI*
Dependent variable:	*Savings 'rate'*	*ln per capita assets*	*ln per capita assets*	*ln per capita assets*	*ln per capita assets*	*ln per capita assets*
Explanatory variable:	*OLS*	*OLS*	*2SLS*	*OLS*	*OLS*	*2SLS*
Savings 'rate'					0.113 (0.058)	0.821 (0.256)
Ln per capita income		0.602 (0.049)	1.493 (0.118)			
Average years of schooling of the adults in the household	0.028 (0.011)			0.081 (0.018)	0.101 (0.015)	0.091 (0.017)
Number of members with technical training	0.006 (0.039)			0.246 (0.063)	0.221 (0.062)	0.237 (0.068)
Number of members with apprentice training	−0.032 (0.040)			0.117 (0.064)	0.100 (0.063)	0.120 (0.069)
Fraction of land suffering adverse shock	−0.408 (0.158)			−0.563 (0.252)		
R-squared	0.17	0.28	–	0.27	0.23	0.07

Notes: (1) Savings is measured as ln(income) – ln (expenditure); (2) Assets are measured as ln (per capita assets); (3) All specifications include village fixed effects. (4) For specification I and IV, additional controls are the same as in the other Tables). For specification II, only the village fixed effects are included, as well as In*pcy*; (6) For specification III, ln*pcy* is instrumented with ln*pcx*. For specification V, only the education, log household size, and land indicators, as well as the village fixed effects are included as controls. (8) In specification VI, the savings rate is instrumented by the shock variable, farm size, and the ratio of kids and teens. The overidentification test is 1.96 (distributed • 2(5) under the null hypothesis of no correlation between identifying instruments and error term) which is insignificant at conventional levels.

4.7 Overview of village-level inequality

In this final section, we summarize some of the key determinants of inequality within villages, focusing on possible interlinkages between the distribution of human capital and market development. While we use regressions to conduct this summary exercise, we are especially cautious in interpreting the coefficients causally: almost certainly these village characteristics evolved simultaneously. Instead, the regression coefficients should be treated as slightly sophisticated tabulations. The dependent variable is the Gini coefficient of village inequality, where the village Gini's range from under 0.2 to over 0.5, with most lying on either side of 0.3. Our focus is on how the distribution of education interacts with market development. Before turning to the results, it is first worth asking in what dimensions educational attainment varies across the households within the sample.

Educational attainment increased significantly with the expansion in the basic education system through much of the first three decades of the PRC.[25] Both literacy and average years of schooling increased, while differences between males and females narrowed considerably with each successive cohort.[26] There is considerable debate over the impact of the restructuring of the education system in the post-Mao era and the post-1978 economic reforms on educational attainment in rural China. On the one hand, the re-introduction of family farming with the HRS and the rapid development of off-farm opportunities increased the returns to labour, and thus the opportunity cost of families keeping their children in school. Decentralizing fiscal reforms, on the other hand, shifted much of the responsibility for primary school funding to rural communities. This gave rise to differences in funding levels and possibly school quality. In poorer areas with weaker tax bases, high school fees reportedly discouraged enrolment.

Some observers suggest that these developments contributed to growing differences across communities and regions in average levels of educational attainment. Possibly counteracting these effects are the potential effects of increased household income and an increase in the returns to schooling on the demand for education.[27]

We cannot address these issues here, but are interested in the potential effect of differences in educational attainment on inequality. First, differences in schooling levels across villages can be an important source of intervillage differences in income, especially in an environment in which the returns to education are positive. There are also differences in educational attainment levels across families within villages. These differences can be a product of differences across age–sex cohorts in educational attainment and differences in the demographic composition of households, or can arise from differences within age–sex cohorts in schooling levels. The source of the inequality in educational attainment has potentially important implications for our interpretation of inequality in China and for policy.

Using as our measure of household schooling the average number of years of completed schooling of all household members 16 years and older that are not currently enrolled, we carried out decomposition exercises analogous to those performed for income. We are interested in assessing the contribution of intervillage and intercohort differences to overall school inequality. Several findings emerge. Differences in average years of schooling across villages explains about only 10 per cent of the differences in schooling levels across households in our sample. In other words, most of the differences are within villages, and either arise from differences across age cohorts or within age cohorts. An examination of our household data reveal that differences across age cohorts are very stark; average schooling increases from 1.8 years for individuals 61+ to 5.1 for individuals 46–60, 6.2 for age group 31–45, 7.1 for 21–30 and 7.6 years for the cohort aged 16–20.[28] These differences are the source of another 25 per cent of the variation in average household schooling. Together, these factors explain slightly more than a third of the variation in household schooling, leaving nearly two-thirds unexplained by age-cohort or village.

Returning to the income inequality summaries, Table 5.9 shows the regression results, with a variety of control variables. In columns (I) and (III), we show results from a 'lean' specification with simple summaries of factor inequality: the Gini coefficient for *per capita* land and the Gini coefficient for average household education inequality, as well as some simple market/institutional variables. The market variables are: (1) The estimated rate of return to schooling; (2) The distance to major markets (county seat); (3) The share of income from non-agricultural sources; (4) The share of the village labour force employed in TVEs; and (5) the fraction of output sold (as opposed to self-consumed). The village marketing variables (distance, employment in TVEs, and the share of crops sold to markets) are taken from a separate village questionnaire, while the remaining variables are estimated from the household survey. Very few coefficients in the lean specification are significant, though the sign patterns are in line with what we expect given a simple model linking income to factor endowments and prices. Income inequality is

Table 5.9 Summarizing patterns of village inequality (standard errors in parentheses)[1,2]

	Gini per capita income		*Gini of per capita expenditure*	
	OLS (I)	*OLS (II)*	*OLS (III)*	*OLS (IV)*
Gini of education	0.105	−1.667	0.251 (0.220)	0.200 (0.882)
Gini of *per capita* land	0.162 (0.101)	0.871 (0.325)	0.061 (0.071)	0.748 (0.337)
Gini of land × Gini of education		−5.885 (1.933)		−4.819 (1.983)
Rate of return to schooling (income)[3]	0.301 (0.161)	−2.486 (0.607)		
Rate of return to schooling (expend)[3]			0.006 (0.197)	1.430 (0.998)
Gini of education × rate of return		17.038 (3.565)		−8.983 (6.031)
Share of income from Non-ag business	0.167 (0.082)	−0.140 (0.090)	−0.065 (0.065)	−0.147 (0.118)
Share of non-ag × Gini of education		0.000 (0.000)		0.000 (0.000)
Distance from country seat	0.000 (0.000)	0.004 (0.001)	0.000 (0.000)	0.001 (0.001)
Distance × Gini of education		−0.015 (0.004)		−0.008 (0.005)
Fraction of ag output sold	−0.001 (0.000)	−0.008 (0.002)	−0.001 (0.000)	−0.007 (0.002)
Fraction sold × Gini of education		0.039 (0.009)		0.034 (0.011)
Fraction employed in rural enterprises	−0.060 (0.083)	0.603 (0.230)	−0.012 (0.070)	1.110 (0.342)
TVE × Gini of education		−3.673 (1.327)		−6.628 (1.968)
R^2	0.610	0.920	0.340	0.7

Notes: 1. The coefficients are estimated from a regression of the village-level Gini coefficient for *per capita* income and expenditure on the variables listed above. 2. All regressions are weighted by village population. 3. The rate of return to schooling at the village level is estimated from the interaction effects in the income and expenditure regressions reported in Table 5.5.

higher in those villages where a higher fraction of income is earned from non-agricultural activities; and lower the closer a village is to the county seat, the more commercialized is agriculture, and the higher the fraction of the labour force employed by TVEs. The coefficients in the consumption inequality equation are generally less significant than the income regressions.

The most interesting results appear when we add interactions between the human capital distribution and the 'institutional' measures. One way to think of these variables is that they proxy various dimensions of market opportunities. It comes as no surprise that there are interactions between the distribution of human capital, and the degree of market opportunity (reflecting the level of economic development, or the extent of 'transition'). Interpreting interaction effects can be tricky, so we discuss the coefficients in some detail. Consider first the distribution of education. To help with interpretation, note that inequality of education is negatively correlated with the average level of schooling; that is, in villages where average schooling levels are higher, the Gini of education is lower. The total effect of education on income inequality depends on all of the interaction effects.

We begin with the separate partial effects, which show where the inequality of schooling is more or less disequalizing. First, where land inequality is higher, the disequalizing effect of education is lower. This may be a product of the land allocation process, where higher land inequality results from land being allocated from the more educated households with better off-farm opportunities. Second, there is a strong positive interaction between the distribution and returns to schooling: where education is unequally distributed, and its return highest, inequality is also highest. This suggests that policies that reduce the returns to schooling, or decrease education inequality (increasing school attainment should do both) will reduce inequality. We return to this point shortly. Third, the institutional variables affect the impact of schooling on inequality. The further a village is from a county seat, the smaller is the disequalizing effect of human capital. In other words, the distribution of education matters less in more remote villages. A similar interpretation applies to the commercialization variable. Unequal educational outcomes adversely affect income inequality most when accompanied by commercial development. On the other hand, employment opportunities in TVEs reduce the adverse effect of education inequality, presumably by providing income opportunities for the less educated.

The institutional variables and their interactions with education can also be viewed on their own (as opposed to partial effects of education). The total institutional effects include the interaction terms, evaluated at some level of schooling inequality. For example, the median Gini coefficient of education inequality is 0.16 (it ranges from 0.08 to 0.28, with most lying between 0.15 and 0.21). The total effect of an increase in the rate of return to schooling on the Gini coefficient of income inequality is $-2.486 + (17.038 \times 0.16) = 0.24$, so that an increase in the rate of return to schooling by 1 percentage point (0.01) adds 0.0024 points to the Gini coefficient in a village with a median level of education inequality.[29] We obtain several interesting and statistically significant results. First, inequality is higher the further away a village is from the county seat. Economic opportunity, as represented by distance to markets, has an equalizing effect on income. However, inequality of education erodes the positive effect of market integration, and inequality worsens when opportunities exist in villages with unequal distributions of schooling. Second, the more commercialized a village, the lower its Gini coefficient. Again, this indicator of market transition worsens inequality when combined with education inequality. Viewed differently, commercialization reinforces the positive effects of a more equal distribution of human capital. Finally, TVE employment worsens inequality if education inequality is zero, but it improves the income distribution for any Gini coefficient above 0.17, which means any Gini above the median.

In summary, there are important interactions between human capital and market development in determining the level of inequality at the village level. Generally, commercialization and economic opportunity equalize incomes. However, the effects are less benign when accompanied by an unequal distribution of education, whereby these opportunities will presumably be taken advantage of most by the more educated, at the expense of a higher income inequality.

5 Conclusions

Our empirical explorations yield a number of suggestive results linking economic transition to income inequality in China. Two important themes emerge. First, is the apparent role that 'economic opportunity' plays in determining the relative position of winners and losers in transition. Second, is the role that human capital plays in allowing households to access these opportunities. Inequality of economic development interacts with the unequal distribution of human capital, leading to more inequality within villages than differences of income across villages. One relatively pessimistic implication of our results is that rural inequality is likely to worsen before it improves. The distribution of human capital likely changes quite slowly, while market institutions and opportunities may change rapidly. Given the current distribution of education, many of these institutional developments will disproportionately benefit the higher educated. Compounding this, current patterns of capital accumulation suggest that the rich will be better positioned to increase their incomes, and thus their future wealth.

Of course, many questions remain unanswered, and our results provoke more questions than they answer. For example, we ignore the role of households as an economic institution. We also ignore cohort dimensions to inequality. For example, is education primarily unequally distributed among generations (cohorts), or is there considerable inequality of education within all age groups? The answers to these questions have important implications for the likely speed with which the education distribution, and thus the income distribution, will evolve. Nevertheless, our explorations suggest a number of important avenues for future empirical work, and highlight the importance of collecting new household survey data.

Notes

1 For an extended discussion of the allocation of land rights, see Turner, Brandt and Rozelle (2001).
2 See Lin (1992).
3 See Sicular (1995), Park and Rozelle (1998).
4 Justin Lin (1992), citing Ministry of Agriculture estimates.
5 See Byrd and Gelb (1990); Naughton (1996).
6 State Statistical Bureau (1998).
7 See the collection of papers edited by West and Zhao (1999).
8 Ministry of Agriculture (1995).
9 This is the 'ecological' model of inequality described by Riskin (1994), whereby Chinese inequality is driven by differences in geographic endowments. The contrasting model (or emphasis) is provided by the 'socioeconomic' model, described by Riskin, which emphasizes local institutions.
10 This is a simplification: markets were not totally absent in the collectivist period, and in the market-based economy, there remain restrictions on price-setting behaviour.
11 Of course, endowments are likely to change with transition as well. Some reshuffling of endowments like land (or other entitlements) may occur as a direct consequence of government policy. As well, individuals will respond to the changed economy by acquiring factors of production, like human or physical capital. Our simplification is really a glossing over of the fact that there are few true 'endowments' that correspond to the economist's usual theoretical notion.
12 For an excellent description of the impact of transition on 'social differentiation' (inequality), applied in a comparative perspective to China and Vietnam, see Van Luong and Unger (1998).

13 See Hare (1994); Khan and Riskin (1998); Guojia Jiwei (1995); Knight and Song (1993); Knight and Shi (1997).
14 State Statistical Bureau (1998).
15 The low return in the wage sector may reflect differences in the wage determination between workers who are assigned to jobs (non-market group) versus those who find jobs themselves (market group). Gregory and Meng (1995) find a significant return to schooling for the latter group, but no return for the non-market job-holders. They are not, however, able to explain the assignment of workers to these sectors.
16 <http://www.cpc.unc.edu/projects/ china/china_home.html>.
17 On this point, see Lardy (1994).
18 Income from family-run businesses represents both profits plus the implicit returns to family labour. We do not try to break up these two components.
19 Slightly more than a third (36.2 per cent) of these jobs were in the villages in which these households lived; 43.1 per cent were in either the county or township seat; and the remainder (20.7 per cent) were in the cities. Most of these jobs households found on their own and were not 'allocated' or 'rationed'.
20 See Putterman (1993); Vermeer (1982).
21 The public-use version of the CHNS data set for 1993 does not provide an estimate for household income. We constructed a measure using the definitions of alternative income sources provided for the 1989 and 1991 data.
22 See Shorrocks (1983).
23 We exclude the value of capital services from our instrument to minimize any mechanical overlap in the measurement of income and expenditure.
24 These estimates are well in line with those reported in Psacharopolous (1985).
25 Schooling was severely disrupted during the famine between 1959 and 1961, and again in the mid-1960s, which explains some of the differences between later cohorts.
26 See Tsui (1997), Lavely *et al.* (1990); Hannum (1998).
27 As noted in our previous discussion, returns to education appear to have been zero, prior to the reforms.
28 These numbers probably slightly underestimate differences in schooling levels across cohorts because these calculations exclude village migrants who tended to be both younger and better educated.
29 In fact, 0.01 is a small change in the rate of return to schooling given the variation in our sample. While the sampling variation is also large (see Table 5.5), we estimate village rates of return to education at an average of 0.07 for income, with a standard deviation of 0.08 (the 25–75 percentile split is 0.03 and 0.10); and an average of 0.04 for expenditure, with a standard deviation of 0.04 (the 25–75 percentile split is 0.02–0.07).

References

An, M. and D. Yang (1998) 'Human Capital, Entrepreneurship, and Farm Household Earnings', Duke University, mimeo.

Benjamin, D. and L. Brandt (1997) 'Land, Factor Markets, and Inequality in Rural China: Historical Evidence', *Explorations in Economic History*, vol. 34, no. 4 (October), pp. 460–94.

Benjamin, D. and L. Brandt (1999) 'Markets and Inequality in Rural China: Parallels with the Past', *American Economic Review*, vol. 89, no. 2 (May), pp. 292–5.

Byrd, W. and A. Gelb (1990) 'Township, Village and Private Enterprise in China's Economic Reform', World Bank, Policy Research and External Affairs Working Papers Series, no. 406.

Cheng, Y.-S. (1996) 'A Decomposition Analysis of Income Inequality of Chinese Rural Households', *China Economic Review*, vol. 7, no. 2, pp. 155–67.

Deaton, Angus (1997) *The Analysis of Household Surveys*, Washington, DC: The World Bank.

Deaton, Angus and Christina Paxson (1994): "Intertemporal Choice and Inequality," *Journal of Political Economy*, 102(3), June, pp. 437–67.

Glewwe, P. and M. Grosh (1998) 'The World Bank's Living Standards Measurement Study Household Surveys', *Journal of Economic Perspectives*, vol. 12, no. 1 (Winter), pp. 187–96.

Gregory, R. and X. Meng (1995) 'Wage Determination and Occupational Attainment in the Rural Industrial Sector of China', *Journal of Comparative Economics*, vol. 21, pp. 353–74.

Guojia Jiwei Yanjiu Suo Ketizu (Chinese State Planning Commission, Economic Research Institution Research Group) (1995) 'Woguo dongzhongxi san da diqu nongcun jingji fazhan chaju de fenxi' (Analysis of Uneven Rural Economic Development of the Eastern, Central and Western Regions of China), *Jingji Yanjiu Cankao* (References on Economic Research), vol. 30, pp. 2–42.

Hannum, E. (1998) 'Educational Inequality: Hidden Consequences of the Reform Era in Rural China', PhD Dissertation, University of Michigan.

Hare, D. (1994) 'Rural Nonagricultural Activities and their Impact on the Distribution of Income: Evidence from Farm Households in Southern China', *China Economic Review*, vol. 41, pp. 59–82.

Ho, S. (1994) *Rural China in Transition* (New York: Oxford University Press).

Howes, S. and A. Hussain (1994) 'Regional Growth and Inequality in Rural China', London School of Economics, mimeo.

Hussain, A., P. Lanjouw and N. Stern (1994) 'Income Inequalities in China: Evidence from Household Survey Data', *World Development*, vol. 22, no. 12, pp. 1947–57.

Khan, A. and C. Riskin (1998) 'Income and Inequality in China: Composition, Distribution and Growth of Household Income, 1988 to 1995', *China Quarterly*, no. 154, pp. 221–51.

Knight, J. and L. Shi (1997) 'Cumulative Causation and Inequality Among Villages in China', *Oxford Development Studies*, vol. 25, no. 2, pp. 149–72.

Knight, J. and L. Song (1993) 'The Spatial Contribution to Income in Inequality in Rural China', *Cambridge Journal of Economics*, vol. 17, pp. 195–213.

Lardy, N. (1994) *China in the World Economy* (Washington, DC: Institute for International Economics).

Lavely, W., Z. Xiao, B. Li and R. Freedman (1990) 'The Rise in Female Education in China: National and Regional Patterns', *China Quarterly*, vol. 121, pp. 61–93.

Li T. and J. Zhang (1998) 'Returns to Education under Collective and Household Farming in China', *Journal of Development Economics*, vol. 56, no. 2, pp. 307–35.

Lin, J. (1992) 'Rural Reforms and Agricultural Growth in China', *American Economic Review*, vol. 82, no. 1, pp. 34–51.
Ministry of Agriculture (1995) *Zhongguo Nongye Fazhan Baogao '95* (China's Agricultural Development Report, 1995) (Beijing: Zhongguo Nongye Chubanshe).
Morduch, J. and T. Sicular (2000) 'Politics, Growth, and Inequality in Rural China: Does It Pay to Join the Party?, *Journal of Public Economics*, vol. 77, no. 3, pp. 331–56.
Naughton, B. (1996) *Growing out of Plan* (New York: Cambridge University Press).
Orazem, P. and M. Vodopivec (1995) 'Winners and Losers in Transition: Returns to Education, Experience, and Gender in Slovenia', *World Bank Economic Review*, vol. 9, no. 2, (May), pp. 201–30.
Park, A. and S. Rozelle (1998) 'Reforming State–Market Relations in Rural China', *Economies of Transition*, vol. 6, no. 2, pp. 461–80.
Psacharapoulos, G. (1985) 'Returns to Education: Further International Update and Implications', *Journal of Human Resources*, vol. 20, no. 4 (December), pp. 583–604.
Putterman, L. (1993) *Continuity and Change in China's Rural Development: Collective and Reform Eras in Perspective* (New York: Oxford University Press).
Ravallion, M. and S. Chen (1996) 'Data in Transition: Assessing Rural Living Standards in Southern China', *China Economic Review*, vol. 7, no. 1 (Spring), pp. 23–56.
Riskin, C. (1994) 'Chinese Rural Poverty: Marginalized or Dispersed?', *American Economic Review*, vol. 84, no. 2 (May), pp. 281–4.
Rosenzweig, M. (1995) 'Why Are There Returns to Schooling?', *American Economic Review*, vol. 85, no. 2 (May), pp. 153–8.
Rozelle, S. (1994) 'Rural Industrialization and Increasing Inequality: Emerging Patterns in China's Reforming Economy', *Journal of Comparative Economics*, vol. 19, pp. 362–91.
Schultz, T. W. (1975) 'The Ability to Deal with Disequilibria', *Journal of Economic Literature*, vol. 13, no. 3 (September), pp. 827–46.
Shorrocks, A. (1982) 'Inequality Decomposition by Factor Components', *Econometrica*, vol. 50, no. 1 (January), pp. 193–211.
Shorrocks, A. (1983) 'The Impact of Income Components on the Distribution of Family Incomes', *Quarterly Journal of Economics*, vol. 98, no. 2 (May), pp. 311–26.
Sicular, T. (1995) 'Redefining State, Plan, and Market: China's Reforms in Agricultural Commerce', *China Quarterly*, vol. 144, pp. 1020–46.
State Statistical Bureau (selected years) *Zhongguo Tongji Nianjian* (Statistical Yearbook of China) (Beijing: State Statistical Bureau).
Tsui, K.-Y. (1991) 'China's Regional Inequality, 1952–1985', *Journal of Comparative Economics*, vol. 15, no. 1 (March), pp. 1–21.
Tsui, K.-Y. (1997) 'Economic Reform and Attainment in Basic Education in China', *China Quarterly*, vol. 149, pp. 104–12.
Tsui, K.-Y. (1998) 'Factor Decomposition of Chinese Rural Income Inequality: New Methodology, Empirical Findings, and Policy Implications', *Journal of Comparative Economics*, vol. 26, pp. 502–28.
Turner, M., L. Brandt and S. Rozelle (2001) 'Local Government Behavior and Property Rights Formation in Rural China', University of Toronto, mimeo.

Van Luong, H. and J. Unger (1998) 'Wealth, Power, and Poverty in the Transition to Market Economies: The Process of Socio-Economic Differentiation in Rural China and Northern Vietnam', *The China Journal*, no. 40 (July), pp. 61–93.
Vermeer, E. B. (1982) 'Income Differentials in Rural China', *China Quarterly*, vol. 111, pp. 1–33.
West, L. and Y. Zhao (eds.) (1999) *The Flow of Rural Labor in China* (Berkeley: University of California Press).
Yang, D. (1997) 'Education and Off-Farm Work', *Economic Development and Cultural Change*, vol. 45, pp. 613–32.
Yang, D. (1999) 'Urban-Biased Policies and Rising Income Inequality in China', *American Economic Review*, vol. 89, no. 2, pp. 306–10.
Zhao Y. (1999) 'Leaving the Countryside: Rural to Urban Migration Decisions in China', *American Economic Review*, vol. 89, no. 2, pp. 281–6.

6
Inequality in Latin America during the 1990s

Miguel Székely
Chief of the Office for Regional Development, Presidency of the Republic, Mexico

and

Marianne Hilgert
Research Department, Inter-American Development Bank, Washington DC, USA

1 Introduction

This chapter takes a close look at the changes in income distribution in Latin America during the 1990s. We have three specific objectives. First, we document the changes in the region. Second, we explore if the changes we observe are an 'illusion' created by differences in the characteristics of the data or by the way in which the data are treated for measuring inequality; and third, we verify what is behind the changes that have taken place.

The Latin American case is especially relevant for at least three reasons. The first is that it is the most unequal region in the world, and the changes in the 1990s give some indication about the prospects for the future.[1] The second is that the 1990s were years of economic recovery and macro stability, as compared to the 'lost decade' of the 1980s, which was characterized by high economic volatility and stagnation, and by a sharp deterioration in income distribution.[2] Macroeconomic volatility and inflation usually have larger negative effects on the poor, but it is still not clear if a more stable environment leads to reductions in inequality or simply to a deceleration or an end in the deterioration.[3] Latin America is a good case to verify if there is a tendency for income distribution to improve after adverse macro conditions, which is important in light of the recent financial turmoil in East Asia, and of the unstable macroeconomic environment in several Eastern European countries.[4]

The third reason is that during the 1980s the Latin American economies started an intense transformation process through trade, financial and fiscal liberalization and reform, and through privatization.[5] These kinds of measures imply an intense reallocation of resources in the economy that is likely to have short-term and longer-term effects over income distribution. Several eastern European economies are going through the initial phases of the same process at the moment, so it is of interest to know if there is a tendency for the distribution to improve or worsen after their implementation.

The chapter is divided into five sections. Section 2 documents the changes in inequality in Latin America in the 1990s by using 31 household surveys from nine countries, and compares them with changes in countries of other regions in the world in recent years. Sections 3 and 4 look at what is behind the changes from a statistical point of view. Section 3 verifies if our impression about the changes in inequality is modified when accounting for differences in sample size, population coverage, and geographic and income source coverage. Section 4 checks for the robustness of the changes to the use of different assumptions about adult equivalence scales, economies of scale in consumption, and the use of alternative inequality measures. Section 5 explores what is behind the changes from an economic point of view, but still with the sole idea of illustrating what aspects of the distribution have been changing, rather than explaining the causes of the shifts. Section 6 concludes.

2 Changes in inequality in the 1990s

To explore the dynamics of income distribution in Latin America in the 1990s we process the micro data in household surveys from Brazil, Chile, Costa Rica, Honduras, Mexico, Panama, Peru, Uruguay, and Venezuela. These countries cover 71 per cent of the total population in the Latin American region (see the Appendix tables for a description of the data), and they are selected under two criteria. The first is that the countries should have surveys that are nationally representative. This is to assure that a sufficiently large proportion of the population is covered and that composition effects owing to migration do not drive the shifts we observe. The only exception we make is Uruguay, where household surveys cover only urban areas, but are used because they include more than 90 per cent of the population of the country.[6] The second, and most important requirement is that household surveys for the 1990s for each country and for different years are strictly comparable in terms of questionnaires, sampling techniques, and institutional origin. For instance, in the case of Venezuela, household surveys are available for each year since 1990. We only use two of those surveys because the questionnaire and the instruments to capture the information were changed in 1994. Thus, the only surveys that are strictly comparable are those held either before 1994 or from 1995 on.[7] This is to make sure that the changes we observe are genuine changes and not shifts due simply to differences in the way the different data points are constructed.

As shown in Figures 6.1 and 6.2, we are left with 31 observations covering the years between 1989 and 1998.[8] Uruguay and Costa Rica are the only cases where the comparison does not go beyond 1995. For seven of the nine countries in our sample, inequality increased during the 1990s (see Figure 6.1), while in two of them inequality remained practically unchanged (Figure 6.2). The largest increases between the two end-points are observed in Peru, Honduras, Venezuela, Brazil, and Uruguay. In Brazil and Uruguay most of the deterioration took place in the early years of the decade, while in Honduras there was a reduction in inequality between 1992 and 1996, but a sharp increase thereafter. In Peru and Venezuela the trend is positive between all the years for which comparable information is available.[9]

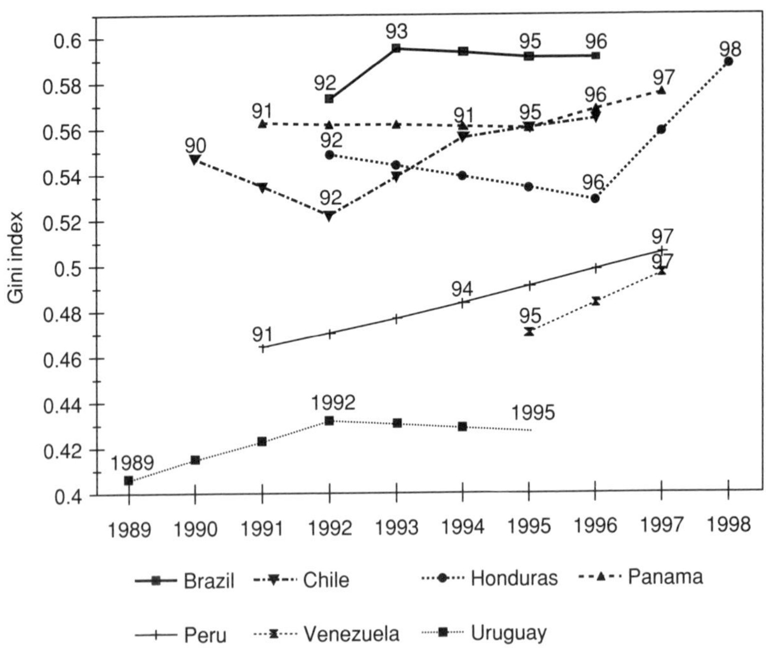

Figure 6.1 Inequality in Latin America, 1989–98 (countries with increasing inequality)

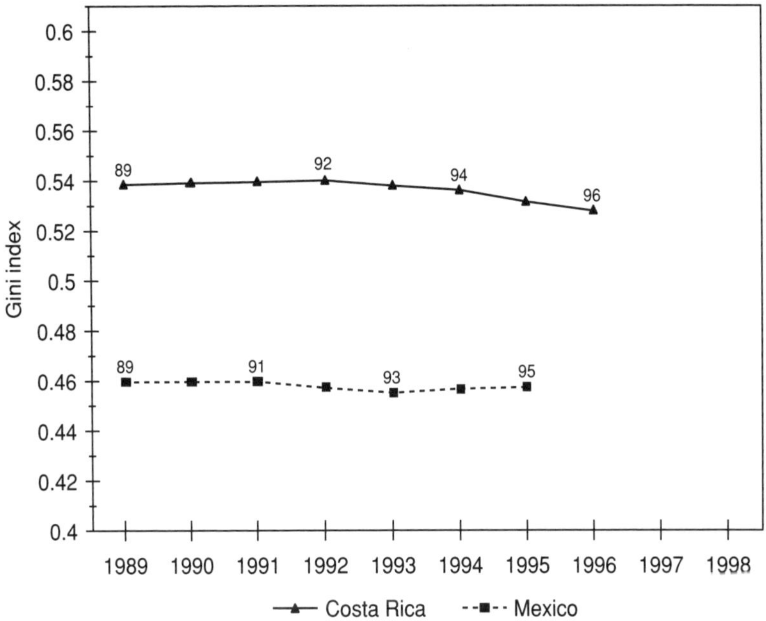

Figure 6.2 Inequality in Latin America, 1989–98 (countries with constant inequality)

Panama and Chile are the other two cases where there is an increase in inequality. In these cases most of the deterioration in income distribution took place some years after the first observation (1995 and 1992, respectively). In Chile there was even a statistically significant improvement in distribution between 1990 and 1992, but the increase in the Gini coefficient thereafter eliminated these gains.

In Costa Rica and Mexico, there is no statistically significant change in the Gini coefficient for the years under study, and in fact, it can be said that none of the nine countries in our sample registers statistically significant reductions in inequality. It can be said confidently that income distribution has not improved in Latin America during the 1990s, at least for the countries where adequate data to examine the changes are available.

Londoño and Székely (1997) (hereafter, LS) show that for six of the countries in Figure 6.1 the Gini coefficient increased during the 1980s. Our results show that in the 1990s there has been a continuation of this trend, although there seems to be a slight deceleration in the deterioration. LS consider only countries with surveys that are nationally representative, so they do not include information for Uruguay. To compare the results in Figure 6.1 with previous years, we compute the Gini coefficient from the 1981 household survey for this country, and find that inequality declined from 0.4329 in 1981 to 0.4064 in 1989. As Figure 6.2 shows, the Gini coefficient for Uruguay for 1992 is about 0.43, and remained at almost the same level in 1995. So, the slight improvement observed during the 1980s seems to have ended during the 1990s.

With respect to the countries in Figure 6.2, LS show that there was a sharp increase in inequality during the 1980s in Mexico. In the 1990s inequality has remained at practically the same high level. Costa Rica is the only country in our sample where LS show that the Gini coefficient declined during the 1980s. During the 1990s the distribution did not continue to improve.

To place these changes in a wider context, we access household survey data from the *Luxembourg Income Study* for two points in time for 12 countries from outside the Latin American region, and check whether inequality has failed to improve in these countries as well. Table 6.1 presents the results, and includes the change between the first and last survey for each of the Latin American countries in our sample.[10] The Gini coefficients refer to the distribution of household *per capita* income.

Of the 21 countries in Table 6.1 there is not a single case where there is a statistically significant reduction in inequality in the 1990s. There are four cases where the Gini coefficient for the second year is smaller than the first, but in all these cases the reduction is only marginal. On average, the smallest yearly increase is observed in the group of countries comprised by Latin America, followed by North America (note, however, that the change in the US is much greater than in Canada) and Western Europe. Eastern Europe is the region with the sharpest deterioration. The *percentage* yearly change in the Gini coefficient is also lowest in Latin America because the other regions started out with much lower inequality.

With respect to individual countries the largest yearly increases are registered in Poland (0.017 points), Hungary (0.015), Venezuela (0.013) and Italy (0.013 points). With the exception of Venezuela, the increase in the rest of the Latin American countries does not deviate considerably from the pattern in countries outside the region. In fact, in eight out of the nine Latin American countries, the yearly change in inequality has been smaller than in the US in the 1990s.

It should be noted that the eastern European countries that register the largest increases in inequality are still going through a period of

Table 6.1 Changes in income inequality around the world, 1989–98

Country	*Years*	*Gini year 1*	*Gini year 2*	*Change (Gini points)*	*Yearly change (Gini points)*	*Yearly change (%)*
Brazil	(1992,1996)	0.5728	0.5906	0.018	0.004	0.779
Chile	(1990,1996)	0.5470	0.5638	0.017	0.002	0.439
Costa Rica	(1989,1995)	0.4595	0.4571	−0.002	−0.000	−0.085
Honduras	(1992,1998)	0.5489	0.5876	0.039	0.006	1.177
Mexico	(1989,1996)	0.5309	0.5300	−0.001	−0.000	−0.023
Panama	(1991,1997)	0.5625	0.5755	0.013	0.002	0.385
Peru	(1991,1997)	0.4643	0.5055	0.041	0.007	1.479
Uruguay	(1989,1995)	0.4064	0.4209	0.014	0.002	0.595
Venezuela	(1995,1997)	0.4703	0.4963	0.026	0.013	2.761
Average, Latin America				0.018	0.004	0.834
Canada	(1991,1994)	0.3501	0.3544	0.004	0.001	0.411
US	(1991,1994)	0.4157	0.4404	0.025	0.008	1.987
Average N. America				0.015	0.005	1.199
Australia	(1989,1994)	0.3809	0.3915	0.011	0.002	0.558
Germany	(1989,1994)	0.3266	0.3464	0.020	0.004	1.213
Italy	(1991,1995)	0.3107	0.3621	0.051	0.013	4.136
Luxembourg	(1991,1994)	0.2694	0.2694	−0.000	−0.000	−0.005
Norway	(1991,1995)	0.2883	0.2935	0.005	0.001	0.450
Average Western Europe				0.017	0.004	1.270
Hungary	(1991,1994)	0.2874	0.3320	0.045	0.015	5.178
Poland	(1992,1995)	0.3250	0.3749	0.050	0.017	5.122
Russia	(1992,1995)	0.4404	0.4525	0.012	0.004	0.915
Average Eastern Europe				0.036	0.012	3.738
Australia	(1989,1994)	0.3809	0.3915	0.011	0.002	0.558
Taiwan	(1991,1995)	0.3049	0.3027	−0.002	−0.001	−0.174

Notes: The results for the Latin American countries were obtained with direct access to household survey data; household surveys from the rest of the countries were accessed through the Luxembourg Income Study.
Source: Authors' calculations from household survey data.

economic liberalization and macroeconomic instability, which is similar to the macro context during the second half of the 1980s in Latin America. In contrast, the latest observation for Taiwan 1995 is several years before the recent financial crisis in East Asia. So, we are comparing changes in inequality post-crisis and during-crisis in Latin America and Eastern Europe, respectively, with inequality pre-crisis in Taiwan. More recent data for Taiwan and Eastern Europe would perhaps change this picture.

3 Changes in inequality and survey characteristics

Results such as those presented in Figures 6.1 and 6.2 are commonly used to evaluate economic performance and they influence our impression about the effectiveness of the policies that countries pursue. Usually, countries where income distribution improves over time are regarded as successful, while the contrary occurs for countries where inequality increases. As mentioned in the introduction, the objective of this chapter is *not* to explain the changes documented so far but, rather, to illustrate what is behind these numbers. In this section we explore whether taking into account changes in the characteristics of the household surveys through time, or across countries, modifies our impression about how successful countries have been in improving the distribution of income. We start by looking at population coverage, and we then look into income source and geographic coverage.

3.1 Precision of survey estimates

Although the household surveys we use are strictly comparable within each individual Latin American country, they can change in subtle ways over time for the same country and there may be differences across countries that blur the picture about the changes in inequality. For instance, survey coverage in terms of sample size can vary, and this modifies the precision of the estimates. Table 6.2 shows the number of observations in each survey, as well as the coverage in terms of proportions of the population. Since sample sizes in household surveys are typically large, standard errors in all cases are relatively low.

However, there are large differences across countries. In Costa Rica, Panama, and Uruguay the surveys cover around 1 per cent of the total population, which is quite high. The precision of any estimate will be greater in these countries. Countries with the smallest relative samples are Mexico and Peru. The only two cases where there are significant variations in survey coverage during the 1990s are Chile – where the 1994 survey is much larger – and Uruguay – where the last survey is twice as large as previous ones. In Chile the Gini coefficient increases precisely from the 1994 survey, but our conclusions about the changes hold even if we restrict our analysis to the other years for which data are available and sample sizes are more similar. Usually, having larger samples covering wider sectors of the population implies more inequality, but in the case of Uruguay there is no increase in the Gini coefficient between 1992 and 1995 although the 1995 survey is more than twice the size of the 1992 survey. Thus, it seems unlikely that our conclusion depends on these sampling differences.

Another way of looking into the issue of population coverage is to obtain some indicator about the sectors of the population represented in each survey. A country may have two surveys with exactly the same sample size, but still a larger proportion of the observations may be focused on particular groups. To verify to what extent the surveys convey information on the individuals at the top of the income distribution (to which inequality measures are specially sensitive) we trace down the richest individual and the 10 richest households in each survey and compare their incomes across countries. The last two columns in Table 6.2 include the results.

The first of the two columns shows the monthly income in US dollars for the richest individual in the household survey, while the second presents the income *per capita* for the individuals in the 10 households with the highest income. Some of these results are striking. For instance, in the case of Venezuela, which is a middle income country, the richest person in the household survey registers a monthly income of $8,610 and $14,878 in 1995 and 1997, respectively, which is clearly an underestimate of the income of the richest individual in the country. Similar low incomes are found in Peru, Panama, Honduras and Costa Rica.

But the most impressive feature of Table 6.2 is that the income of the richest individual changes significantly, and in some cases dramatically, between surveys. In Brazil, Chile, Honduras, Uruguay, and Venezuela, it seems that the most recent surveys might be capturing better the upper part of the distribution. It is possible that part of the increase in inequality during the 1990s in these countries is reflecting a better coverage of socio-economic subgroups. However, in all these cases the incomes of the richest sectors of the population are still clearly grossly underestimated.

The only case where the coverage of the upper part of the distribution seems to have been reduced is Mexico. This is an upper middle income country where inequality levels are high by international standards, and it is difficult to believe that the richest person in the country earned in 1996 a monthly income of about $40,000. The income of the richest person in the survey and the *per capita* income of all individuals in the 10 richest households are much higher in the 1989 survey than in any subsequent year. Thus, it is possible that part of the relative stability in the income distribution in this country in the 1990s is just a reflection of the lack of coverage of the richest sectors of society in the household surveys.

Table 6.2 Population coverage of household, 1992–97

Country	*Year*	*Conventional Gini index*	*Precision of survey estimates*			*Highest income in the survey (monthly $US)*	
			Sample size (num. obs.)	*Sample size as % total population*	*Standard error Gini coeff.*	*Richest person in the survey*	*Individuals in 10 richest households*
Brazil	1992	0.5728	317,145	0.21	0.0028	50,200	18,887
Brazil	1993	0.5952	322,011	0.21	0.0030	53,667	14,954
Brazil	1995	0.5911	334,106	0.21	0.0025	41,848	32,899
Brazil	1996	0.5906	331,142	0.21	0.0025	62,871	44,117
Chile	1990	0.5470	105,189	0.80	0.0044	31,152	20,698
Chile	1992	0.5220	110,555	0.82	0.0038	16,787	13,360
Chile	1994	0.5558	178,057	1.27	0.0066	26,432	8,051
Chile	1996	0.5638	134,262	0.93	0.0042	65,510	32,489
Costa Rica	1989	0.4595	34,368	1.16	0.0050	7,730	4,474
Costa Rica	1991	0.4598	35,565	1.13	0.0053	7,261	4,414
Costa Rica	1993	0.4550	37,703	1.12	0.0048	6,193	4,340
Costa Rica	1995	0.4571	40,613	1.14	0.0045	7,121	5,798
Honduras	1992	0.5489	24,704	0.48	0.0081	3,455	2,562
Honduras	1996	0.5284	33,172	0.57	0.0080	7,600	5,015
Honduras	1998	0.5876	32,696	0.53	0.0075	15,213	12,480
Mexico	1989	0.5309	57,289	0.07	0.0080	74,367	17,148
Mexico	1992	0.5341	50,862	0.06	0.0059	23,941	16,246
Mexico	1994	0.5361	60,402	0.07	0.0054	40,642	16,765
Mexico	1996	0.5276	64,916	0.07	0.0052	39,210	14,321

Panama	1991	0.5625	38,000	1.55	0.0062	21,686	8,655
Panama	1995	0.5602	40,320	1.53	0.0059	11,600	10,254
Panama	1997	0.5755	39,706	1.46	0.0067	17,548	13,213
Peru	1991	0.4643	11,507	0.05	0.0096	7,729	4,463
Peru	1994	0.4832	18,662	0.08	0.0084	8,989	5,651
Peru	1997	0.5055	19,575	0.08	0.0085	10,302	6,451
Uruguay	1989	0.4064	31,766	1.03	0.0055	37,483	16,085
Uruguay	1992	0.4319	29,927	0.95	0.0049	26,556	11,544
Uruguay	1995	0.4209	64,930	2.02	0.0030	42,914	21,839
Venezuela	1995	0.4703	92,450	0.42	0.0033	8,610	6,813
Venezuela	1997	0.4963	76,965	0.34	0.0039	14,878	8,737

Note: *From UN Population Statistics, 1998 revision.
Source: Authors' calculations from household survey data.

3.2 Income source and geographic coverage

One of the main differences across countries is the emphasis of household surveys on capturing the range of possible income sources. The most complete surveys capture non-monetary incomes, labour incomes, income from capital, government transfers, property rents, and other incomes. As shown in Appendix Table 6 A.2, most surveys capture some non-labour incomes, but (as indicated in the last column) it is common to capture these sources through a single question in the questionnaires rather than gathering information on each of them separately. This difference undoubtedly reduces the precision of estimation of non-labour incomes.

Table 6.3 presents the Gini coefficient for different income concepts. The last column contains the Gini coefficient for labour incomes (including labour income from self-employment). This is the income source with the highest degree of comparability across countries and through time. If we restrict our comparison to this source, we would conclude that in all nine countries inequality increased during the 1990s (comparing the first and last points).

These differences also modify our impression about individual country performance. For instance, as shown in Figure 6.1, Honduras is one of the countries with the largest increases in inequality. However, the Honduran surveys mainly capture labour incomes (in fact, for 1992 and 1996 the questionnaires capture only labour incomes). If we restrict the Gini coefficient to measure inequality by using the same income sources in Costa Rica and Mexico, some of our conclusions would change. In Costa Rica, the Gini coefficient increases by 1 point, and in Mexico by 4, which is similar to the shift registered in Honduras. In Mexico, the overall distribution remained practically unchanged because the inequality of non-labour incomes declined, but if we compare only the income concept that is most comparable across countries, we would conclude that inequality in this country has increased significantly in the 1990s.[11]

The second most important difference is that there are only four cases where household surveys provide information on non-monetary incomes. Our impression about the changes in inequality actually changes for Peru and Uruguay if we limit the comparison to monetary incomes (which are more comparable across countries). In Peru inequality increases more if we consider only monetary incomes, while in Uruguay we would conclude that inequality has been increasing continuously during the 1990s if we limit the comparison to this same concept.

Since our sample of countries has one survey that is not nationally representative, it is also of interest to compare the change in national inequality in each country to the change in urban areas only. Table 6.4 presents the Gini coefficient for urban and rural areas separately, as well as the relation between the average urban and rural incomes, and the proportion of urban population.[12] According to the results, the only two

Table 6.3 Gini coefficient, by income source, 1992–97

Country	*Year*	*Total income*	*Monetary income*	*Non-labour income*	*Labour income*
Brazil	1992		0.5728	0.6753	0.5809
Brazil	1993		0.5952	0.6837	0.6064
Brazil	1995		0.5911	0.6609	0.5991
Brazil	1996		0.5907	0.6541	0.5965
Chile	1990	0.5470	0.5565	0.6774	0.5587
Chile	1992	0.5219	0.5308	0.7539	0.5428
Chile	1994	0.5558	0.5742	0.7154	0.5767
Chile	1996	0.5638	0.5724	0.7131	0.5845
Costa Rica	1989		0.4596	0.6475	0.4526
Costa Rica	1991		0.4613	0.6271	0.4605
Costa Rica	1993		0.4549	0.6449	0.4509
Costa Rica	1995		0.4570	0.6397	0.4582
Honduras	1992				0.5489
Honduras	1996				0.5302
Honduras	1998		0.5876	0.7178	0.5947
Mexico	1989	0.5309	0.5465	0.6817	0.5408
Mexico	1992	0.5341	0.5631	0.6643	0.5671
Mexico	1994	0.5361	0.5579	0.6424	0.5669
Mexico	1996	0.5276	0.5461	0.6338	0.5800
Panama	1991		0.5625	0.6744	0.5355
Panama	1995		0.5602	0.6893	0.5466
Panama	1997		0.5755	0.7060	0.5678
Peru	1991	0.4643	0.4910	0.7124	0.4917
Peru	1994	0.4832	0.4963	0.7084	0.5003
Peru	1997	0.5055	0.5333	0.8325	0.5301
Uruguay	1989	0.4064	0.4114	0.5623	0.4461
Uruguay	1992	0.4319	0.4230	0.5686	0.4562
Uruguay	1995	0.4209	0.4316	0.5647	0.4683
Venezuela	1995		0.4703	0.6686	0.4664
Venezuela	1997		0.4963	0.6310	0.4951

Source: Authors' calculations from household survey data.

Table 6.4 Inequality, by geographic coverage, 1992–97

Country	*Year*	*Gini index*		*Urb/rur ratio*	*% urban population*
		Urban	*Rural*		
		(1)	*(2)*	*(3)*	*(4)*
Brazil	1992	0.5512	0.5380	2.83	0.78
Brazil	1993	0.5755	0.5780	2.62	0.78
Brazil	1995	0.5695	0.5364	3.00	0.79
Brazil	1996	0.5691	0.5470	2.97	0.79
Chile	1990	0.5370	0.5742	1.34	0.81
Chile	1992	0.5161	0.4719	1.84	0.81
Chile	1994	0.5499	0.5097	1.92	0.83
Chile	1996	0.5546	0.5006	2.30	0.84
Costa Rica	1989	0.4431	0.4256	1.77	0.44
Costa Rica	1991	0.4332	0.4449	1.58	0.44
Costa Rica	1993	0.4336	0.4333	1.65	0.44
Costa Rica	1995	0.4292	0.4374	1.72	0.44
Honduras	1992	0.5153	0.4956	2.36	0.42
Honduras	1996	0.4917	0.4817	2.29	0.44
Honduras	1998	0.5356	0.6065	2.22	0.44
Mexico	1989	0.5201	0.4576	2.46	0.62
Mexico	1992	0.5021	0.4535	2.83	0.59
Mexico	1994	0.5018	0.4403	2.83	0.58
Mexico	1996	0.4892	0.4560	3.02	0.59
Panama	1991	0.5127	0.5512	3.03	0.53
Panama	1995	0.5147	0.5321	2.74	0.59
Panama	1997	0.5287	0.5507	3.14	0.60
Peru	1991	0.4294	0.4139	3.09	0.77
Peru	1994	0.4487	0.4478	2.81	0.70
Peru	1997	0.4484	0.4330	2.45	0.65
Uruguay	1989	0.4064			
Uruguay	1992	0.4319			
Uruguay	1995	0.4209			
Venezuela	1995	0.4634	0.4346	1.71	0.82
Venezuela	1997	0.4963			

Source: Authors' calculations from household survey data.

cases where our impression about the change in inequality would be modified by restricting the samples to the same geographic areas would be Mexico and Costa Rica. In these two countries, but especially in Mexico, urban inequality declines between the first and last observation, rather than remaining constant.

In Brazil and Honduras, rural inequality has increased, but in the remaining countries inequality in these areas has either remained unchanged, or has declined. The differences in average income between urban and rural areas have remained at similar levels in Brazil, Costa Rica, Honduras, Panama, and Peru, and increased only in Chile and Mexico, while the proportion of the population in urban areas has been very stable also (the exceptions are Panama and Peru).

4 Do the conclusions survive some robustness tests?

The Gini coefficients presented so far are computed by assuming that there are no economies of scale in consumption and that each individual in the household has the same relative weight (adult equivalence scales are equal to unity for all ages). This is the standard way in which inequality estimates are computed in Latin America,[13] but there are equally valid alternative assumptions that could be used. In this section we check whether our conclusions about the changes in inequality in Latin America depend on specific methodological choices about economies of scale in consumption, adult equivalence scales, and the selection of inequality index.

4.1 Economies of scale and adult equivalence scales

With regard to economies of scale in consumption, the assumption when computing income *per capita* is that there are no economies of scale. As argued by Lanjow and Ravallion (1994) this assumption might be especially pertinent among poorer households because when an additional member joins the household it is not necessary to duplicate many of the basic expenditures such as infrastructure. There can even be economies of scale in food production and consumption.

Income *per capita* is computed by dividing total income (y) over the number of individuals in the household (n), y/n^{α}, where α is a parameter indicating the extent to which there are economies of scale. *Per capita* income is obtained when $\alpha = 1$. Unfortunately, there is no convincing theoretical argument to decide what should the value of α be in different contexts, so the parameter is usually given a range of values with which the sensitivity to the choice can be verified. For the purposes of this work we chose four values for α, 0.975, 0.95, 0.925, and 0.9, which still imply rather conservative assumptions about economies of scale. If we assume the most extreme of these values $\alpha = .90$, a household of five members (the size of the average Latin American household) is equivalent to a household size of 4.2 individuals. This yields a greater income for each member as compared to the assumption that $\alpha = 1$.

Column (1) in Table 6.4 presents the Gini coefficient calculated with $\alpha = 0.90$ (we do not present the results using other values of α for brevity). In the case of Brazil and Peru, the change in inequality is slightly smaller with $\alpha = 0.90$ than the change in the conventional Gini in Table 6.2, while in Chile the change is slightly larger. For the rest of the countries, our conclusions about the change in inequality remain unchanged when using the range of parameters to account for economies of scale in consumption.

Apart from the possible existence of economies of scale, it is normally argued that different individuals have different needs. For instance, in the analysis of income distribution in developed countries equivalence scales are widely used to adjust for differences in needs by age.[14] In Latin America, the use of equivalence scales has been much more limited, mainly because adequate estimates are not readily available. To check for the robustness of the results in Section 1 to adjusting the data for differences in needs, we use two equivalence scales. The first is the 'Amsterdam' scale in Deaton and Muellbauer (1980), which has been widely used in developed countries, and the second is a recent scale estimated by Contreras (1996) with data from Chile. Column (2) in Table 6.5 presents the results using the equivalence scale by Contreras.[15]

If rather than focusing on the conventional Gini coefficient we allow for the use of equivalence scales, our conclusions from Section 1 change only marginally. The increase in inequality is slightly smaller in Honduras, Panama, and Peru. There is a slight decline in Mexico, and the increase is greater in Uruguay.

4.2 Use of different indexes for measuring inequality

Undoubtedly the Gini coefficient is the most commonly used measure of inequality. However, there is a long list of equally acceptable measures. The main difference is that different measures apply different weights to different sections of the distribution (for instance, the Gini applies more weight to the middle). The family of Generalized Entropy Inequality measures (*E*) explained by Cowell and Jenkins (1995) and Foster and Sen (1997) are some of the most transparent measures, in the sense that they explicitly allow different weights to be applied to different sections of the distribution through the choice of a simple parameter.[16]

Table 6.5 shows the changes in inequality by using two members of the entropy family of indexes; one that applies greater weight to

Table 6.5 Robustness tests to methodological preferences, 1993–97

Country	*Year*	*Economies of scale*	*Adult equivalent*	*Entropy* $a = -1$	*Entropy* $a = +1$	*Dominance tests**
Brazil	1992	0.5655	0.5522	2.6400	0.6534	
Brazil	1993	0.5882	0.5759	2.1747	0.7256	
Brazil	1995	0.5840	0.5700	1.3625	0.6915	
Brazil	1996	0.5839	0.5712	1.3420	0.6853	–
Chile	1990	0.5423	0.5329	0.9980	0.6076	
Chile	1992	0.5169	0.5043	0.8104	0.5588	
Chile	1994	0.5504	0.5397	0.8902	0.5974	
Chile	1996	0.5578	0.5358	1.0452	0.6556	–
Costa Rica	1989	0.4519	0.4391	0.7657	0.3838	
Costa Rica	1991	0.4532	0.4361	0.7065	0.3890	
Costa Rica	1993	0.4479	0.4338	0.7446	0.3761	
Costa Rica	1995	0.4499	0.4366	0.7130	0.3799	–
Honduras	1992	0.5407	0.5252	1.1126	0.5862	
Honduras	1996	0.5203	0.5056	0.8311	0.5655	
Honduras	1998	0.5825	0.5698	2.5395	0.6687	1992
Mexico	1989	0.5280	0.5016	0.8064	0.5247	
Mexico	1992	0.5310	0.5116	0.7676	0.5734	
Mexico	1994	0.5258	0.5088	0.7556	0.5729	
Mexico	1996	0.5300	0.4916	0.7500	0.5900	–
Panama	1991	0.5547	0.5438	2.0983	0.5907	
Panama	1995	0.5523	0.5387	1.9680	0.5896	
Panama	1997	0.5686	0.5543	1.8195	0.6401	–
Peru	1991	0.4568	0.4411	0.6062	0.4076	
Peru	1994	0.4747	0.4540	0.7125	0.4520	
Peru	1997	0.4983	0.4791	0.7993	0.4995	1991
Uruguay	1989	0.3979	0.3843	0.3748	0.2514	
Uruguay	1992	0.4227	0.4085	0.4769	0.2816	
Uruguay	1995	0.4116	0.3966	0.4437	0.2671	–
Venezuela	1995	0.4613	0.4425	1.3546	0.4036	
Venezuela	1997	0.4873	0.4722	1.4700	0.4682	1995

Source: Authors' calculations from household survey data.
Note: *Year in which Lorenz dominates the distribution of current year.

changes at the lower tail of the distribution ($\beta = -1$), and another that applies more weight at the top ($\beta = 1$). According to these results, our conclusions about the change in inequality for Chile, Costa Rica, Honduras, Peru, and Venezuela hold for any of these two indexes. In the case of Brazil, Panama, and Mexico the bottom-sensitive index declines while the top-sensitive index increases. Overall, inequality measured by the Gini coefficient in these countries does not decline significantly because the improvements at the bottom of the distribution are counterbalanced by the greater concentration at the top. In the case of Uruguay, the increase in inequality has been the outcome of slight improvements at the top of the distribution that have been counterbalanced by deteriorations in income distribution at the lower end.

In three out of nine cases, our impression about the changes in inequality depends on the way in which we choose to summarize the income distribution; but in Table 6.5 we restrict the choice of measure to only two entropy indexes. For a more general approach we perform first order stochastic dominance tests with the micro data to determine whether the distribution for the first year is more unequal than the distribution for the last year available.[17] Column (5) of Table 6.5 shows the year that Lorenz dominates (is more equal) the distribution of the current year (blank spaces indicate that there is no first order stochastic dominance between the year in question and other years). The test is performed only for the end-points. In Brazil, Chile, Costa Rica, Mexico, Panama, and Uruguay the Lorenz curves for the first and last years intersect at some point, so the direction of the change in inequality is ambiguous. In the case of Honduras, Peru and Venezuela, the last year is dominated by the first, so there is an unambiguous increase in inequality.

5 What is behind the changes?

This section explores what is driving the changes in inequality in Latin America in the 1990s. First we look into the role played by some specific socio-economic groups and we then focus on the role of the different income sources. We stress that our objective is not to explain the shifts but rather provide an idea about what aspects of the data are driving the changes.

5.1 Who is behind the changes?

We are especially interested in determining which parts of the distribution have been shifting in Latin America in the 1990s because theoretically it is not clear if after periods of macroeconomic instability and economic reform there are specific groups of the population that are able to take advantage of the opportunities that are being generated. To look into this issue, we first focus on the influence of the richest sectors of the population and secondly we try to establish the effect of other groups, characterized by their years of schooling.

A simple way to verify if the lack of distributive progress is due to a continuation of the concentration of resources in few hands, is to re-compute the Gini coefficient by truncating the distribution at the top.[18] Specifically, we estimate inequality by excluding the richest 10 households, the richest one per cent of the population, the richest two per cent, the richest five per cent, and the richest 10 per cent, respectively, and verify if the direction and magnitude of the distributive shift is similar to the results in Table 6.2. Table 6.6 presents the results.

In Chile, Costa Rica, Honduras, and Venezuela, truncating the distribution at the richest 10 per cent or above does not make much of a difference. The change in inequality in these four cases is practically the same as in Table 6.2. However, there are countries where the conclusion about the change in inequality is very sensitive to the sample chosen for the estimation. In Brazil, for instance, if the 10 richest households were excluded, the conclusion is that inequality changed by 0.09 Gini points between 1992 and 1996, rather than by 0.02 points. This would be one of the greatest shifts observed in the 1990s in Latin America and even in the countries from outside the region. A similar result is obtained if the distribution is truncated anywhere above the richest decile. The main reason behind the increase in inequality in the 1990s in this country is the deterioration in the distribution of income among the first nine deciles. In fact, the other two elements affecting the change in total inequality, which are the distribution within the richest 10 per cent and the differences between the average income of the richest decile and the rest of the population, contributed to reduce inequality. A similar, although much less extreme result is obtained for Uruguay. If we exclude the 10 richest households from the calculation, the conclusion is that inequality increased much more during the present decade.

The opposite appears to be the case in Mexico, Panama, and Peru. In Mexico, excluding the richest two per cent, five per cent, and 10 per cent from the computation of the Gini leads to the conclusion that inequality declined significantly between 1989 and 1996. Most of the shift is given by the change between 1994 and 1996. During these two years, the distribution among the first nine deciles actually improved markedly, but due to the top 10 per cent overall inequality failed to decline in a significant way. A similar situation arises in Panama. The increase in 0.02 Gini points in this country is mainly due to the distributional changes among the richest one per cent of the population. In Peru, about two-thirds of the overall shift is accounted for by the richest five per cent of the population.

Another way of looking at the influence of specific subgroups is to divide the population according to years of schooling rather than to the

Table 6.6 Inequality with truncated income of distribution, 1992–97

Country	*Year*	*Excluding*				
		Richest 10 households	*Richest 1%*	*Richest 2%*	*Richest 5%*	*Richest 10%*
Brazil	1992	0.4981	0.4705	0.4475	0.4098	0.3685
Brazil	1993	0.5921	0.5424	0.5188	0.4736	0.4276
Brazil	1995	0.5901	0.5447	0.5222	0.4781	0.4317
Brazil	1996	0.5891	0.5460	0.5240	0.4814	0.4375
Chile	1990	0.5429	0.4958	0.4738	0.4290	0.3793
Chile	1992	0.5199	0.4719	0.4471	0.4010	0.3581
Chile	1994	0.5383	0.4906	0.4675	0.4250	0.3802
Chile	1996	0.5575	0.5110	0.4839	0.4347	0.3871
Costa Rica	1989	0.4516	0.4287	0.4140	0.3866	0.3568
Costa Rica	1991	0.4497	0.4263	0.4126	0.3843	0.3538
Costa Rica	1993	0.4476	0.4251	0.4105	0.3802	0.3493
Costa Rica	1995	0.4517	0.4241	0.4079	0.3789	0.3488
Honduras	1992	0.5435	0.5024	0.4809	0.4432	0.4062
Honduras	1996	0.5175	0.4760	0.4557	0.4218	0.3868
Honduras	1998	0.5818	0.5435	0.5235	0.4893	0.4566
Mexico	1989	0.5236	0.4735	0.4494	0.4078	0.3671
Mexico	1992	0.5200	0.4892	0.4664	0.4241	0.3800
Mexico	1994	0.5295	0.4887	0.4646	0.4189	0.3740
Mexico	1996	0.5300	0.4600	0.4200	0.3900	0.3400
Panama	1991	0.5556	0.5275	0.5098	0.4785	0.4454
Panama	1995	0.5555	0.5237	0.5046	0.4667	0.4302
Panama	1997	0.5698	0.5315	0.5112	0.4744	0.4389
Peru	1991	0.4479	0.4248	0.4095	0.3800	0.3509
Peru	1994	0.4695	0.4385	0.4215	0.3918	0.3620
Peru	1997	0.4938	0.4589	0.4375	0.4003	0.3684
Uruguay	1989	0.3934	0.3696	0.3570	0.3316	0.3046
Uruguay	1992	0.4263	0.4010	0.3859	0.3564	0.3270
Uruguay	1995	0.4189	0.3942	0.3810	0.3540	0.3250
Venezuela	1995	0.4673	0.4317	0.4150	0.3841	0.3529
Venezuela	1997	0.4897	0.4560	0.4386	0.4051	0.3706

Source: Authors' calculations from household survey data.

position in the distribution. This has the advantage that most individuals in Latin America do not continue their formal schooling after age 20 and makes it possible to follow the same group of individuals across surveys.[19] Table 6.7 presents our estimations by excluding different groups of individuals at the top of the schooling (rather than

Table 6.7 Inequality, by excluding education groups, 1992–97

Country	*Year*	*Excluding*			
		Years of educ > 19 (1)	*Years of educ > 17 (2)*	*Years of educ > 14 (3)*	*Years of educ > 11 (4)*
Brazil	1992	0.5702	0.5690	0.5452	0.5377
Brazil	1993	0.5930	0.5912	0.5648	0.5565
Brazil	1995	0.5887	0.5868	0.5562	0.5477
Brazil	1996	0.5884	0.5860	0.5576	0.5506
Chile	1990	0.5472	0.5415	0.5266	0.5268
Chile	1992	0.5220	0.5099	0.4872	0.4852
Chile	1994	0.5566	0.5492	0.5270	0.5075
Chile	1996	0.5634	0.5554	0.5349	0.5296
Costa Rica	1989	0.4590	0.4573	0.4445	0.4383
Costa Rica	1991	0.4614	0.4571	0.4464	0.4379
Costa Rica	1993	0.4542	0.4507	0.4372	0.4318
Costa Rica	1995	0.4569	0.4542	0.4370	0.4286
Honduras	1992	0.5507	0.5437	0.5323	0.5114
Honduras	1996	0.5295	0.5243	0.5077	0.4913
Honduras	1998	0.5865	0.5857	0.5841	0.5869
Mexico	1989	0.5355	0.5352	0.5126	0.5056
Mexico	1992	0.5383	0.5383	0.5139	0.5032
Mexico	1994	0.5328	0.5329	0.5035	0.4871
Mexico	1996	0.5143	0.4983	0.4881	0.4668
Panama	1991	0.5621	0.5558	0.5444	0.5364
Panama	1995	0.5555	0.5474	0.5291	0.5270
Panama	1997	0.5720	0.5544	0.5300	0.5430
Peru	1991	0.4584	0.4583	0.4404	0.4368
Peru	1994	0.4806	0.4785	0.4518	0.4439
Peru	1997	0.5025	0.5003	0.4706	0.4633
Uruguay	1989	0.3992	0.3992	0.3952	0.3905
Uruguay	1992	0.4306	0.4255	0.4161	0.4105
Uruguay	1995	0.4196	0.4143	0.4043	0.3969
Venezuela	1995	0.4706	0.4702	0.4537	0.4457
Venezuela	1997	0.4863	0.4841	0.4693	0.4644

Source: Authors' calculations from household survey data.

the income) distribution. Column (1) excludes individuals over around 20 years of age with at least 20 years of formal schooling (typically these individuals have post-graduate education). The second column excludes those with at least 18 years (with college degree), the third column truncates the schooling distribution at 15 years (some college education), while the last column refers to the Gini coefficient computed for individuals with at least 12 years (some post-secondary). The change in overall inequality is the result of the inequality within the group we are considering (those below each schooling threshold), plus the inequality among those in the subgroup excluded from the calculation, plus the inequality due to the difference in average income between the two groups. In Table 6.7 we are considering the distribution only within one specific group.

In Brazil, Chile, Costa Rica, and Uruguay, the conclusion about the magnitude of the change in inequality remains practically unchanged after truncating the schooling distribution. In Honduras, excluding all individuals with schooling over 11 years would lead to the conclusion that inequality changed more than when we consider the whole sample. Thus, the subgroup of individuals with more than 14 years of schooling actually contributes to reduce inequality during the 1990s. However, in Panama and Venezuela, and especially in Mexico and Peru, the opposite is the case. In Panama, Venezuela, and Peru excluding the highly educated from the estimation would lead to the conclusion that inequality increased less, while in Mexico, the conclusion would be that there was a sharp decline. Thus, in these four countries, the dynamics among individuals with more than14 years of schooling are one of the main reasons why income distribution has not improved.

5.2 Which income sources are behind the changes?

In a similar way to that of the previous section it is possible to ask which types of income sources have been behind the changes in inequality. We have already presented some information on this in Table 6.3, but to provide a more precise idea about the contribution of each source to total inequality we apply the decomposition suggested by Székely (1998). This method allows us to identify the effect on total inequality of changes in the distribution within each source and changes in the factor shares.[20]

Table 6.8 presents the decomposition of the change between the first and the last year available for each country. We divide total income into four different sources: labour income for employees, labour income for self-employed, non-labour income, and non-monetary income. The split of labour income into self-employment and employees is because, presumably, one of the effects of economic reform is the creation of market opportunities which could be reflected in a surge in self-employment.

Table 6.8 Decomposition of the change in inequality by income source

Country	*Effect*	*Total*	*(%) contribution by source*			
			Labour income employees	*Labour income self-emp*	*Non-labour income*	*Non-monetary income*
Brazil	Factor share effect	5.5	23.2	−16.5	−1.3	
	Inequality effect	94.5	95.1	−43.4	42.9	
	Total	100	118.3	−59.9	41.6	
Chile	Factor share effect	4.6	−15.7	−11.2	13.7	17.8
	Inequality effect	95.4	51.6	−13.1	28.3	28.6
	Total	100	35.9	−24.3	42.0	46.3
Costa Rica	Factor share effect	2.5	15.0	−4.8	−7.7	
	Inequality effect	97.5	168.4	−90.8	19.9	
	Total	100	183.4	−95.6	12.2	
Honduras	Factor share effect	47.8	−186.6	246.0	−11.6	
	Inequality effect	52.2	274.3	−210.4	−11.6	
	Total	100	87.6	35.6	−23.2	
Mexico	Factor share effect	0.4	−0.3	4.1	0.7	−4.2
	Inequality effect	99.6	134.6	−42.0	14.6	−7.6
	Total	100	134.4	−37.9	15.3	−11.8
Panama	Factor share effect	3.7	15.0	−4.4	−6.9	
	Inequality effect	96.3	88.2	−20.8	28.9	
	Total	100	103.2	−25.2	22.0	
Peru	Factor share effect	9.9	−6.4	−0.8	1.3	15.9
	Inequality effect	90.1	11.2	−13.8	2.5	90.2
	Total	100	4.7	−14.6	3.8	106.1
Uruguay	Factor share effect	4.6	6.1	3.0	−8.2	3.7
	Inequality effect	95.4	111.2	−25.6	9.1	0.7
	Total	100	117.3	−22.6	0.9	4.4
Venezuela*	Factor share effect	1.3	7.0	−4.3	−1.4	
	Inequality effect	−0.3	−82.1	112.5	−30.7	
	Total	1	−75.1	108.1	−32.1	

Note: *Results are divided by 100 owing to the low value of the denominator.
Source: Authors' calculations from household survey data.

In all cases but Honduras and Venezuela, the factor share effect, which accounts for changes in the relative weight of each income source, plays a minor role in the change in income distribution. In Honduras, the relative importance of labour income from self-employment increased sharply during the 1990s. Since this source has a more unequal distribution than labour income for employees, the shift has a positive contribution to the increase in inequality. A similar situation arises in Mexico and Uruguay, although the factor share effect is much smaller. In the case of Venezuela, we observe the opposite dynamics. The share of labour income by employees increases substantially, and since this source has a less egalitarian distribution, the shift results in a contribution to increased inequality.

In all cases but Venezuela, there is deterioration in the distribution of labour incomes for employees, which accounts for a major inequality increasing effect, and there is a strong inequality reducing effect from the improvement in the distribution of labour income from the self-employed. These two shifts may be responding to the same incentives. The inequality increasing effect may be reflecting a rise in the return to skills, while the negative effect from the self-employed may be associated with a displacement of individuals with relatively high incomes and education, who might have shifted toward the jobs with the highest remuneration among employees.

Non-labour incomes have had unequalizing effects in all countries but Honduras and Venezuela. In both of these cases, the factor share and inequality effects have contributed to reducing inequality, but the effect has been totally counterbalanced by the regressive effects of labour incomes from employees. In the rest of the countries, non-labour incomes have been part of the reason why inequality has failed to decline in the 1990s. It should be stressed however, non-labour incomes tend to be captured with lower precision than labour income. So, part of the reason why this source does not play a predominant role may simply be that household surveys are not able to register them appropriately.

Only four countries have information for non-monetary incomes. In Chile and Uruguay these sources have had a modest contribution to the increase in inequality, while in Peru they have been the main cause of the shift. In Mexico, non-monetary incomes have had a modest contribution for reducing inequality.

In sum, there is no very clear pattern about the role of different income sources over the changes in inequality. The only main regularity we find for most of the countries is a substantial contribution of labour incomes of employees to the increase in inequality, which is counterbalanced to some extent by the improvement in the distribution of labour incomes from self-employment.

6 Conclusions

We can say confidently that income distribution in Latin America has not improved in the 1990s, at least for the countries where comparable household surveys covering most of the population are available. There are three cases – Honduras, Peru and Venezuela – where inequality has definitely increased sharply, and in seven of nine cases the Gini coefficient estimated in a conventional way, shows a statistically significant rise.

However, the lack of distributive progress in Latin America is not an exclusive feature of this region. There are 12 countries from outside the region with data for at least two points during the 1990s that show similar trends. In fact, the percentage increase in inequality in Latin America is among the smallest, and in eight out of the nine countries covered the shift has been smaller than the increase in inequality in the US.

The shifts we document are genuine shifts. They do not seem to be due to changes in sample size or coverage of different socio-economic subgroups in the surveys. There are even cases, such as Mexico, where there are reasons to believe that the coverage of the richest individuals has declined across surveys, so that the apparent stability in the income distribution may simply be an illusion created by an underrepresentation of the incomes at the top tail of the distribution.

Although the household surveys used for our estimation are strictly comparable within each country, undoubtedly there are differences across countries. If we limit the comparison to the income concepts that are most widely comparable (labour incomes) we conclude that inequality in all nine countries has increased during the 1990s.

The above conclusions are robust to the use of a range of parameters accounting for possible economies of scale in consumption and to the use of alternative adult equivalence scales. However, our impression about the changes in inequality is modified if we use inequality measures other than the Gini coefficient. If an index that is more sensitive to redistributions at the bottom of the distribution is used, inequality declines in four out of nine cases, while when a top-sensitive index is employed, inequality increases in all the countries in our sample. If the whole distribution is compared, there are only three cases where inequality in the last year for which observations are available is unambiguously greater than in the first year. In the remaining six countries our impression about the change depends on the section of the distribution on which we focus. Even so, the conclusion is that the distribution has *not* improved unambiguously in any of the nine countries holds.

In Mexico, Panama, and Peru the lack of distributive progress is accounted for by the top 10 per cent of the distribution. Excluding this subgroup from the calculation would lead to the conclusion that inequality declined. In Brazil, the opposite is the case, while in the other five countries the change in inequality is similar when including or excluding this group. In Panama and Venezuela, but specially in Mexico and Peru, the lack of distributive progress is mainly attributed to the income changes among highly educated individuals.

One interesting conclusion is that the changes in labour incomes earned by employees have been the main force driving the distributional shifts in Latin America in the 1990s. The distribution of labour income by the self-employed improved during the decade, and the relative importance of this source of income declined in most cases. This might be reflecting that the self-employed with higher incomes and education could have shifted to the salaried activities where the returns to skills have been rising.

There are no signs of reductions in the Gini coefficient in the nine countries under study. Does this mean that we should not expect major improvements in distribution in other regions, such as eastern Europe, where countries are facing similar conditions to Latin America in the 1980s? Or that it is likely that the distribution will worsen in East Asia after the financial crisis, and that the trends will persist even with more stable macroeconomic conditions? The evidence presented here leads us to think that the answer might be 'yes'.

Appendix

Table 6A.1 Description of the data, 1992–97

Country	*Year*	*Name of the survey*	*Coverage*	*Sample size*	
				Households	*Individuals*
Brazil	1992	Pesquisa Nacional por Amostra de Domicilios	National	78,188	317,145
	1993	Pesquisa Nacional por Amostra de Domicilios	National	80,054	322,011
	1995	Pesquisa Nacional por Amostra de Domicilios	National	85,167	334,106
	1996	Pesquisa Nacional por Amostra de Domicilios	National	84,862	331,142
Chile	1990	Encuesta de Caracterización Socioeconómica Nacional	National	25,793	105,189
	1992	Encuesta de Caracterización Socioeconómica Nacional	National	27,666	110,555
	1994	Encuesta de Caracterización Socioeconómica Nacional	National	45,379	178,057
	1996	Encuesta de Caracterización Socioeconómica Nacional	National	33,636	134,262
Costa Rica	1989	Encuesta de Hogares de Propósitos Múltiples	National	7,637	34,368
	1991	Encuesta de Hogares de Propósitos Múltiples	National	8,002	35,565
	1993	Encuesta de Hogares de Propósitos Múltiples	National	8,696	37,703
	1995	Encuesta de Hogares de Propósitos Múltiples	National	9,631	40,613
	1997	Encuesta de Hogares de Propósitos Múltiples	National	9.923	41,277
Honduras	1992	Encuesta Permanente de Hogares de Propósitos Múltiples	National	4,757	24,704
	1996	Encuesta Permanente de Hogares de Propósitos Múltiples	National	6,428	33,172

(*continues*)

Table 6A.1 (Continued)

Country	*Year*	*Name of the survey*	*Coverage*	*Sample size*	
				Households	*Individuals*
	1998	Encuesta Permanente de Hogares de Propósitos Múltiples	National	6,493	32,696
Mexico	1989	Encuesta Nacional de Ingreso Gasto de los Hogares	National	11,531	57,289
	1992	Encuesta Nacional de Ingreso Gasto de los Hogares	National	10,530	50,862
	1994	Encuesta Nacional de Ingreso Gasto de los Hogares	National	12,815	60,365
	1996	Encuesta Nacional de Ingreso Gasto de los Hogares	National	14,042	64,916
Panama	1991	Encuesta Continua de Hogares – Mano de Obra	National	8,867	38,000
	1995	Encuesta Continua de Hogares	National	9,875	40,320
	1997	Encuesta de Hogares	National	9,897	39,706
Peru	1991	Encuesta Nacional de Hogares sobre Medición de Niveles de Vida	National	2,308	11,507
	1994	Encuesta Nacional de Hogares sobre Medición de Niveles de Vida	National	3,623	18,662
	1997	Encuesta Nacional de Hogares sobre Medición de Niveles de Vida	National	3,843	19,575
Uruguay	1989	Encuesta Continua de Hogares	Urban	9,684	31,766
	1992	Encuesta Continua de Hogares	Urban	9,282	29,927
	1995	Encuesta Continua de Hogares	Urban	20,057	64,930
	1997	Encuesta Continua de Hogares	Urban	20,003	64,028
Venezuela	1995	Encuesta de Hogares por Muestra	National	18,702	92,450
	1997	Encuesta de Hogares por Muestra	National	15,948	76,965

Table 6A.2 Description of the data, 1992–97

Country	Year	Name of the survey	Income						All non-lab. inc.
			Labour	*Property rent*	*Capital rent*	*Transfers*	*Non-monetary*	*Imputed rent*	*Repor, as 1 source*
Brazil	1992	Pesquisa Nacional por Amostra de Domicilios	X	X	X[c]	X	n.a.	n.a.	
	1993	Pesquisa Nacional por Amostra de Domicilios	X	X	X[c]	X	n.a.	n.a.	
	1995	Pesquisa Nacional por Amostra de Domicilios	X	X	X[c]	X	n.a.	n.a.	
	1996	Pesquisa Nacional por Amostra de Domicilios	X	X	X[c]	X	n.a.	n.a.	
Chile	1990	Encuesta de Caracterización Socioeconómica Nacional	X	X[b]	X[b]	X[b]	X	X	X
	1992	Encuesta de Caracterización Socioeconómica Nacional	X	X	X	X	X	X	
	1994	Encuesta de Caracterización Socioeconómica Nacional	X	X[b]	X[b]	X[b]	X	X	X
	1996	Encuesta de Caracterización Socioeconómica Nacional	X	X[b]	X[b]	X[b]	X	X	X
Costa Rica	1989	Encuesta de Hogares de Propósitos Múltiples	X	X[b]	X[b]	X[b]	n.a.	n.a.	X
	1991	Encuesta de Hogares de Propósitos Múltiples	X	X[b]	X[b]	X[b]	n.a.	n.a.	X
	1993	Encuesta de Hogares de Propósitos Múltiples	X	X[b]	X[b]	X[b]	n.a.	n.a.	X

(*continues*)

Table 6A.2 (Continued)

Country	*Year*	*Name of the survey*	*Income*						*All non-lab. inc.*
			Labour	*Property rent*	*Capital rent*	*Transfers*	*Non-monetary*	*Imputed rent*	*Repor, as 1 source*
	1995	Encuesta de Hogares de Propósitos Múltiples	X	X[b]	X[b]	X[b]	n.a.	n.a.	X
	1997	Encuesta de Hogares de Propósitos Múltiples	X	X[b]	X[b]	X[b]	n.a.	n.a.	X
Honduras	1992	Encuesta Permanente de Hogares de Propósitos Múltiples	X	n.a.	n.a.	n.a.	n.a.	n.a.	
	1996	Encuesta Permanente de Hogares de Propósitos Múltiples	X	n.a.	n.a.	n.a.	n.a.	n.a.	
	1998	Encuesta Permanente de Hogares de Propósitos Múltiples	X	X[b]	X[b]	X[b]	n.a.	n.a.	X
Mexico	1989	Encuesta Nacional de Ingreso Gasto de los Hogares	X	X	X	X	X	X	
	1992	Encuesta Nacional de Ingreso Gasto de los Hogares	X	X	X	X	X	X	
	1994	Encuesta Nacional de Ingreso Gasto de los Hogares	X	X	X	X	X	X	
	1996	Encuesta Nacional de Ingreso Gasto de los Hogares	X	X	X	X	X	X	
Panama	1991	Encuesta Continua de Hogares – Mano de Obra	X	X[a]	X[a]	X	n.a.	n.a.	

	1995	Encuesta Continua de Hogares	X	X[a]	X[a]	X	n.a.	n.a.	
	1997	Encuesta de Hogares	X	X[a]	X[a]	X	n.a.	n.a.	
Peru	1991	Encuesta Nacional de Hogares sobre Medición de Niveles de Vida	X	X[b]	X[b]	X[b]	X	X	X
	1994	Encuesta Nacional de Hogares sobre Medición de Niveles de Vida	X	X[b]	X[b]	X[b]	X	X	X
	1997	Encuesta Nacional de Hogares sobre Medición de Niveles de Vida	X	X[b]	X[b]	X[b]	X	X	X
Uruguay	1989	Encuesta Continua de Hogares	X	X	X	X	X	X	
	1992	Encuesta Continua de Hogares	X	X	X	X	X	X	
	1995	Encuesta Continua de Hogares	X	X	X	X	X	X	
	1997	Encuesta Continua de Hogares	X	X	X	X	X	X	
Venezuela	1995	Encuesta de Hogares por Muestra	X	X[b]	X[b]	X[b]	n.a.	n.a.	X
	1997	Encuesta de Hogares por Muestra	X	X[b]	X[b]	X[b]	n.a.	n.a.	X

Notes: [a] Cannot separate between property and capital rent.
[b] Cannot separate other sources.
[c] Cannot separate capital rent from other sources
n.a. = Not available.

Notes

1 See Székely and Hilgert (1999) for the most updated comparison of inequality indicators in 18 Latin American countries and countries from other regions.
2 See Londoño and Székely (1997) for evidence on the changes in inequality and poverty, and IDB (1997) for information on macro conditions.
3 There is a large list of works documenting a deterioration in the distribution of income during recession, volatility and stabilization. Some examples are Székely (1998) and the collection of country studies in Ganuza, Taylor and Morley (1998).
4 One of the best examples of why stable economic conditions do not necessarily imply improvements in the distribution is inflation. It is well known that high inflation rates affect the poor more because they do not have access to financial instruments to protect their assets and because their incomes are more closely tied to minimum wages, which tend to deteriorate in these conditions. However, if inflation is controlled this normally means that the additional pressure on inequality will be released. Inequality will not continue to grow, but there is no reason to expect that it will decline.
5 See IDB (1997).
6 Countries with a tradition of producing household surveys are left out. Two notable cases are Argentina, where most of the surveys refer only to Gran Buenos Aires, and cover only around 33 per cent of the population of the country, and Bolivia, which has several urban surveys, but which contain less than 50 per cent of the population.
7 The only exceptions we make are one survey for Peru and two surveys for Honduras. The 1991, 1994 and 1997 Peruvian surveys are nationally representative, but the 1991 survey excludes the geographic areas of Costa Rural, Selva Urbana and Selva Rural, which account for 16 per cent and 18 per cent of the total population in 1994 and 1997, respectively. Throughout this work we do not restrict the 1994 and 1997 samples to the same geographic areas as 1991 mainly because of the loss of information that this would convey. However, we checked if our conclusions about the changes in inequality in Peru are modified when restricting the last surveys to the geographic areas covered in 1991, but none of them are modified. In fact, the Gini coefficient computed with and without these geographic areas in 1994 and 1997 is not statistically significantly different from the Gini for the whole population. In the case of Honduras, the three surveys we use are strictly comparable. However, the 1998 survey includes additional questions in the questionnaire to capture non-labour incomes. We have used the three surveys for our analysis and in Section 3 we show that the conclusions about the changes in inequality in this country hold when we use only the incomes that are strictly comparable throughout.
8 We end up with four observations for Brazil, Chile, Costa Rica, Honduras, and Mexico, three for Panama, Peru and, Uruguay, and two for Venezuela.
9 As mentioned previously, household surveys for Venezuela are available for years previous to 1995. We have not used this information here because the data is not comparable with the surveys for 1995 and 1997 (the main difference is a change in the questionnaire). We do have access to household surveys for Venezuela for 1989 and 1993. The Gini indexes computed from

those data are 0.44 and 0.43, respectively. Including them in the picture would lead to the conclusion that inequality in this country increased by even more than is apparent in Figure 6.1, but this conclusion should be taken cautiously for the reasons just mentioned.

10 Note that the comparison does not refer to the same years for each country. In all cases, with the exception of Venezuela, there is a gap of at least four years between the first and last observation. Note also that the last year in the comparison for the Latin American countries, is generally closer to 1999 than in the other regions.

11 It should be noted that non-labour income is a greater proportion of total income among the richest households. This, added to the results in Table 6.2, shows that the coverage of the richest sectors has in fact been declining in Mexico, and suggests that one of the reasons why inequality in this country has remained fairly stable in the 1990s is because of changes in the coverage of the surveys rather than genuine distributional stability.

12 We present the data in this way, rather than through the traditional decomposition of the change in inequality into between and within group effects (by using members of the general entropy family of inequality measures) because our objective is to determine whether our impression of the change in inequality depends on the geographic area that the surveys cover. For Venezuela the 1997 household survey does not contain a variable indicating the geographic location of each observation. For this reason we do not separate the data in this particular case.

13 Londoño and Székely (1997) review 111 studies measuring poverty and inequality in Latin America between 1970 and 1997. In the vast majority of the studies, inequality is computed as described in the main text.

14 See for instance Gottschalk and Smeeding (1997).

15 This equivalence scale is taken from Ferreira and Litchfield (1997), who adjust the original scale by Contreras (1996). The composition of the average household in Latin America is two adults, one child between 11 and 15 years of age, one child between five and 10, and one under five. For the typical five-member household, applying the Contreras equivalence scale implies reducing household size from five to 3.5. We present the results with the method by Contreras only because by using this scale we get higher variation in the income distribution estimates than with the 'Amsterdam' scale.

16 These indexes take the following form:

$$E = 1 - \left[(1/n_x) \sum_{i=1} (y_i/\mu_x)^{\beta} \right]^{(1/\beta)}$$

where β is a parameter that can be assigned any real value, n_x is the size of the population, and y_i and μ_x are the income of each individual and average income of population x, respectively. Specifying a high positive value yields an index that is more sensitive to redistributions at the upper tail of the distribution, while a negative value yields indices attaching larger weights to changes at the lower tail.

17 In fact, we computed the entropy measures with a wide variety of values for the parameter α. We present the cases only for $\beta = 1$ and $\beta = -1$ here because

these are enough to make the point that different measures may lead to different conclusions.

18 The standard way to measure the influence on a change in inequality of certain subgroups of the population is to classify the population according to certain personal characteristics and decompose the change in inequality into the effect of the redistribution within and between groups, respectively, and the effect of population shifts from one group to another (see, for instance, Mookherjee and Shorrocks (1982) and Tsakloglou (1993)). For the purposes of this chapter we focus exclusively on the redistribution within groups.

19 There will be changes in composition owing to the incorporation of individuals who were below 20 in the first survey, but since we are not looking at long periods of time, these composition effects are not expected to be strong.

20 The decomposition consists on expressing a change in inequality as:

$$\Delta I = \sum_{i=1} I_k \Delta \beta_k + \sum_{i=1} \beta_k \Delta I_k$$

where I is overall inequality, I_k is inequality within source k and β_k is the income share of source k. The first term on the right-hand side of the equation is the 'factor share effect', while the second term is the 'inequality effect'. The equation provides an exact decomposition that can be applied equally well to any inequality measure.

References

Contreras, D. (1996) 'Household and Individual Welfare: Evidence from Less Developed Economies', University of California, Los Angeles, mimeo.

Cowell, F. A. and S. P. Jenkins (1995) 'How Much Inequality Can We Explain? A Methodology and an Application to the United States', *Economic Journal*, vol. 105, pp. 421–30.

Deaton, A. and J. Muellbauer (1980) *Economics and Consumer Behaviour* (Cambridge: Cambridge University Press).

Ferreira, F. and J. Litchfield (1997) 'Income Distribution and Poverty: A Statistical Overview', Annex 1 in *Chile, Poverty and Income Distribution in a High-Growth Economy: 1987–1995* (Washington, DC: The World Bank).

Foster, J. and A. Sen (1997) 'On Economic Inequality after a Quarter Century' (with Amartya Sen) in Amartya Sen's *On Economic Inequality*, enlarged edition (Oxford: Clarendon Press).

Ganuza, E., L. Taylor and S. Morley (1998) *Politica Macroeconómica y Pobreza en America Latina y el Caribe* (Madrid: Mundi Prensa for UNDP, IDB and ECLAC).

Gottschalk, P. and T. Smeeding (1997) 'Cross-National Comparisons of Earnings and Income Inequality', *Journal of Economic Literature*, vol. 35, pp. 633–87.

Inter-American Development Bank (IDB) (1997) *Latin America After a Decade of Reforms: Economic and Social Progress in Latin America* (Baltimore: United States: Johns Hopkins University Press).

Lanjow, P. and M. Ravallion (1994) 'Poverty and Household Size', Policy Research Working Paper, no. 1332 (Washington, DC: The World Bank).

Londoño, J. L. and M. Székely (1997) 'Persistent Poverty and Excess Inequality: Latin America, 1970–1995', Working Paper, no. 357, Office of the Chief Economist, Inter American Development Bank, Washington, DC.
Mookherjee, D. and A. Shorrocks (1982) 'A Decomposition Analysis of the Trend in UK Income Inequality', *Economic Journal*, vol. 92, pp. 886–902.
Székely, M (1998) *The Economics of Poverty, Inequality and Wealth Accumulation in Mexico* (London: Macmillan–now Palgrave).
Székely, M. and M. Hilgert (1999) 'What's Behind the Inequality We Measure: An Exploration with Latin American Data for the 1990s', Research Department, Inter American Development Bank, Washington DC, mimeo.
Tsakloglou, P. (1993) 'Aspects of Inequality in Greece', *Journal of Development Economics*, vol. 40, pp. 53–74.

7

Inequality and Mortality during Russia's Economic Transition

*Elizabeth Brainerd**
Williams College and Center for International Development, Harvard University, USA

1 Introduction

As the twentieth century drew to a close, few Russians mourned its departure. A centenarian born at the turn of the century in Russia would have experienced in her lifetime an extraordinary range of events, encompassing civil war, revolution, famine, political purges, a devastating world war, and finally a traumatic if hopeful attempt to introduce capitalism into an economy previously run by central planning. Concurrently with the latter event, she would have witnessed an upsurge in mortality and decline in life expectancy of a magnitude never experienced by a country at peace. Russia's struggles in the 1990s seem only a continuation of the difficulties of the past, as the reforms intended to improve the country's standard of living have instead, at least initially, impoverished part of the population and led to continuing economic instability.

What is the relationship, if any, between the economic reforms implemented in Russia in the 1990s and the mortality crisis that occurred during the same period? The mortality upsurge has been heavily concentrated among men in their prime working ages – children and pensioners have emerged remarkably unscathed from the recent demographic catastrophe – which suggests that rising mortality rates may at least in part be linked with the substantial changes in the labour market that occurred in Russia during this period. In particular, could there be a link between the tremendous increase in inequality in Russia in the early

* The author thanks Richard Freeman and Katherine Terrell for helpful suggestions. Financial support from the German Marshall Fund of the United States is gratefully acknowledged.

1990s and the mortality crisis that occurred simultaneously with this increase? This is the question addressed in this chapter.

The relationship between inequality and mortality both within and across countries has become a subject of much interest and debate in recent years, with most of the literature on the issue examining the relationship across countries, or across US states or British regions. Analysing this relationship for Russia affords a unique opportunity to examine the question in the context of a sharp and rapid decline in life expectancy, in contrast to the US and other developed countries in which life expectancy evolves slowly over time and follows a gradual upward trend. It also provides an opportunity to examine the relationship during a time of rapidly increasing income inequality.

The chapter is organized as follows. Section 2 briefly summarizes the literature on inequality and mortality, and discusses the possible mechanisms through which the two might be related in the Russian context. Section 3 describes the trends in inequality and mortality that have characterized the Russian population in the 1990s. Section 4 describes the empirical work that tests the hypothesis of a positive correlation between inequality and death rates in Russia and analyses the results. Section 5 concludes.

2 Previous research

As noted above, the possible link between inequality and mortality has been an area of active research and debate in recent years. This literature has primarily been within the realm of public health specialists and demographers, although it is an area of increasing interest to economists as well. One of the earliest studies of the issue is Rodgers (1979), which showed that income inequality (measured by the Gini coefficient) was negatively related to life expectancy across 56 countries in the mid-1970s.[1] Waldmann (1992) reported a positive relationship between infant mortality and the share of income going to the rich across 57 countries in 1960 and 1970 after controlling for the income of the poor and other factors; and Wilkinson (1996) demonstrated a strong correlation between inequality and mortality across countries in the 1970s and 1980s. Researchers studying the US have found that the relationship also holds across US states (Kaplan *et al.* (1996); Kennedy, Kawachi and Prothrow-Stith (1996)).

Many of these studies have been criticized on a number of grounds, including sensitivity of the results to the inequality measure used, and the 'ecological fallacy', i.e. that positive cross-region correlations between inequality and mortality fail to prove that inequality affects the probability of dying at the individual level. In response to this criticism, researchers have turned to individual-level data to study the issue. Daly *et al.* (1998), for example, test the correlation between state-level inequality and mortality risk using the Panel Study of Income Dynamics. Like other researchers using individual-level data (for example, Mellor and Milyo (1999)), these authors failed to find a clear relationship between inequality and mortality. While Kennedy *et al.* (1998) did find a statistically significant relationship between self-reported health status and mortality using a large survey of individuals conducted by the Centers for Disease Control, this study has been criticized for methodological problems (see Mellor and Milyo (1999)).

Researchers also continue to debate the specific mechanisms that might generate a positive correlation between mortality rates and income inequality within or across countries. One possibility is that increased income inequality may result in greater frustration and stress, which in turn may lead to higher death rates (particularly due to cardiovascular disease). The positive correlation between inequality and mortality may also reflect increasingly unequal access to medical care and education; or it could operate through crime rates, with higher inequality inducing more crime. One possibility particularly relevant for Russia is the idea that one's relative ranking in society may affect health: a sense of relative deprivation may create feelings of hopelessness or induce individuals to engage in risky behaviour. Researchers have found, for example, that middle-aged men who feel despair or consider themselves failures are more likely to develop atherosclerosis (a condition that leads to heart attacks and strokes) than men who do not have such feelings, even controlling for individual risk factors such as smoking and drinking (Everson *et al.* (1997)). The Russian mortality crisis has most severely affected men in their prime working ages (this is discussed in Section 3), and this same group has experienced a substantial loss in wages, both real and relative, since the beginning of the reforms in Russia. For example, in 1991 men with 21–30 years of potential labour market experience earned 16 per cent more on average than new entrants to the labour market. By 1994 this ratio had fallen to −4 per cent, and men who would be at their peak earning years in other industrialized countries actually earned lower wages on average than did new entrants to the labour market (Brainerd (1998)). These changes in relative wages may be important in explaining rising mortality rates among older men of working age since they reflect a substantial devaluation of the human capital of these workers. The uncertainty in the labour market for older men combined with their loss of relative standing may also explain the astonishing suicide rates recorded for men in older age groups (described in Section 3). Given the profound and rapid changes experienced by the Russian population in the 1990s, it is likely that increased stress is at least in part responsible for the upsurge in mortality rates, and increased stress may in turn be due in part to increased inequality.

3 Trends in inequality and mortality in Russia in the 1990s

Russia's economic reforms began in earnest on 2 January 1992, when most prices and wages were freed from central control. Although this decisive move emulated the Polish 'Big Bang' implemented two years earlier, in contrast to Poland the reform process in Russia quickly deteriorated into an indecisive and erratic effort that resulted in high inflation and steep declines in GDP for several years. The government achieved a partial stabilization in 1995, when the inflation rate fell below 200 per cent annually and real GDP fell 'only' four per cent compared to the 12.6 per cent decline in the previous year (EBRD (1997)).

The economic instability exacted a toll on many workers. It is estimated that real GDP *per capita* fell by over one-quarter between 1990 and 1994 (EBRD (1997)), and official statistics indicate that nearly a quarter of the population earned incomes below the subsistence level in 1995 (Goskomstat (1998)). Unemployment has remained relatively low compared with some east European countries, but it has risen steadily throughout the 1990s, from 4.7 per cent of the labour force in 1992 to 8.8 per cent in 1995, eventually reaching double-digit levels in 1997 at 11.2 per cent (Goskomstat (1998)).[2]

And as Russia has joined the community of market economies, so too have Russia's workers joined the community of populations experiencing rising wage and income inequality. While this was to be expected given the collapse of the centralized wage setting system and the new opportunities to earn rents in the Russian economy, the speed and extent of the increase in inequality has nevertheless been remarkable.

Several measures of income and wage inequality in Russia are shown in Table 7.1 and in Figures 7.1a–c. The official published measures are limited to the Gini coefficient for household income and to income shares by quintile. The Gini coefficient rose slightly between 1980 and 1991, from 0.245 to 0.260, then jumped dramatically to 0.398 in 1993 and 0.409 in 1994 before declining slightly in 1995–97. This trend is illustrated in Figure 7.1a, which also shows the change in the Gini coefficient in the US since 1980. The increase in inequality in Russia in

Table 7.1 Measures of income and wage inequality in Russia, 1990–97

	1990	*1991*	*1992*	*1993*	*1994*	*1995*	*1996*	*1997*
Official measures								
Gini coefficient[a]	n.a.	0.26	0.289	0.398	0.409	0.381	0.375	0.375
Income shares by quintile:[a]								
First (poorest)	9.8	11.9	6	5.8	5.3	5.5	6.2	6.2
Second	14.9	15.8	11.6	11.1	10.2	10.2	10.7	10.6
Third	18.8	18.8	17.6	16.7	15.2	15	15.2	15.1
Fourth	23.8	22.8	26.5	24.8	23.0	22.4	21.5	21.4
Fifth (richest)	32.7	30.7	38.3	41.6	46.3	46.9	46.4	46.7
Survey-based measures								
90–10 for wages[b]	n.a.	1.079	n.a.	1.919	1.938	n.a.	n.a.	1.875
90–50 for wages[b]	n.a.	0.511	n.a.	0.956	0.995	n.a.	n.a.	0.916
50–10 for wages[b]	n.a.	0.568	n.a.	0.963	0.943	n.a.	n.a.	0.959
Variance of log wages[b]	n.a.	0.189	n.a.	0.614	0.59	n.a.	n.a.	0.641

Note: na = Not available.

[a] *Sources*: *Rossiiskii statisticheskii ezhegodnik 1998*, p. 223.

[b] Household surveys conducted by the All-Russian Centre for Public Opinion Research. Sample sizes are 2,068, 6,724, 4,923, and 2,231 for 1991, 1993, 1994, and 1997, respectively. For the latter three years, monthly surveys for three months were combined and monthly wages were deflated into rubles for the first month using regional monthly price indices.

the early 1990s dwarfs the rise in inequality in the US since 1980; the latter development has been much analysed in recent years.[3] Similar trends are evident in the quintile shares (Figure 7.1b, 7.1c), which show a large drop in the share of income earned by the poorest 20 per cent of the population in Russia and a dramatic increase in the share earned by the richest 20 per cent of the population, the latter reaching the US level in 1994. These official series indicate that the largest increase in inequality in Russia occurred between 1991 and 1993, and that income inequality peaked around 1994.

Similar trends in wage inequality are evident using household surveys to track these measures. Although these surveys are much smaller than those available in the US and the earliest survey available is for 1991, they nevertheless indicate that wage inequality rose substantially between 1991 and 1993 and followed a pattern similar to that of income inequality (Table 7.1). For example, the 90/10 log wage differential[4] rose from 1.08 in 1991 to 1.92 and 1.94 in 1993 and 1994, respectively, then declined slightly between 1994 and 1997. The one important difference between the official measures of inequality and the survey-based measures is that the former indicate a level of income inequality in Russia roughly similar to that of the US, whereas the latter suggest that wage inequality is higher in Russia than in the US.[5] Although this discrepancy may arise in part from differences in government transfers in the two countries, it may also reflect the (probable) poor quality of the official inequality measures published in Russia's statistical yearbooks. It is likely that these measures are calculated from Russia's Family Budget Survey,[6] which have been widely criticized as unrepresentative. In particular, it is reported that this survey omits individuals who work in the private sector, whereas the households surveys include such individuals.[7]

In any case, despite the weaknesses of the inequality measures – both the official measures and the survey-based measures – it is clear that the Russian population experienced a remarkably rapid and substantial increase in income and wage inequality in a few short years in the early 1990s, after living for decades in a country in which the income distribution appeared to be relatively equal.

Concurrently with these developments in the labour market occurred an equally astonishing decline in life expectancy in Russia. Between 1990 and 1994 (the apparent peak of the mortality crisis) male life expectancy at birth fell from 63.8 years to 57.6 years – a decline of over six years in the course of less than half a decade. Female life expectancy at birth declined as well, although less dramatically, from 74.3 years in 1990 to 71.2 years in 1994.

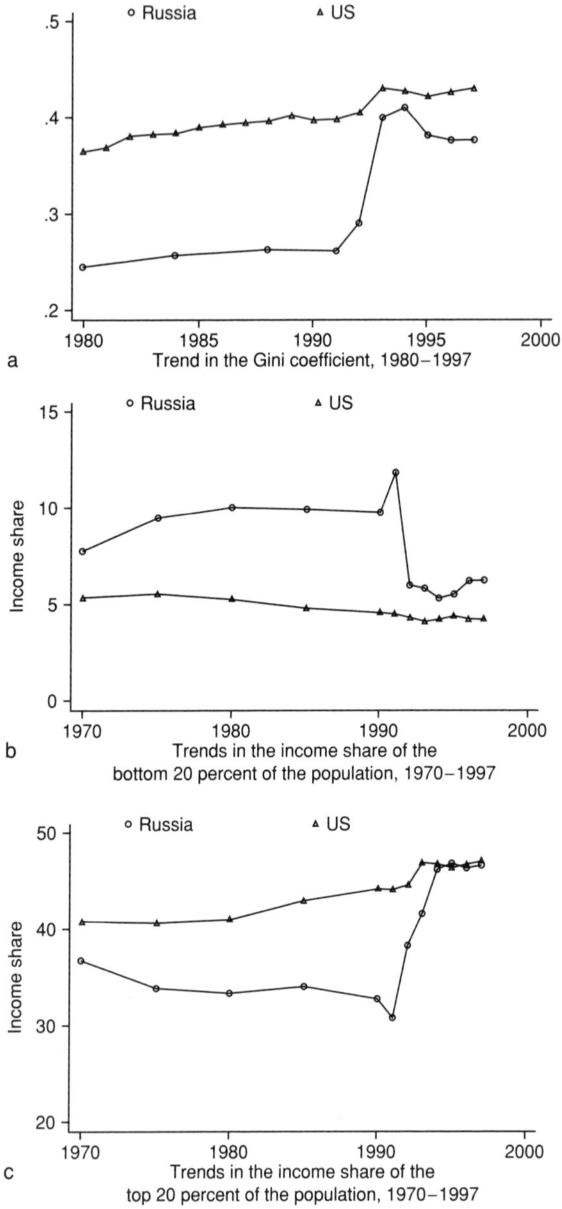

Figure 7.1 Trends in Gini coefficient, 1980–1997, and income share, 1970–1997
Sources: *Rossiiskii statisticheskii ezhegodnik 1998*; Atkinson and Micklewright (1992); US Census Bureau website, Table F-2.

Unfortunately for Russia, the 1990s were not the country's first experience of declining life expectancy. After a decade of progress in the 1950s during which life expectancy in Russia converged rapidly with that of western countries (owing largely to declining infant mortality rates), in the mid-1960s female life expectancy began to stagnate and male life expectancy entered a period of long-term decline that continued until 1984. Figures 7.2a and 7.2b illustrate this deterioration by contrasting the trends in Russian life expectancy with those of the US. In 1964 female life expectancy had nearly reached the US level, and male life expectancy was improving as well. After that year, however, Russian life expectancy stagnated while US life expectancy continued to rise, creating a

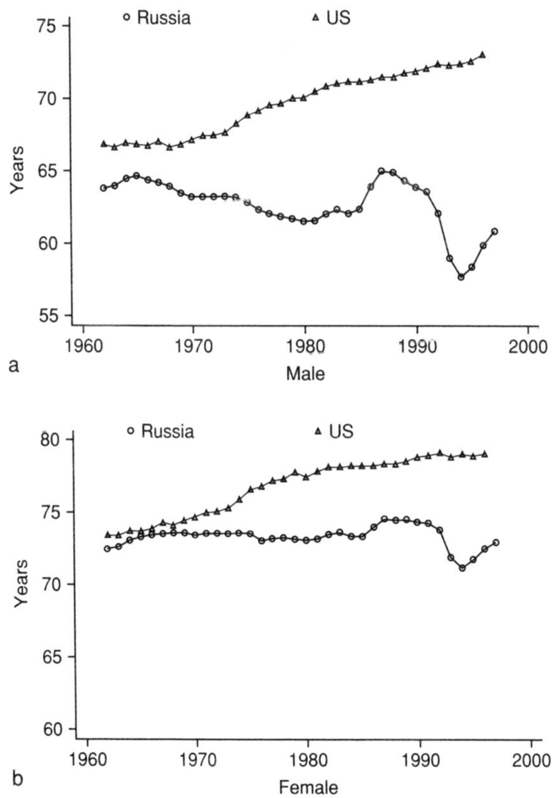

Figure 7.2 Male and female life expectancy at birth, 1962–97
Sources: *Demograficheskii ezhegodnik Rossii 1998; Statistical Abstract of the United States 1998; Historical Statistics of the United States.*

substantial life expectancy gap between the two countries. The one bright spot in Russia occurred in 1985–87 during Mikhail Gorbachev's anti-alcohol campaign. Male life expectancy improved dramatically and reached a peak of 64.9 years in 1986–87; female life expectancy reached 74.6 years in the same year.[8] Deteriorating mortality resumed in 1988 as alcohol sales returned to previous levels, and in 1991 the pace of deterioration accelerated sharply. The population began to decline in absolute terms in 1992 owing to rising mortality and falling birth rates (the birth rate fell from 13.4 to 9.6 per 1,000 population from 1990 to 1994). Mortality rates fell slightly in 1995 and declined through 1997, although the mortality rate remains extremely high by the standards of industrialized countries, and the population continues to decline in absolute terms.

Figure 7.3 illustrates the percentage increase in age-specific death rates from 1990 to 1994 for all age groups.[9] Mortality rates have increased the most for men aged 40–44, although the mortality increases are extremely high across the broad 25–54 age group. A similar group of women – those aged about 20–54 – have been most affected by rising mortality. It is striking that the working age population rather than the most vulnerable groups – children and the elderly – is bearing the burden of excess mortality.[10] It is also striking that these same age groups bore the burden of excess mortality in the 1960s and 1970s (Anderson and Silver (1990)).

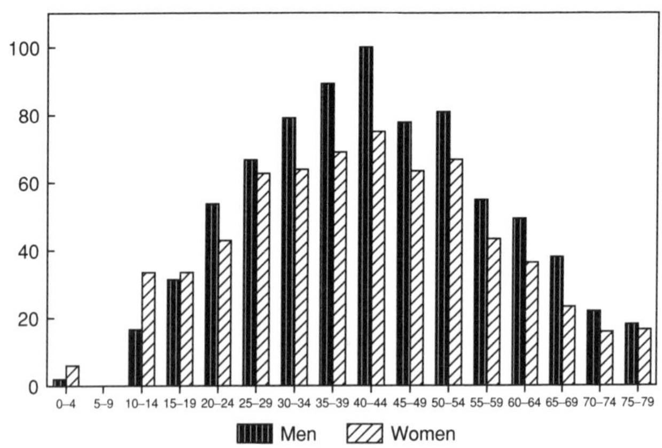

Figure 7.3 Percentage increase in age-specific death rates, men and women, 1990–94
Source: *Demograficheskii ezhegodnik Rossii 1998.*

In both the earlier and recent periods the most important cause of death has been cardiovascular diseases, followed by deaths owing to external causes (accidents, suicides, and homicides). In 1994 53.5 per cent of all deaths were owing to cardiovascular disease; 16.0 per cent were owing to external causes and 13.2 per cent were owing to cancer. Deaths from all causes except cancer increased sharply over the 1990–94 period (Table 7.2, top panel), with the largest increase occurring in deaths owing to external causes (87.5 per cent). Deaths owing to cardiovascular disease, however, explain the largest share of the *increase* in

Table 7.2 Increased death rates in Russia by cause of death, 1990–94 (death rates per 100,000 population)

All population 1990–94	*1994 number dying*	*1990 number dying*	*Extra deaths 1994 over 1990*	*% increase in deaths, this cause*	*% increase in deaths due to this cause*
All causes	1566.1	1116.7	449.4	40.2	100.0
Cardiovascular	837.3	617.4	219.9	35.6	48.9
Cancer	206.6	194.0	12.6	6.5	2.8
External causes	250.7	133.7	117.0	87.5	26.0
Resp. diseases	80.8	59.3	21.5	36.3	4.8
Digestive diseases	44.1	28.7	15.4	53.7	3.4
Infectious diseases	20.1	12.1	8.0	66.1	1.8
Other*	126.5	71.5	55.0	76.9	12.2
Men, working age					
All causes	1323.7	759.2	564.5	74.4	100.0
Cardiovascular	394.6	220.6	174.0	78.9	30.8
Cancer	145.2	142.7	2.5	1.7	0.4
External causes	534.4	284.7	249.7	87.7	44.2
Resp. diseases	68.7	30.9	37.8	122.3	6.7
Digestive diseases	51.5	23.2	28.3	122.0	5.0
Infectious diseases	39.2	19.6	19.6	100.0	3.5
Other*	90.1	37.5	52.6	140.3	9.3
Women, working age					
All causes	312.9	198.1	114.8	58.0	100.0
Cardiovascular	82.0	47.9	34.1	71.2	29.7
Cancer	60.2	60.5	–0.3	–0.5	–0.3
External causes	103.9	51.7	52.2	101.0	45.5
Resp. diseases	10.8	6.1	4.7	43.5	4.1
Digestive diseases	15.9	7.1	8.8	123.9	3.7
Infectious diseases	6.0	2.9	3.1	106.9	2.7
Other*	34.1	21.9	12.2	55.7	10.6

Note: * Calculated as a residual.
Source: Calculated from *Demograficheskii ezhegodnik Rossii 1996*.

deaths over this period. Deaths owing to infectious diseases also increased a great deal, but these deaths explain only 1.8 per cent of the increase in all deaths because infectious disease deaths comprise a relatively small share of all deaths. The increase in deaths due to 'other' (unexplained) reasons is difficult to interpret but may reflect a loosening of state controls over doctors.

The bottom panels of Table 7.2 record cause-of-death data for men and women of working age. Male deaths in that age group increased an astonishing 74 per cent from 1990 to 1994, with deaths owing to external causes comprising 44 per cent of the increase. Deaths owing to external causes were the leading cause of death for both men and women in this age group; deaths owing to cardiovascular disease also contributed a large share of deaths.

Figure 7.4 illustrates the dramatic increase in deaths owing to suicides, murder and accidental alcohol poisoning over the period. As with all deaths, deaths owing to these causes peaked in 1994 and declined somewhat since, although the levels remain astonishingly high.[11] The highest levels and largest increases in suicide rates were concentrated among older men in the working ages: the suicide rate among men aged 50–59 increased by over 80 per cent from 1990 to 1994 (reaching an astronomical level of 125.7 suicides per 100,000 population in that age group); the suicide rate increased by roughly 70 per cent across all men aged 20–49. For women the largest increase in suicides (63 per cent) occurred in the 25–29 age group.

Figure 7.4 Male deaths in the working ages, various causes, 1990–98
Source: *Demograficheskii ezhegodnik Rossii, 1998.*

Is it possible that the increased death rates in Russia are simply an artifact of improved statistical reporting in a more open era? This is unlikely; in general the quality of vital statistics in the Russian Federation is considered to be relatively high, i.e. registration of vital events is believed to be nearly complete both before and after the recent reforms (Murray and Bobadilla (1994)). Russia's mortality statistics, however, probably suffer from problems common to those of mortality statistics in most developed countries, such as age exaggeration at older ages on death certificates and underregistration of births. These sources of error lead to an underestimation of older age mortality rates and of infant mortality rates. As a result, if the vital registration system in Russia has improved in recent years, the increasing mortality rates could simply be a statistical artifact of improved death registration.

The death registration system in Russia has changed little over time, however,[12] and the mortality data appear to be internally consistent (Anderson and Silver (1990)). While inconsistencies in the reporting of older age and infant mortality may remain, given the few changes in the vital registration system it is unlikely that rising mortality is an artifact of improved reporting.

To summarize, Russia experienced a tremendous increase in mortality rates in the early 1990s. Increased deaths were concentrated among men and women of working ages and were largely owing to external causes and cardiovascular disease. The patterns of death are strikingly similar to those that characterized the Russian republic during the 1965–80 period of high mortality.

4 Empirical analysis

The time trends discussed above indicate that the mortality crisis occurred nearly simultaneously with the increase in inequality in Russia, and that, moreover, the mortality crisis eased in the same years that inequality began to decline. One can test this apparent correlation between inequality and mortality more formally by investigating whether this relationship holds at a more disaggregated level. For example, is there any evidence at the individual level that a region's inequality affects the probability of dying? Does an individual's relative position in the income distribution affect the probability of death? This section attempts to answer these questions using data from a large panel household survey taken in Russia between 1992 and 1994.

Before turning to that analysis, however, it should be noted that previous researchers have found a negative and statistically significant correlation between income inequality and the change in life expectancy in Russia between 1990 and 1994, using regional data for the European regions of the Russian Federation (Walberg *et al.* (1998)); this finding is similar to those that found a statistically significant correlation between inequality and mortality across US states. While this does provide supportive evidence of a relationship between inequality and mortality in Russia, as noted above cross-region regressions such as these have been criticized on the grounds that they may be subject to an 'ecological fallacy', i.e. that correlations that hold at an aggregate level do not necessarily provide a convincing test of the relationship between inequality and mortality. If such a relationship exists, it is argued, it should also appear as a factor explaining individual deaths such as those that occur during the course of a panel household survey.

The Russian Longitudinal Monitoring Survey (RLMS) is a nationally representative panel household survey that began in Russia in the summer of 1992; this is the one source of individual-level data that may help a researcher investigate this question. In the first phase of the survey, which is used here, households were surveyed four times between August–September 1992 and November–December 1993.[13] The RLMS provides detailed information on income, expenditures, and demographic characteristics of individuals and families, as well as on individual behaviour such smoking and drinking. During the first phase of the survey, 14,205 individuals were followed, of whom 211 died during the period. While this is a small sample with which to work, it is the only source of individual-level data on deaths available.

Given the small sample size, the analysis here takes the simplest possible approach to identifying correlates of the individual deaths that occurred during the period: Probit regressions are estimated with the dependent variable equal to one if the individual died, zero if not. Independent variables are taken from the first round of the survey (1992) and include the individual's sex, age, marital status, education level, income, whether or not they smoke, and the amount of vodka they 'usually' drink, in grams. The first set of regressions tests the hypothesis that an individual's probability of dying is affected by the level of income inequality within the region; the measure of regional income inequality used is the variance of log income in the region during the first round of the survey.[14] The results of these regressions are summarized in Table 7.3, columns (1)–(4). The strongest correlates of deaths are gender and age, as would be expected, as well as the usual amount of vodka the respondent reported drinking. The level of inequality in the region appears to have little relationship to the probability

Table 7.3 Probit regressions for individuals dying in the RLMS, August 1992–December 1993; variance of log income in region as independent variable (robust standard errors corrected for clustering in parentheses)

	Dep. variable: died (1 = yes)				*Dep. variable: poor health status (1 = yes)*			
	(1)	*(2)*	*(3)*	*(4)*	*(5)*	*(6)*	*(7)*	*(8)*
Female (1 = yes)	–	–	–	–				
	0.0548***	0.568***	0.378***	0.403***	0.371***	0.324***	0.238***	0.238***
	(0.063)	(0.069)	(0.112)	(0.108)	(0.032)	(0.037)	(0.041)	(0.041)
Age	0.033***	0.032***	0.041***	0.043***	0.034***	0.033***	0.030***	0.030***
	(0.002)	(0.002)	(0.003)	(0.003)	(0.001)	(0.001)	(0.001)	(0.001)
Log(income)	–	–0.072	–0.033	–0.064	–	–	–	–
		(0.045)	(0.048)	(0.049)		0.129***	0.112***	0.113***
						(0.016)	(0.015)	(0.014)
Variance of log	–0.172	–0.146	–0.287	–	0.098	0.192	0.245	
income	(0.895)	(0.224)	(0.302)	1.628***	(0.216)	(0.204)	(0.219)	0.727***
in region				(0.268)	(0.249)			
Smokes	–	–	0.153	0.114	–	–	0.055	0.059
(1 = yes)			(0.112)	(0.121)			(0.038)	(0.039)
Vodka (grams)	–	–	–	–	–	–		
			0.0006***	0.0007***	0.0005***			0.0005***
				(0.0002)	(0.0002)		(0.001)	(0.0001)
Married	–	–	0.056	0.056	–	–	–0.050	–0.045
(1 = yes)			(0.073)	(0.070)			(0.043)	(0.042)

(continues)

Table 7.3 (Continued)

	Dep. variable: died (1 = yes)				*Dep. variable: poor health status (1 = yes)*			
	(1)	*(2)*	*(3)*	*(4)*	*(5)*	*(6)*	*(7)*	*(8)*
Ever unemployed in 1992–4 (1 = yes)	–	–	0.188 (0.177)	0.174 (0.188)	–	–	0.058 (0.079)	0.058 (0.075)
Includes education variables	No	no	yes	yes	No	no	yes	yes
Includes large region dummies	No	no	no	yes	No	no	no	yes
Pseudo R^2	0.174	0.162	0.236	0.297	0.165	0.156	0.168	0.172
No. of obs.	14205	10911	10911	10911	14205	10911	10911	10911

Notes: *** Significant at the 1% level or less.

of dying, except in the specification in column (4) which includes regional dummy variables. In this case the variance of log incomes is statistically significant, but the sign is the opposite that one would expect: inequality appears to be negatively correlated with mortality in this specification. It is difficult to imagine how one might explain such a relationship, although one possibility is suggested in Deaton (1999). In discussing a simple model he develops to explain the relationship between inequality and health, he notes that it is generally implicitly assumed that it is the income gap from the top that matters for health, i.e. that the 'reference person' is the wealthiest person and one measures his ranking relative to that person. As a result, as the income gap widens this is detrimental to health for all but the top person. In contrast, if instead the reference person is the bottom person and the health of all others improves as the income gap from the bottom widens, then increased income inequality would improve health on average and one would expect a negative relationship between inequality and mortality rates. While this theory is plausible, its relevance for Russia is unclear and the negative coefficient on the inequality measure remains difficult to explain.

Given the small number of deaths in this sample, it is unsurprising that these results appear to be imprecisely estimated. A potentially better way of using the RLMS data to investigate the relationship between inequality and mortality is instead to test the correlation between inequality measures and individuals' self-reported health status. Self-reported health status has been shown to be a strong predictor of subsequent mortality, even controlling for individual behavioural and social risk factors,[15] and many researchers have used this measure to test the relationship between inequality and mortality (see, for example, Kennedy *et al.* (1998) and Mellor and Milyo (1999)). In the first round of the RLMS, respondents were asked to evaluate how their health affects their ability to work and carry out everyday activities. If they answered that their health 'often' affects their ability to work and carry out everyday activities, or that they were unable to work and carry out everyday activities due to their health, these responses were coded into a 0–1 dummy variable for poor health status. Over 5,500 respondents in the sample (39 per cent of the adult respondents) had poor health status by this measure, and a much larger share of those who died during the course of the survey (61 per cent) reported poor health status in the first round.

The same Probit regressions as in Table 7.3, columns (1)–(4) were estimated using 'poor health status' as the dependent variable. The results are somewhat different than those using mortality status as the dependent variable and are reported in columns (5)–(8) of Table 7.3. Women are more likely to report poor health status than are men, and income is negatively and significantly related to poor health status. Surprisingly, respondents appear to be less likely to report poor health status the more vodka they drink. While this may reflect the protective effect that alcohol is said to have on health (at least in moderate amounts), it directly conflicts with the results reported in columns (3) and (4) which indicate that drinking more vodka increases the probability that one will die. The inequality measure is positively correlated with poor health status, and the coefficient is statistically significant in the final specification given in column (8). These results do suggest that higher inequality in a region is related to poorer health and, therefore, higher mortality rates in Russia, and these results are also consistent with the cross-region evidence discussed above on inequality and mortality. However, given the conflicting results using actual deaths as the dependent variable in the RLMS regressions, the evidence of a link between inequality and health status in Russia is inconclusive.

An alternative approach to this issue is suggested by the potential links between inequality and mortality discussed earlier in the chapter. As noted in that discussion, rising inequality may increase death rates because it implies a relative loss in standing for at least some members of society; the subsequent feelings of despair or hopelessness can increase the risk of death owing to cardiovascular diseases. This mechanism may affect older Russian men in particular who appear to have lost in the reforms relative to younger workers and who are dying at unprecedented rates.

A test of this hypothesis is to include a variable in the Probit regressions for how the individual's status or ranking changed over the course of the survey. One way to approximate an individual's ranking is to assign him or her a percentile in the income distribution in each period during the panel. Calculating the change in the individual's percentile in the income distribution will give one measure of the change in the individual's relative economic status over the period.

Table 7.4 presents the results of regressions that include the level of (rather than the change in) the individual's percentile in the income distribution as an independent variable. The sign on this coefficient is negative and statistically significant in all specifications, indicating that the lower one's position in the income distribution, the more likely one was to die during the course of the survey (or, the more likely one was to report poor health status). While these results appear to support the

Table 7.4 Probit regressions for individuals dying in the RLMS, August 1992–December 1993, individual's percentile in income distribution as an independent variable (robust standard errors corrected for clustering in parentheses)

	Dep. variable: died (1 = yes)				Dep. variable: poor health status (1 = yes)			
	(1)	*(2)*	*(3)*	*(4)*	*(5)*	*(6)*	*(7)*	*(8)*
Female (1 = yes)	–	–	–	–				
	0.587***	0.596***	0.405***	0.420***	0.318***	0.318***	0.236***	0.229***
	(0.069)	(0.069)	(0.106)	(0.104)	(0.037)	(0.037)	(0.041)	(0.043)
Age	0.032***	0.032***	0.041***	0.042***	0.032***	0.032***	0.030***	0.029***
	(0.002)	(0.002)	(0.003)	(0.003)	(0.001)	(0.001)	(0.001)	(0.001)
Percentile in	–	–	–0.010**	–0.010**	–	–	–	–
income	0.003***	0.012***	(0.004)	(0.005)	0.004***	0.008***	0.008***	0.008***
distribution	(0.001)	(0.004)			(0.001)	(0.002)	(0.002)	(0.002)
Log(income)	–	0.326**	0.302**	0.252	–			
		(0.133)	(0.148)	(0.166)		0.140***	0.143***	0.145***
						(0.048)	(0.052)	(0.051)
Smokes	–	–	0.157	0.139	–	–	0.054	0.052
(1 = yes)			(0.120)	(0.120)			(0.039)	(0.040)
Vodka (grams)	–	–			–	–	–	–
			0.0006***	0.0006**			0.0005***	0.0005***
			(0.0002)	(0.0002)			(0.001)	(0.0001)
Married	–	–	0.052	0.050	–	–	–0.048	–0.045
(1 = yes)			(0.073)	(0.068)			(0.043)	(0.042)

(*continues*)

Table 7.4 (*Continued*)

	Dep. variable: died (1 = yes)				*Dep. variable: poor health status (1 = yes)*			
	(1)	*(2)*	*(3)*	*(4)*	*(5)*	*(6)*	*(7)*	*(8)*
Ever unemployed in 1992–4 (1 = yes)	–	–	0.196 (0.182)	0.186 (0.186)	–	–	0.060 (0.081)	0.058 (0.076)
Includes education variables	No	no	yes	yes	No	no	yes	yes
Includes large region dummies	No	no	no	yes	No	no	no	yes
Pseudo *R*2	0.163	0.165	0.28	0.291	0.157	0.157	0.169	0.172
No. of obsv.	10911	10911	10911	10911	10911	10911	10911	10911

Notes: *** Significant at the 1% level or less.
** Significant at the 5% level or less.

theory that the 'losers' of the transition faced an increased probability of death, it should be pointed out that the results are likely affected by multicollinearity owing to the close relationship between log income and the percentile ranking in the income distribution; this problem may be reflected in the surprising positive sign on the log income variable in these specifications.

A more compelling test of the theory, in any case, is to examine whether the change in one's relative economic status affects the probability of dying. Table 7.5 presents the results of regressions that include the change in the individual's percentile in the income distribution as an independent variable, defined as the individual's percentile ranking in the income distribution in the second round of the RLMS minus their ranking in the first round of the survey. In three of the four specifications that use 'died' as the dependent variable, the coefficient on this variable is negative as would be expected: the more an individual gained in terms of relative ranking during the transition, the lower the individual's probability of death during the RLMS, and vice versa. While the standard errors are estimated imprecisely in these regressions, this is likely due at least in part to the small number of deaths in these samples (108) which results from the exclusion of individuals who died in the second round of the RLMS and therefore did not report an income. Using 'poor health status' as the dependent variable avoids this problem; these results are reported in columns (5)–(8). The change in percentile ranking variable is negative and statistically significant at the 1.2 per cent, 5.8 per cent, and 2.7 per cent levels, respectively, in the columns (5)–(8) of Table 7.5. This indicates that individuals who experienced a loss in relative standing are more likely to report poor health status and will therefore likely experience elevated mortality rates.

5 Conclusion

The 1990s, much like the twentieth century, has been a time of extraordinary upheaval for Russians. While researchers will continue for years to try to understand the country's mortality crisis of the 1990s, the evidence presented above suggests that one piece of the puzzle may be found in the dramatic and rapid loss in relative ranking in society experienced by some members of the population during the transition. A loss in relative ranking increases the probability that an individual reports poor health status, and may increase the probability of death.

Table 7.5 Probit regressions for individuals dying in the RLMS, August 1992–December 1993, change in individual's percentile in income distribution as an independent variable, (robust standard errors corrected for clustering in parentheses)

	Dep. variable: died (1 = yes)				*Dep. variable: poor health status (1 = yes)*			
	(1)	*(2)*	*(3)*	*(4)*	*(5)*	*(6)*	*(7)*	*(8)*
Female (1 = yes)	–0.489***	–0.533***	–0.315***	–0.334***	0.397***	0.339***	0.227***	0.218***
	(0.081)	(0.086)	(0.108)	(0.110)	(0.038)	(0.039)	(0.050)	(0.050)
Age	0.029***	0.028***	0.038***	0.038***	0.035***	0.034***	0.031***	0.031***
	(0.003)	(0.003)	(0.003)	(0.003)	(0.001)	(0.001)	(0.001)	(0.001)
Change in percentile in inc. distribution	0.0003	–0.001	–0.001	–0.001	–0.0006	–0.0016***	–0.0013*	–0.0014**
	(0.0012)	(0.001)	(0.002)	(0.002)	(0.0005)	(0.0006)	(0.0007)	(0.0006)
Log(income)	–	–0.123**	–0.091	–0.123*	–	–0.172***	–0.143***	–0.150***
		(0.061)	(0.060)	(0.065)		(0.024)	(0.024)	(0.019)
Smokes (1 = yes)	–	–	0.185	0.182	–	–	0.051	0.050
			(0.150)	(0.153)			(0.043)	(0.042)
Vodka (grams)	–	–	0.0007**	0.0007**	–	–	–0.0007***	–0.0008***
			(0.0003)	(0.0003)			(0.002)	(0.0002)
Married (1 = yes)	–	–	0.011	0.013	–	–	–0.083	–0.084
			(0.086)	(0.086)			(0.051)	(0.052)

Ever	–	–	0.245	0.267	–	–	0.014	0.012
unemployed in 1992–4 (1 = yes)			(0.246)	(0.252)			(0.087)	(0.084)
Includes education variables	No	no	yes	yes	No	no	yes	yes
Includes large region dummies	No	no	no	yes	No	no	no	yes
Pseudo *R2*	0.131	0.133	0.226	0.238	0.157	0.163	0.168	0.17
No. of obs.	8390	8390	8390	8390	8390	8390	8390	8390

Notes: *** Significant at the 1% level or less.
** Significant at the 5% level or less.
* Significant at the 10% level or less.

One is reluctant to draw strong conclusions on the basis of this evidence, however. Besides the weaknesses of the data discussed above which make it difficult to discern the impact of inequality or relative status on mortality rates, data limitations have prevented perhaps the most telling test of the hypothesis that inequality and mortality are related: this would be to test whether the probability of a dying at the individual level is related to the change in inequality that occurred before 1992, i.e. before wages and prices were liberalized. If changes in one's relative status are linked with mortality, presumably the most dramatic changes in individual status occurred between the period preceding the beginning of reforms, when the wage and income distributions were still relatively equal, and the period after the decentralization of wages. Because the RLMS began only in the summer of 1992, however, such a test is impossible. Further research into inequality and mortality in Russia may yield more insights on the issue, but it appears that few other sources will enable analysis of Russia's mortality crisis at the individual level, at least for the early 1990s.

Notes

1 Rodgers (1979) avoided the claim that there is a causal relationship between inequality and mortality, and pointed out that the positive correlation between income inequality and life expectancy could simply be due to the concave relationship between life expectancy and income (so that life expectancy is related to both the mean and distribution of income).
2 Unemployment rates are calculated based on the ILO definition of unemployment from a large labour force survey conducted by Goskomstat in October of each year. Goskomstat is the statistical agency of the Russian government.
3 See Levy and Murnane (1992) for an overview of the literature on rising inequality in the United States.
4 The 90–10 log wage differential is the log monthly wage at the 90th percentile minus the log monthly wage at the 10th percentile of the wage distribution.
5 For example, the 90–10 log wage differential in the US was 1.40 for men in 1990 (Katz, Loveman and Blanchflower (1995)).
6 The source of the income inequality measures is not given in Goskomstat's publications.
7 Atkinson and Micklewright (1992) and Zohoori *et al.* (1998) describe and critique these surveys in detail.
8 Shkolnikov and Nemtsov (1997) describe the anti-alcohol campaign and its effects on male and female mortality rates; see also Leon *et al.* (1997) on this topic.
9 The 1990–4 period is used in Figure 7.3 and in Table 7.2 because death rates peaked in 1994. Results are similar (although less dramatic) using more recent years as an end-point.

10 The working age population in Russia comprises men aged 16–59 and women aged 16–54.

11 The overall murder and suicide rates in Russia in 1994 were roughly three times higher than those in the US in the same year.

12 The primary exception is the change in the definition of infant mortality. The Russian definition of infant mortality used to exclude children born before 28 weeks, or weighing less than 1000 grams or less than 35 centimetres in height. These infants were not counted as live births or infant deaths if the infant died within the first seven days of life. On 1 January, 1993 the definition was revised to include these births and deaths in accordance with the WHO definition. It is estimated that this change led to a 25 per cent increase in the infant mortality rate. Correcting for this underreporting over the 1958–93 period decreases life expectancy for men and women slightly (e.g. .3 year in 1992) and has little effect on the trends over time (Shkolnikov and Nemtsov 1997).

13 A detailed description of the sampling design and implementation of the RLMS is available at the RLMS website at <http://www.cpc.unc.edu/rlms>. See Zohoori *et al.* (1998) for a description of the survey and an overview of the economic and demographic trends in Russia based on the RLMS.

14 Twenty 'sites' are used to calculate this measure. The average sample size for the sites is 613, with a range from 535 to 898 observations. Standard errors are corrected for including a group-level variable in an individual-level regression, and for clustering within sites (i.e. that the assumption that observations within sites are independent is violated).

15 See Idler and Benyamini (1997) for a survey of 27 studies on the relationship between self-rated health and mortality.

References

Anderson, B. A. and B. D. Silver (1990) 'Trends in Mortality of the Soviet Population', *Soviet Economy*, vol. 6, no. 3, pp. 191–251.

Atkinson, A. B. and J. Micklewright (1992) *Economic Transformation in Eastern Europe and the Distribution of Income* (Cambridge: Cambridge University Press).

Brainerd, E. (1998) 'Winners and Losers in Russia's Economic Transition', *American Economic Review*, vol. 88, no. 5, pp. 1094–1116.

Daly, M. C., G. J. Duncan, G. A. Kaplan and J. W. Lynch (1998) 'Macro-to-Micro Links in the Relation between Income Inequality and Mortality', *The Milbank Quarterly*, vol. 76, no. 3, pp. 315–39.

Deaton, A. (1999) 'Inequalities in Income and Inequalities in Health', NBER Working Paper, no. 7141.

European Bank for Reconstruction and Development (EBRD) (1997) *Transition Report 1997* (London: European Bank for Reconstruction and Development).

Everson, S. A., G. A. Kaplan, D. E. Goldberg, R. Salonen and J. T. Salonen (1997) 'Hopelessness and 4-year Progression of Carotid Atherosclerosis: The Kuopio Ischemic Heart Disease Risk Factor Study', *Arteriosclerosis, Thrombosis and Vascular Biology*, vol. 17, no. 8, pp. 1490–5.

Goskomstat (1993–98) *Demograficheskii ezhegodnik Rossii* (*The Demographic Yearbook of Russia*) (Moscow: Goskomstat of Russian Federation).

Goskomstat (1998) *Rossiisski statisticheskii ezhegodnik 1998* (*Russian Statistical Yearbook 1998*) (Moscow: Goskomstat of Russian Federation).
Idler, E. and Y. Benyamini (1997) 'Self-Rated Health and Mortality: A Review of Twenty-Seven Community Studies', *Journal of Health and Social Behaviour*, vol. 38, no. 1, pp. 21–37.
Kaplan, G., E. R. Pamuk, J. M. Lynch, R. D. Cohen and J. L. Balfour (1996) 'Inequality in Income and Mortality in the United States: Analysis of Mortality and Potential Pathways', *British Medical Journal*, vol. 312, pp. 999–1003.
Katz, L. F., G. W. Loveman and D. G. Blanchflower (1995) 'A Comparison of Changes in the Structure of Wages in Four OECD Countries', in R. B. Freeman and L. F. Katz (eds), *Differences and Changes in Wages Structures* (Chicago: University of Chicago Press), pp. 25–65.
Kennedy, B. P., I. Kawachi and D. Prothrow-Stith (1996) 'Income Distribution and Mortality: Cross-Sectional Ecological Study of the Robin Hood Index in the United States', *British Medical Journal*, vol. 312, pp. 1004–7.
Kennedy, B. P., I. Kawachi, R., Glass and D. Prothrow-Stith (1998) 'Income Distribution, Socioeconomic Status, and Self-Rated Health in the United States: Multilevel Analysis', *British Medical Journal*, vol. 317, pp. 917–21.
Leon, D. A., L. Chenet, V. M. Shkolnikov, S. Zakharov, J. Shapiro, G. Rakhmanova, S. Vassin and M. McKee (1997) 'Huge Variation in Russian Mortality Rates 1984–94: Artefact, Alcohol, or What?', *The Lancet*, vol. 350, pp. 383–8.
Levy, F. and R. J. Murnane (1992) 'US Earnings Levels and Earnings Inequality: A Review of Recent Trends and Proposed Explanations', *Journal of Economic Literature*, vol. 30, no. 3, pp. 1333–81.
Mellor, J. M. and J. Milyo (1999) 'Income Inequality and Health Status in the United States: Evidence from the Current Population Survey', Department of Economics, The College of William and Mary and Tufts University, mimeo.
Murray, C. and J.-L. Bobadilla (1994) 'Epidemiological Transitions in the Formerly Socialist Economies: Divergent Patterns of Mortality and Causes of Death', Harvard Center for Population and Development Studies, Health Transition Working Paper Series, no. 94.07.
Rodgers, G. B. (1979) 'Income and Inequality as Determinants of Mortality: An International Cross-Section Analysis', *Population Studies*, vol. 3, pp. 343–51.
Shkolnikov, V. M., F. Mesle, and J. Vallin (1997) 'Recent Trends in Life Expectancy and Causes of Death in Russia (1970–1993)', in J.-L. Bobadilla, C. A. Costello and F. Mitchell (eds), *Premature Death in the New Independent States* (Washington, DC: National Academy Press), pp. 34–65.
Shkolnikov, V. M. and A. Nemtsov (1997) 'The Anti-Alcohol Campaign and Variations in Russian Mortality', in J.-L. Bobadilla, C. A. Costello and F. Mitchell, F. (eds), *Premature Death in the New Independent States* (Washington, DC: National Academy Press), pp. 239–61.
Walberg, P., M. McKee, V. Shkolnikov, L. Chenet and D. A. Leon (1998) 'Economic Change, Crime and Mortality Crisis in Russia: Regional Analysis', *British Medical Journal*, vol. 317, pp. 312–8.
Waldmann, R. J. (1992) 'Income Distribution and Infant Mortality', *Quarterly Journal of Economics*, vol. 107, no. 4, pp. 1283–302.
Wilkinson, R. G. (1996) *Unhealthy Societies: The Afflictions of Inequality* (London: Routledge).

Zohoori, N., T. A. Mroz, B. Popkin, E. Glinskaya, M. Lokshin, D. Mancini, P. Kozyreva, M. Kosolapov and M. Swafford (1998) 'Monitoring the Economic Transition in the Russian Federation and its Implications for the Demographic Crisis – The Russian Longitudinal Monitoring Survey', *World Development*, vol. 26, no. 11, pp. 1977–93.

8
The Impact of Minimum Wages on Wage Inequality and Employment in the Formal and Informal Sector in Costa Rica*

Fatma El-Hamidi
University of Pittsburgh, USA

and

Katherine Terrell
Business School and William Davidson Institute, University of Michigan, USA

1 Introduction

Minimum wage policies have always been controversial among economists and policy-makers and the debate has become more heated following the publication of the book by Card and Krueger (1995) and related papers (e.g. Katz and Krueger (1992), Card and Krueger (1994)). Supporters of minimum wages justify them as a way of improving the living conditions of the poor, unskilled, and unorganized workers. Critics emphasize the efficiency losses associated with their use, and disqualify them as an adequate way of affecting inequality. They argue that in developing countries minimum wages are the principal source of labour market segmentation and unemployment.

The traditional view, using the standard two-sector model which assumes a perfectly competitive labour market with homogeneous and mobile labour, is that an increase in the minimum wage, reduces employment in the covered sector, creates unemployment, and has 'negative' spillover effects in the uncovered sector (i.e. increasing employment there and putting downward pressure on wages at the lower end of the distribution).[1] Hence increasing the minimum wage should increase income inequality in the uncovered sector and reduce it in the covered sector.

* This chapter benefited from comments and suggestions made by Richard Freeman and Gary Solon.

On the other hand if minimum wages do not reduce employment in the covered sector and hence have no spillover effects (the outcome in a monopsonistic model of the labour market), changes in minimum wages will not have an efficiency loss and may not effect wage inequality in the uncovered sector.[2] If employment actually increases in the covered sector as a result of minimum wage increase, and draws low wage workers from the uncovered sector, then one might expect earnings inequality to fall in the uncovered sector. Until the Card and Krueger (1994, 1995) and related research, which found a positive effect of the minimum wage on employment in the US, monopsony was not a very popular model of the labour market. Dickens, Machin and Manning. (1999, p. 2) argue that monopsony may be more common than we have traditionally believed from the one-company-town examples: 'For example, in most labour markets employers that cut wages do not instantaneously lose all their workers, so the supply of labour to a firm is not perfectly elastic, and firms therefore possess some monopsony power... in the short and long run.'

Our chapter examines the effects of changes in the minimum wage on earnings inequality and aggregate level of employment in Costa Rica's covered and uncovered sectors over the 1980–92 period. We also examine whether changes in the minimum wage lead to a reallocation of labour between the covered and uncovered sector.

There are a number of features about Costa Rica that make it an interesting country for the analysis of minimum wages and inequality in the two sectors. For one there is a significant group, approximately one-fifth of the employed, who are not covered by minimum wages. These are self-employed ('informal sector') workers.[3] Second, unlike most countries, Costa Rica has multiple minimum wages, set for various occupations and industries. In the 1970s and early 1980s there were approximately 350 minimum wages and in 1990 the number was reduced to about 80. Setting the minimum at different levels by occupation and industry could but need not be more a more effective instrument for raising the wage floor and reducing wage inequality than one minimum wage. However, the Costa Rican National Salary Council took an additional step of systematically raising the lowest minimum wages by a greater percentage than it raised the higher minimum wages over the 1980s and 1990s. Moreover, the Council did not allow minimum wages to erode over the 1980s as was the case in most Latin American countries, especially Ecuador, Mexico, and Peru (Bell (1997), de Villareal and Breach (1988), Drobny and Wells (1983)). As seen in Figure 8.1, the plot of the lowest minimum wage in each industry as a per cent

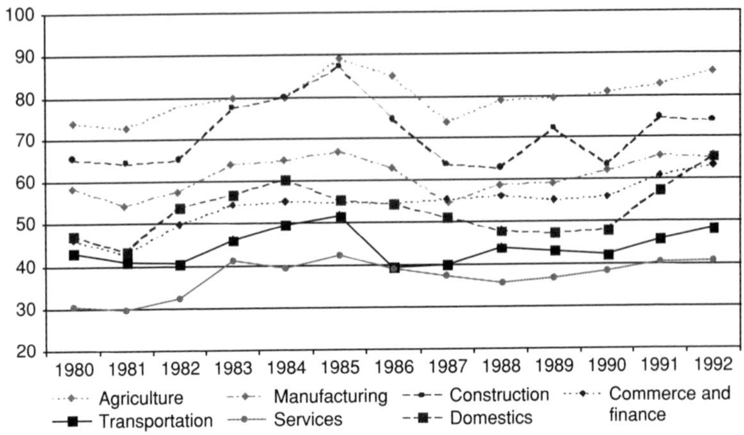

Figure 8.1 Minimum wage/wage 'toughness', by industry, 1980–92

of the average wage of covered sector workers in each industry over the 1976–92 period reveals that minimum wages have been fairly stable and relatively high (the median is 55 per cent of the average wage) when compared to other countries. Hence, one would expect from the manner in which minimum wages are designed and changed over time that minimum wages would reduce inequality among Costa Rican workers in the covered sector. Their impact on the uncovered sector depends on whether the labour market is competitive or monopsonistic.

2 Methodology

2.1 Inequality

There are many ways to measure wage inequality; we have used three widely accepted measures. First, the coefficient of variation:

$$CV = \frac{\sigma_x}{\bar{y}} = \frac{\sqrt{\sum_{i=1}^{n}(\bar{y}_i - \bar{y})^2 n}}{\bar{y}} \qquad (1)$$

where Y_i is the earnings/wage of person i in the population, n represents the number of people in the population, and $\bar{Y}$ is the mean wage in the population.

The second indicator we use is the most common measure of wage inequality, namely the Gini coefficient:

$$G = 1 + 1/n - 2/n^2\bar{Y}\left[Y_1 + 2Y_2 + 3Y_3 + \ldots + nY_{yn}\right] \tag{2}$$

where n and $\bar{Y}$ are as before, and $Y_1,\ 2Y_2,\ \ldots\ nY_n$. is the individual income in decreasing order of size.
The third measure we have selected is the Theil mean logarithmic deviation:[4]

$$T = (1/n)\sum_{i=1}^{n} \log Y_i/\bar{Y} \tag{3}$$

The measures differ in their sensitivity to income variations at different levels of the distribution. For equidistant transfers, the Gini index is considered to be more sensitive to changes around the mode, while the coefficient of variation is more sensitive to transfers at the top of the distribution. The mean logarithmic deviation is relatively more responsive to changes at the lower end of the distribution.

To test whether the level of the minimum wage and changes in the minimum wage affect wage dispersion in the covered and the uncovered sectors, we estimate the following equation separately for the covered and uncovered sectors:

$$\ln D_{it} = \alpha_0 + \alpha_1 (MW_i/W_i)_t + \sum_{i=1}^{6} \beta_i I_i + \sum_{t=1}^{12} \gamma_t T_t + \mu \tag{4}$$

where the subscripts $i = 1 \ldots 7$ are for each industry,[5] and $t = 1 \ldots 13$ for years (1980–92) and:

- $D = CV, G, T$ is a measure of hourly wage dispersion within an industry and sector in each of the 13 years.
- *MW/W* is the lowest average hourly minimum wage set by the government for each industry divided by the average hourly wage in each industry. This variable captures the 'toughness' of the minimum wage.
- *I* are industry specific dummies, with domestics as the base.
- *T* are annual dummies for 1980–92.

Industry and time dummies are added to control for industry and time fixed effects, such as changes in aggregate output and shocks over time. We also test whether the impact of the minimum wage is nonlinear (with a quadratic specification) and whether the minimum wage has a lagged effect, using a one-year lag.

2.2 Employment effects

To estimate the employment effect of the minimum wage we estimate separate regressions for the covered and uncovered sector workers using two different measures as a dependent variable: (a) the log of the number employed (by industry and year) and (b) the total number of hours worked in an average week (by industry and year). These measures allow us to learn about the reallocation of workers and hours worked across industries over time. We also examine whether there is a reallocation of labour within an industry between covered and uncovered employment as the 'toughness' of minimum wages rises. For this we use the per cent working in the covered sector in each industry (and year) as a dependent variable. All three of these measures are regressed on various specifications of the 'toughness' measure with industry and time fixed effects.

2.3 Data

The analysis is based on aggregated data from the Costa Rican annual *Household Survey of Employment and Unemployment (HSEU)*. The minimum wage data were taken from the *Gazetta* published by the Ministry of Labour. Since it was not possible to match the occupational codes in the HSEU with those in the *Gazetta,* we have selected the lowest minimum wage in each one-digit industrial sector as our benchmark. The toughness measure used in our analysis is plotted in Figure 8.1. In the regression analysis we were not able to use the data from the 1976–79 household surveys because no questions were asked to distinguish self-employment from other forms of employment in 1977–79.

3 Findings

3.1 Trend of wage inequality (1976–92)

In Figure 8.2 we present plots of the three measures of inequality in the hourly labour earnings of all workers. In Figure 8.3 we plot these measures for the covered and uncovered workers. The plots reveal the following patterns:

(a) *Earnings inequality for the whole population fell over the 1982–92 period.* This is the case for all three measures of inequality but the decline is most dramatic in the coefficient of variation. (Inequality was very high in 1981–82 when there was very high inflation.)

(b) *The hourly earnings of covered workers are distributed more equally than those of the uncovered sector* in every year.

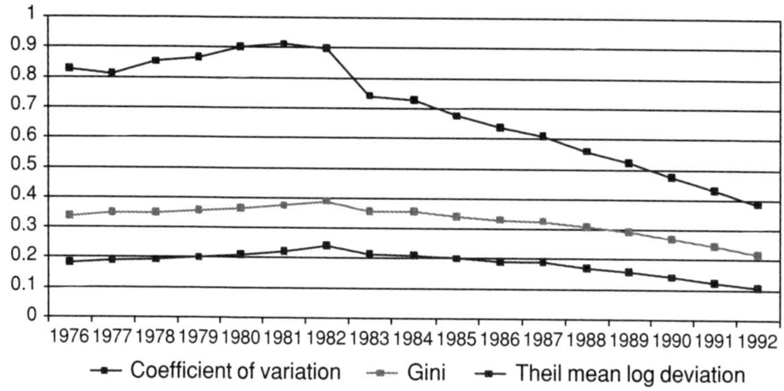

Figure 8.2 Inequalities for Costa Rica, total population, 1976–92

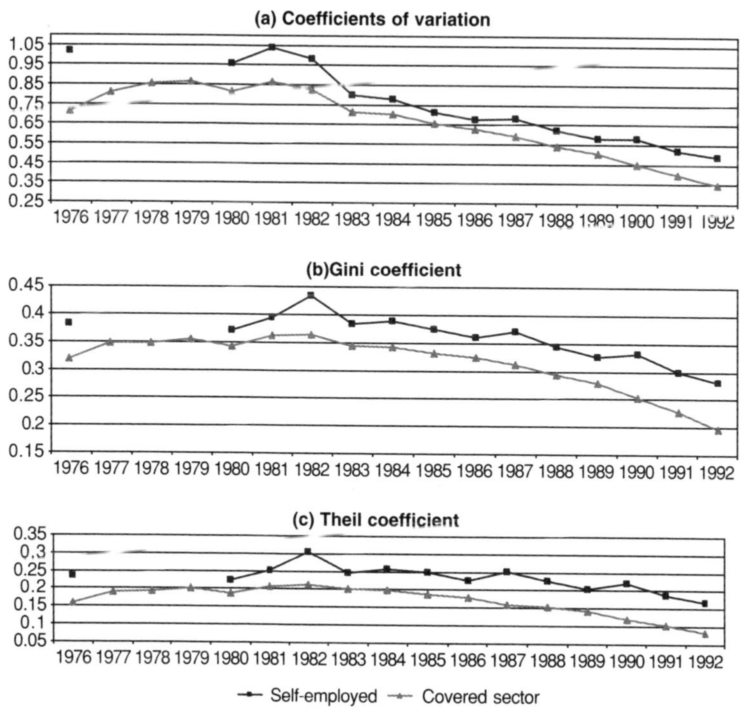

Figure 8.3 Wage inequality in Costa Rica covered sector versus self-employed, 1976–92

(c) The level of earnings inequality fell by a greater percentage in the covered sector than in the uncovered sector.

An examination of the Gini coefficient for the covered and uncovered/self-employed workers in each of the seven industries (Figures 8.4 and 8.5, respectively) indicate the same overall declining pattern, but a more erratic pattern among the industries in 1981 and 1982, when inflation was high. It is also noteworthy that the relative level of inequality among the industries is not consistent across the covered and uncovered sectors.

3.2 Inequality results

The results from estimating (4) with the three measures of wage dispersion are presented in Table 8.1. Panel A contains the coefficients from the regression using the coefficient of variation as the dependent variable, Panel B contains the findings using the Gini and Panel C presents the results for the Theil mean log deviation measure.

The main finding is striking: *up to a point an increase in the industry-specific minimum wage relative to industry average wages, reduces wage inequality in the covered sector when inequality is measured with the Gini and the Theil mean log deviation. However, it has no effect on the covered sector when*

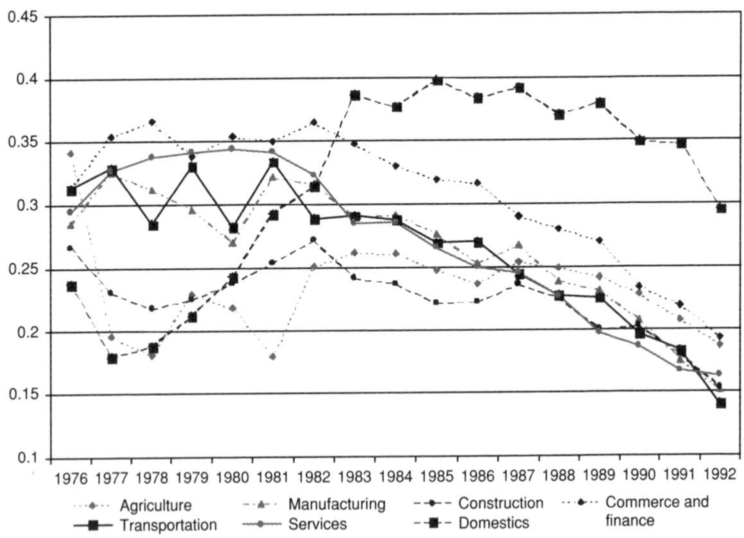

Figure 8.4 Gini for covered sector workers, by industrial activity, 1976–92

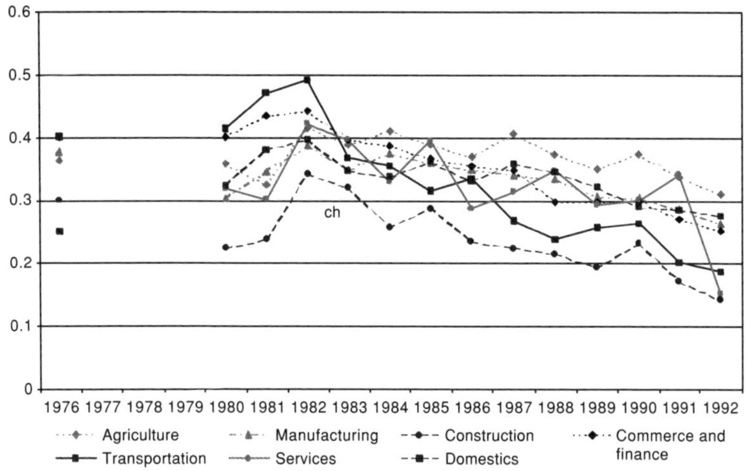

Figure 8.5 Gini for the self-employed by industrial activity, 1976–92

measured with the coefficient of variation. The toughness measure has no impact on the earnings inequality of the self-employed in all three regressions. The effect on the covered sector is non-linear and it is decreasing at a decreasing rate.[6] As seen in Table 8.2, at the lowest level of toughness we find in the data (30 per cent), a 1 percentage point increase in the toughness measure reduces inequality by two to three per cent, depending on which measure is used. A unit increase at the median level of toughness (55.5 per cent) reduces inequality between 0.9 and 1.7 per cent but at the highest level of toughness (89 per cent) a 1 percentage point increase actually *increases* inequality (but only by 0.4–0.6 per cent). Hence as long as the minimum wage is not set 'too high', it reduces inequality.[7] One explanation offered for this is that enforcement is even less stringent when the minimum is very high.

3.3 Employment

Contrary to the traditional view, we find that up to a point minimum wage increases are associated with increases in the level of total and covered sector employment (see Table 8.3). We find no statistically significant correlation between the toughness of the minimum wage and the number of self-employed. The relationship between the minimum wage toughness measure and the level of employment is non-linear (for both total and covered sector): an increase in the toughness of the minimum wage increases employment at a decreasing rate.[8] As seen

Table 8.1 Effect of minimum wage on wage dispersion

	Covered sector	*Self-employed*
Panel A: log of coefficient of variation		
Toughness	−0.015	−0.0039
	(0.015)	(0.0158)
Toughness^2	0.00008	0.00005
	(0.00010)	(0.00011)
Time dummies	Yes	Yes
Industry dummies	Yes	Yes
Adjusted R^2	0.80	0.77
Panel B: log of Gini		
Toughness	−0.0315[a]	−0.015
	(0.013)	(0.013)
Toughness^2	0.0002[b]	0.0001
	(0.0001)	(0.0001)
Time dummies	Yes	Yes
Industry dummies	Yes	Yes
Adjusted R^2	0.73	0.79
Panel C: Theil mean log deviation		
Toughness	−0.055[b]	−0.034
	(0.025)	(0.031)
Toughness^2	0.00034[c]	0.00029
	(0.00018)	(0.00022)
Time dummies	Yes	Yes
Industry dummies	Yes	Yes
Adjusted R^2	0.69	0.60
No. of obs.	91	91

Note: [a]Significant at the 1% level; [b]significant at the 5% level; [c]significant at the 10% level.

Table 8.2 Impact of changes in the toughness of the minimum wage on inequality

	Range of toughness measure		
Increase in	*Lowest (30.0)*	*Median (55.5)*	*Highest (89.0)*
Gini	−0.0195	−0.0093	0.0041
Theil	−0.0346	−0.0173	0.00552

in Table 8.4, total employment rises by 1.1 per cent and covered sector employment rises by 1.3 per cent when the toughness measure rises from 30–31 per cent. The employment effect is positive until the

Table 8.3 Impact of minimum wages on the log of employment

	Total employment	*Covered sector employment*	*Self-employment*
Toughness	0.019[a]	0.0211[a]	0.016
	(0.011)	(0.0118)	(0.19)
$(\text{Toughness})^2$	–0.00014[a]	–0.00014[a]	–0.00018
	(0.00007)	(0.00009)	(0.00014)
Time dummies	yes	yes	yes
Industry dummies	yes	yes	yes
Adjusted R^2	0.97	0.97	0.97
No. of obs.	91	91	91

Note: [a]Significant at the 10% level.

Table 8.4 Impact of changes in the toughness of the minimum wage on employment

	Range of toughness measure		
Increase in	*Lowest (30.0)*	*Median (55.5)*	*Highest (89.0)*
Total emp.	0.0106	0.00346	–0.0059
Cov. emp.	0.0127	0.00556	–0.0038

toughness measure reaches between 68 and 75 per cent (for total employment and covered sector employment, respectively). At that point further increases in the minimum wage *reduce* employment. At the highest level of toughness observed in Costa Rica over this period, a 1 percentage point increase lowers total employment by 0.6 per cent and covered sector employment by 0.4 per cent.

These findings may be interpreted as supporting the monopsonistic model, which predicts that increases in wages can increase employment up to the point where the marginal cost is equal to the marginal revenue. Any increases above that point force the employer to be on her demand curve. However, it is difficult to imagine a labour market for unskilled workers as functioning as in the monopsonistic model. Hence, another plausible interpretation of these findings is that they support the traditional model of the labour market for less skilled workers and the monopsonistic or efficiency wage models for the skilled workers. In particular, industries that use unskilled labour and pay low wages have a high ratio of minimum to actual wage (i.e. high toughness). Firms in these industries face an elastic supply of labour and when a rise in minimum wage forces these firms to move up their demand for labour curves and lay off workers. This is consistent with the negative employment effect documented in Tables 8.3 and 8.4. On the other hand, industries that employ relatively more skilled labour (and where capital intensity may be higher), have a low ratio of the minimum to the average wage (i.e. low toughness). These are also the industries that are likely to face upward sloping supply curve of labour or where employers may pay efficiency wages so as to attract and keep skilled workers. In these industries an increase in the minimum wage may be expected to raise employment under the monopsonistic or efficiency wage scenario. This is consistent with the positive effect of increasing minimum wage on employment found for these industries in Tables 8.3 and 8.4.[9]

Our empirical estimates are hence consistent with the view that the minimum wage increases assist in reallocating labour from the 'traditional' to the 'modern' sector in the spirit of the Lewis model. The high-wage (modern sector) firms would not raise wages and employment unless induced to do so by the minimum wage increase. The low-wage (traditional sector) firms in turn release labour that migrates to the expanding high-wage (modern) sector. The story is appealing but needs fine tuning in terms of explaining skill compatibility between the two sectors.

Turning to our findings on the impact of minimum wages on the number of hours worked in an average week, we find that up to a point, increases in the minimum wage are positively correlated with the toughness of the minimum wage in *both* the covered and uncovered sector (Table 8.5). Moreover, the impact is much greater (and more highly significant) among the self-employed workers. Whereas at the lowest toughness level a 1 percentage point increase in toughness increases number of hours worked by covered sector workers by 0.4 per cent, it increases the number of hours worked in self-employment by 1.2 per cent (see Table 8.6). Hence, although the *number* of self-employed workers does not change with changes in the minimum wage relative to average wage, the number of hours of the self-employed does change. As with the impact on employment, once the minimum wage toughness reaches 66–71 per cent of the average wage in the industry, the number of hours worked in the covered sectors begins to fall and at the highest level it falls by 0.2 per cent in the covered sector and 0.8 per cent among the self-employed. Tests for longer-term effects show that the estimated coefficients on one year lagged toughness variable are

Table 8.5 Impact of minimum wages on the log of the number of hours worked

	Total economy	*Covered sector*	*Self-employment*
Toughness	0.0055	0.0064[c]	0.0223[b]
	(0.0035)	(0.0035)	(0.0091)
(Toughness)^2	–0.00004	–0.000045[c]	–0.00017[b]
	(0.00003)	(0.000025)	(0.000066)
Time dummies	yes	yes	yes
Industry dummies	yes	yes	yes
Constant	3.503[a]	3.508[a]	2.835[a]
	(0.132)	(0.130)	(0.334)
Adjusted R^2	0.80	0.80	0.79
No. of obs.	91	91	91

Note: [a]Significant at the 1% level; [b]significant at the 5% level; [c]significant at the 10% level.

Table 8.6 Impact of changes in the toughness of the minimum wage on hours worked

	Range of toughness measure		
Increase in hours of work of	*Lowest (30.0)*	*Median (55.5)*	*Highest (89.0)*
Covered sector	0.0037	0.00141	–0.0016
Self-employed	0.0121	0.00343	–0.0080

not significant when entered in addition to the current measure of toughness.

3.4 Reallocation of workers between the covered and uncovered sector, within an industry

Our analysis of the allocation of workers between the covered and uncovered sectors within an industry indicates that as minimum wages rise relative to average wages in an industry, the percentage of workers in the covered sector will rise (see Table 8.7). The short-run impact is marginally statistically significant (with a P value of 0.113) and indicates a linear effect of 0.19 per cent increase in the percentage of covered sector workers. This of course relates to the findings in Table 8.1, where increases in the toughness of the minimum wage increases the number of covered sector workers (up to a point) but seems to leave the number of self-employed unchanged. However, we also have the interesting finding that the coefficient on the lagged value of toughness is significant (at the five per cent level) and indicates that a one percentage point increase in toughness in one year will raise the percentage of workers in the covered sector by 0.29 per cent in the following year. Hence the redistribution of labour from the informal to the formal sector within each industry, brought about by increases in the minimum wage, is significant and long term. This is counter to the traditional view that increases in the minimum wage enlarge the informal sector.

4 Summary and conclusions

The purpose of this chapter is to test whether the Costa Rican government is reaching its goal of reducing wage inequality while at the same time not reducing significantly the level of employment in the covered sector with the use of a complicated minimum wage policy. We also examine the redistributive effects of the minimum wage between the covered and the uncovered (self-employed) sectors.

Costa Rica has a complex system of minimum wages that are industry and occupation specific. Over the 1980s and 1990s, the government systematically raised the lowest minimum wages by a higher percentage than the higher minimum wages. We show that minimum wages in

Table 8.7 Impact of minimum wages on the relative level of employment in the covered sector (percentage covered)

	(1)	*(2)*	*(3)*
Toughness	0.019*	0.0018	0.0018
	(0.012)	(0.0035)	(0.0037)
$(\text{Toughness})^2$		3.40e-07	5.89e-06
		(0.000025)	(0.00003)
Lag toughness			0.0029[b]
			(0.0012)
Time dummies	yes	yes	yes
Industry dummies	yes	yes	yes
Constant	4.32[a]	4.33[a]	4.25[a]
	(0.06)	(0.12)	(0.12)
Adjusted R^2	0.89	0.89	0.90

Notes: *$P = 0.113$.
[a]Significant at the 1% level; [b]significant at the 5% level.

Costa Rica have been maintained at relatively high levels with respect to average wages (the median is 55.5 per cent) over this period. Moreover, unlike most of the Latin America countries, this ratio has risen in the 1980s compared to the 1970s. We find a declining trend in overall inequality (using three measures) over the 1980–92 period. We also find that the level of wage (earnings) inequality among covered sector workers is lower than among the uncovered sector workers. Finally, inequality has declined more rapidly in the covered sector than that in the uncovered sector.

Regression analysis reveals that at the median, a unit increase in the minimum wage relative to the average wage in the industry is associated with: (a) a reduction in wage inequality in the covered sector of between 0.9 per cent (using the Gini coefficient) and 1.7 per cent (using the Theil mean logarithmic deviation) and no effect on earnings inequality among the self-employed (using all measures); (b) an increase in the level of covered sector employment by 0.56 per cent and total employment by 0.35 per cent, but has no effect on the number of self-employed; (c) an increase in the average number of hours worked per week by 0.14 per cent in the covered sector and 0.34 per cent in the uncovered sector; and (d) a raise in the percentage of covered sector workers within an industry by 0.29 per cent one year after the minimum wage is increased. Hence, the Costa Rican government does appear to be accomplishing its goal and its policy also seems to be assisting the reallocation of workers from the self-employed (informal) sector to the covered (formal) sectors counter to the traditional view.

From a theoretical perspective, these finds are counter to the traditional competitive two-sector models of the minimum wage. We interpret these findings as supporting the monopsonistic and efficiency wage models of the labour market in those industries where the ratio of the minimum wage to the average wage ('toughness') is low but supports the traditional models in those industries where toughness is high. Hence, workers in traditional industries (with low average wages) are losing jobs whereas workers in more modern industries (with high average wages) are gaining jobs. Given that we found overall employment to have increased, minimum wages could be seen as assisting the reallocation of labour from the traditional to the more modern sectors.

Notes

1 See for example, Brown (1999) for a description of this model. See also Freeman (1996), Machin and Manning (1996) and SATEP-ILO (1988)

2 See for example, Card and Krueger (1995), Fiszbein (1992) and Rebitzer and Taylor (1995).
3 In this chapter we use the terms 'informal sector' and 'self-employed' interchangeably.
4 For further definitions see Coulter; Cowell and Jenkins (1992).
5 The seven industrial sectors are: agriculture, manufacturing, construction, transportation, commerce and finance, services, and domestics. Domestic servants were singled out since they are a large group (about 10 per cent) of the work force.
6 Tests for other specifications of the equation indicated that neither the coefficients for the linear toughness specification nor those for the lagged toughness specification were not significantly different from zero for either sector.
7 The turning point is when minimum wages were about 79–81 per cent of the average wage in the industry.
8 The coefficient on toughness was not significant either in the linear specification or the lagged specification (when the lagged term was entered in addition to the current term).
9 Note that in the monopsonistic model a rise in the minimum wage results in an increase in employment as the firm moves rightward along the supply curve of labour. The positive effect will of course be reversed when one reaches the point of intersection of labour supply and demand and further wage increases will result in a backward movement along the employer's demand curve.

References

Bell, L. (1997) 'The Impact of Minimum Wages in Mexico and Colombia', *Journal of Labor Economics*, vol. 15, pp. S102–S134.

Brown, C. (1999) 'Minimum Wages, Employment, and the Distribution of Income', in O. Ashenfelter and B. Card (eds) *Handbook of Labor Economics* (Amsterdam: Elsevier), pp. 2101–63.

Card, D. and A. B. Krueger (1994) 'Minimum Wages and Employment: A Study of the Fast-Food Industry in New Jersey and Pennsylvania', *American Economic Review*, vol. 84, pp. 772–93.

Card, D. and A. B. Krueger (1995) *Myth and Measurement: The New Economics of the Minimum Wage* (Princeton: Princeton University Press).

Coulter, Fiona, A. E., F. A. Cowell and S. P. Jenkins (1992) 'Differences in Needs and Assessment of Income Distribution', *Bulletin of Economic Research*, vol. 44, no. 2, pp. 77–124.

de Villarreal, N. S. and R. S. Breach (1988) 'Evaluation of the Impact of Minimum Wages on the Mexican Economy', in *Assessing the Impact of Statutory Minimum Wages in Developing Countries: Four Country Studies* (Geneva: International Labour Organization).

Dickens, R., S. Machin and A. Manning (1999) 'The Effects of Minimum Wages on Employment: Theory and Evidence from Britain', *Journal of Labour Economics*, vol. 17, no. 1, pp. 1–22.

Drobny, A. and J. Wells (1983) 'Wages, Minimum Wages, and Income Distribution in Brazil', *Journal of Development Economics*, vol. 13, pp. 305–30.

Fiszbein, A. (1992) 'Do Workers in the Informal Sector Benefit from Cuts in the Minimum Wage?', World Bank Policy Research Working Paper, no. 826.

Freeman, R. B. (1996) 'The Minimum Wage as a Redistributive Tool', *Economic Journal*, vol. 106, pp. 639–49.

Katz, L. and A. Krueger (1992) 'The Effect of the Minimum Wage on the Fast Food Industry', *Industrial and Labour Relations Review*, vol. 46, pp. 6–21.

Machin, S. and A. Manning (1996) 'The Effects of Minimum Wages on Wage Dispersion and Employment', *Industrial and Labour Relations Review*, vol. 47, pp. 319–29.

Rebitzer, J. and L. Taylor (1995) 'The Consequences of Minimum Wage Laws Some: New Theoretical Ideas', *Journal of Public Economics*, vol. 56, pp. 245–55.

South African Team for Employment Promotion (SATEP)–ILO (1988) 'Minimum Wage Fixing in Botswana: Implications for Employment and Income Distribution', in *Assessing the Impact of Statutory Minimum Wages in Developing Countries: Four Country Studies* (Geneva: International Labour Organization).

Part III

Understanding Micro-Behaviour and the Broad Economy of Inequality

9

The Economics of Reciprocity: Evidence and Theory

*Armin Falk and Urs Fischbacher**
Institute for Empirical Economic Research, University of Zurich, Switzerland

1 Introduction

In many social sciences, particularly in economics, a fundamental assumption is that people are rational and selfish. According to this assumption people maximize their material well-being and ignore the well-being of others. In this chapter, we question the omnipresence of the *homo economicus* as assumed by conventional economic theory. We review empirical evidence, which impressively suggests that *reciprocity* is a powerful determinant of human behaviour. Moreover, we demonstrate that reciprocity can fruitfully be incorporated into game theory and economic modelling in general. With our model it is possible to formalize the concept of reciprocity and to organize the empirical evidence.

What do we mean by 'reciprocity'? It is the reward of a kind treatment (*positive reciprocity*) or the punishment of an unkind treatment (*negative reciprocity*). Importantly, reciprocity means that people even punish or reward in one-shot situations and even if it is costly to them. Our empirical review concentrates on two experimental studies, the gift-exchange game and the ultimatum game. The first game is a typical example for positive reciprocity, the latter for negative reciprocity. We will describe these experiments in some detail and discuss the most important experimental findings. Moreover, we point out that the findings of these two

* Financial support by the Swiss National Science Foundation (Project 12–43590.95) and by the MacArthur Foundation (Network on Economic Environments and the Evolution of Individual Preferences and Social Norms) is gratefully acknowledged. We thank Sam Bowles, Herbert Gintis, and the participants of the IEA Congress, Buenos Aires 1999, and particularly Simon Gächter, for helpful discussions.

games are very robust. This holds with respect to (i) variations of the experimental institutions, (ii) the stake size implemented in the experimental sessions, and (iii) a cross-cultural comparison.

An important theme in the psychology of reciprocity concerns the role of attribution and intentions. As we noted above, reciprocity is a behavioural response to perceived kindness. The crucial question to ask is: What determines the kindness of an action? Two aspects are essential here, namely (i) the *consequences* of an action and (ii) the underlying motivation, i.e. the *intentions* involved. We present experimental evidence which indicates that it is not only the consequences that determine the kindness of an action. Rather, people are well aware of the intention behind a particular action. In our model we explicitly allow that people – in determining their dispositions towards others – take account of the motivation that guided their opponents' action. This is novel in the sense that economics usually takes a *consequentialistic* perspective. We think that the non-consequentialistic view put forward in our model can be extended to other economically relevant questions. As an example, think of the economics of crime. The criminal law distinguishes quite carefully between criminal activities that were intended and those that were not. A particular crime is considered less criminal and will be punished less if it was committed negligently and not with criminal intent (compare, e.g. the concepts of manslaughter and second-degree manslaughter). This holds even if the consequences of the criminal activity are exactly the same. As another example, take pay cuts by a firm: As Bewley (1995) shows in his questionnaire study, workers interpret pay cuts as an insult, which adversely affect work morale. This, however, holds to a much lesser degree if workers know that their firm is 'forced' to lower wages, e.g. to avoid bankruptcy. A possible explanation is that if the firm is *forced*, its behaviour does not signal bad intentions. Consequently, the reaction of the workers will be less severe.

What is *not* meant by reciprocity? To avoid terminological confusion we need to specify our concept of reciprocity in two dimensions. *First*, reciprocity means a behaviour that cannot be justified in terms of selfish preferences. Therefore, it sharply distinguishes from 'reciprocal altruism' (Trivers (1971)). The concept of 'reciprocal altruism' is based on repeated game incentives. In repeated games, reciprocal actions like 'tit-for-tat-strategies' can be supported as an equilibrium of an infinitely repeated game (Folk Theorems) or in finitely repeated games with incomplete information (see Kreps *et al.* (1982)). These equilibria may be achieved even among purely *selfish* actors. The distinguishing feature between these 'tit-for-tat' equilibria and reciprocity is that reciprocity prevails even in one-shot-interactions – i.e. in relationships where repeated game incentives are absent.[1] Of course, we do not claim that repeated game incentives are of minor importance. To the contrary, we think that they are of great importance. Moreover, reciprocity and repeated game incentives interact in a complementary manner (on this point see Falk Gächter, and Kovács (1999) and Gächter and Falk (forthcoming)). *Second,* reciprocity is not altruism. An altruist is unconditionally kind whereas a reciprocal person acts kindly only in response to a kind action. In this sense reciprocity means a *conditional* behaviour. The experimental evidence available indicates that altruism is a rather weak phenomenon.

A frequent objection against our and similar approaches is concerned with (i) the arbitrariness of new elements entering the utility functions and (ii) the loss of parsimony. These points are well taken and should be considered seriously. We would like to stress, however, that given the *systematic* evidence on reciprocity the assumption of omnipresent selfishness seems to us no less arbitrary than to assume preferences for fairness. Concerning the parsimony of a theory, one always faces a trade off. It is true that the standard predictions regarding the experimental evidence we look at are nice and simple. However, they are wrong. In our view, parsimony should be viewed as a relative concept, which puts some weight on easiness but *also* on predictive power. Finally, we would like to stress that we explain a wide range of experiments with a *single* utility function. This even includes market experiments where the outcomes are compatible with the standard model.

The chapter is organized as follows. In Section 2 we review some experimental findings on positive and negative reciprocity and on intentions. Section 3 outlines a formal model developed in Falk and Fischbacher (1999). Applications are discussed in Section 4. Section 5 is devoted to the question whether reciprocity can account for selfish outcomes in competitive markets. Section 6 discusses implications of the existence of reciprocity for policy advice and institutional design.

2 Evidence on reciprocity and intentions

In this section we review some important experimental findings on reciprocity. We contrast these findings with the predictions made by 'standard game theory'. These predictions rest on the assumption that people are rational and selfish money maximizers. As we will see, these assumptions are clearly refuted by the experimental data.

2.1 An example for positive reciprocity: the gift-exchange game

The gift-exchange game epitomizes in a very stylized form a principal–agent relationship with incomplete contracts. The contract in this game is incomplete since the principal cannot specify and enforce (via a third party like the court) a particular effort level. The contractual incompleteness is very typical for many principal–agent relations, in particular for labour relations. In a typical labour contract not all contingencies that might arise in the course of the relation can be specified (see for example Milgrom and Roberts (1992)). As a consequence, workers usually have considerable discretion on how much effort they want to put forward.

In the gift-exchange experiment, the first mover (called a firm) offers a wage w to a second mover (called a worker). The worker can either take or leave the wage offer. If the worker rejects the offer, both earn nothing. If the worker accepts the wage offer, she has to make an effort decision e. Providing effort is costly. This is captured by an increasing effort cost function $c(e)$. A firm's payoff function is given by $\pi_F = ve - w$ where v represents an exogenously given redemption value. The payoff function for workers is given by $\pi_W = w - c(e)$. Thus, a firm's payoff is the higher the higher the effort provided by the worker and the lower the wage paid to the worker. A worker's payoff on the other hand is the higher the lower her effort choice and the higher the wage paid to her. Given these payoff functions, the standard game theoretic predictions are straightforward. Since effort is increasingly costly to the worker, a rational and selfish worker will – irrespective of the wage paid – choose the minimum effort level. With backward induction, the firm will offer only the lowest possible wage. Is this prediction borne out by the data?

A typical gift-exchange experiment is reported by Falk, Gächter, and Kovács (1999). In their experiment firms could offer wages from the interval [20,120], the redemption value v was set equal to 120 and the effort cost function as well as the feasible effort choices were given as in Table 9.1. Payoff functions were thus $\pi_F = (120 - w)e$ for firms and $\pi_W = w - c(e)$ for workers.[2] Given these parameters, the unique strict subgame perfect outcome according to standard game theory is $e = 0.1$ and $w = 21$.

In sharp contrast to the standard game theoretic prediction the main experimental findings are that (i) wages clearly exceed the predicted level (60.6 instead of 21) and that (ii) effort levels are on average 0.5, which is well above the predicted level of 0.1. Moreover, there is a positive wage–effort relation. Figure 9.1 shows that, on average, workers provide higher effort levels the higher the wage paid to them. This is

Table 9.1 Effort levels and costs of efforts

e	0.1	0.2	0.3	0.4	0.5	0.6	0.7	0.8	0.9	1
c(e)	20	21	22	24	26	28	30	32	35	38

clear evidence for positive reciprocity. Remember that workers have no pecuniary incentive to provide above minimum effort levels. Reciprocally motivated workers, however, feel a desire to respond in kind, i.e. to reward high wage payments with high effort levels. As suggested by the efficiency wage theory (e.g. Akerlof (1982)) the existence of a positive wage–effort relation makes it profitable for firms to appeal to the workers' reciprocity by paying above minimum wages.

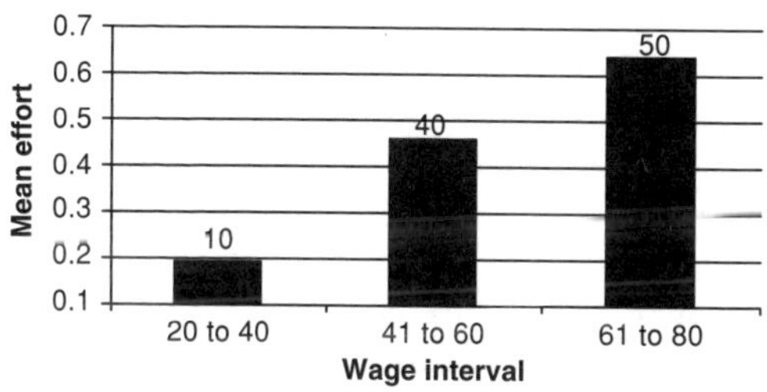

Figure 9.1 Wage effort relation in the gift-exchange game
Note: Relative frequencies (percentages) are on top of the bars.
Source: Falk, Gächter, and Kovács (1999).

It is important to notice that the experimental findings of the gift-exchange game are remarkably robust. In the Falk, Gächter, and Kovács (1999) experiment just outlined, wages were settled in a bilateral trading institution – i.e. there was no competition among the workers. In the experiments by Fehr, Kirchsteiger and Riedl (1993) and Fehr and Falk (1999), on the other hand, wages were settled in a competitive market. In Fehr and Falk (1999), seven firms and 11 workers traded for jobs with each other. Payoff functions and parameters were as outlined above. However, even though there was fierce competition among the workers to get a job (excess supply of four workers) firms paid wages, which were identical to those in the Falk, Gächter, and Kovács (1999) experiment. The reason was again the reciprocal wage–effort relationship: firms could earn more by paying higher wages because this ensured – on average – a higher effort level. Even though there was a lot of underbidding on the side of the workers, firms voluntarily paid rather generous wages. This yields a provocative result. In the presence of incomplete markets and reciprocity competition has no impact on wage formation.

The positive wage–effort relationship is not only robust with respect to competitive forces but also with respect to stake size and across cultures. In their experiment Fehr and Tougareva (1995) performed gift-exchange experiments in Russia where subjects earned on average 2.5 times their monthly income in two hours. Despite this tremendous increase in stake size we find a positive wage effort correlation and generous wages. The gift-exchange game has been performed in different cultures as well. Data were collected in Austria, Switzerland, Hungary, Russia, and the US. The results are qualitatively the same across countries.

There are many other experiments where positive reciprocity is an important motivational factor. For example in the *investment game* studied by Berg, Dickhaut and McCabe (1995) and Miller (1997), first movers are endowed with an amount of money, which they can keep or transfer to the second mover. Any amount y transferred is tripled. The second mover then has to decide on a countertransfer z, with $0 \leq z \leq 3$. If both players are rational and selfish money maximizers, the predicted outcome is $y = z = 0$. However, the authors report that contrary to the standard prediction, first movers on average transfer positive amounts of money and do receive positive countertransfers.

Positive reciprocity is also observed in prisoner's dilemma games and in public goods games. Despite the fact that the dominant strategy is to defect, subjects on average contribute more, the higher the contributions of the other group members (see also our discussion in Section 6).

2.2 An example for negative reciprocity: the ultimatum game

The second game we will focus on is the so-called ultimatum game. This simple two-stage game is the best-known game where negative reciprocity applies. The first mover (called a proposer) is allocated an amount of money from the experimenter. (In the following we normalize this amount of money to unity.) The proposer has to divide this amount between himself and a second mover (called a responder). He may offer any feasible amount c to the responder, i.e. $0 \leq c \leq 1$. This offer is revealed to the responder. The latter can either accept or reject it. If she accepts, the resulting payoffs are $\pi_P = 1 - c$ for the proposer and $\pi_R = c$ for the responder. If the responder rejects the offer, payoffs are zero for both parties. The standard game theoretic prediction is straightforward. The responder prefers accepting any positive amount of money to rejecting and receiving a payoff of zero. Knowing this, the proposer maximizes his income by offering the smallest feasible amount, e.g. 1 cent. Thus, given the standard assumptions, the outcome in the subgame perfect Nash equilibrium is extremely unfair in favour of the proposer.

The ultimatum game has been intensively studied. The reported behavioural regularities are quite robust and can be summarized as follows: concerning the offers there are (i) practically no offers that exceed 0.5, (ii) the modal offers lie in a range between 0.4 and 0.5, and (iii) offers below 0.2 are extremely rare. Table 9.2 gives an overview of 10 ultimatum game experiments. All studies confirm findings (i)–(iii).

Why do proposers not choose the small offers predicted by standard game theory? The reason is simple. Offers that are too low are frequently rejected, leaving the proposer with a zero income: whereas according to the standard prediction responders should be happy with any positive amount of money, they are in fact not. They prefer to turn down a small offer and to punish greedy proposers, rather than accepting and letting the proposers keep their large share. The higher the offers get, the less people are inclined to turn down the offer. Whereas offers close to 0.5 are practically never rejected, the rejection rate for offers below 0.2 is rather high. This reveals that there are individual differences between subjects.

A frequent objection against experimental methods concerns the stake size. Do people really care if the stakes involved are 'peanuts'? Table 9.2 provides an answer to this question (see column (3). It is true that in many experiments the allocated cake is 'only' 10 dollars. However, some experiments implemented very high stakes. As an example, take the second experiment by Hoffman, McCabe, and Smith (1996). In this experiment the cake size was $100 and yet only 4 per cent of all offers were below 20 per cent of the total pie. The 200,000 Rupia in the second experiment reported by Cameron (1999) even involved a pie which is equivalent to a person's three-month income. Again, the results do not differ, which indicates that even if pie sizes are very high, proposers anticipate reciprocal actions.

Table 9.2 reveals yet another important experimental result. Notice that the percentage of offers with $0.4 \leq c \leq 0.5$ is very similar across experiments even though the experiments took place in very different countries and cultures. Besides their cultural differences subjects anticipate reciprocal actions regardless whether they play in Europe, in Asia or in Northern America.

2.3 An example for the importance of intentions

In the gift-exchange game as well as in the ultimatum game we saw reciprocal actions as behavioural responses to an action perceived as

Table 9.2 Percentage of offers below .2 and between .4 and .5 of the total pie in the ultimatum game

Study *(1)*	*No. of observations* *(2)*	*Stake size (country)* *(3)*	*Percentage of offers with $c < 0.2$* (4)	*Percentage of offers with $0.4 \leq c \leq 0.5$* *(5)*
Cameron (1999)	35	Rp 40,000 (Indonesia)	0	66
Cameron (1999)	37	Rp. 200,000 (Indonesia)	5	57
Forsythe *et al.* (1994)	67	$ 5nd 10 (US)	0	82
Güth *et al.* (1982)	79	DM 4–10 (Germany)	8	61
Hoffman *et al.* (1996)	24	$ 10 (US)	0	83
Hoffman *et al.* (1996)	27	$ 100 (US)	4	74
Kahneman *et al.* (1986)	115	$ 10 (US)	?	75[a]
Roth *et al.* (1991)	116[b]	~ $ 10 (USA, Slovakia, Israel, Japan)	3	70
Slonim and Roth (1997)	240[c]	SK 60 (Slovakia)	0.4[d]	75
Slonim and Roth (1997)	250[c]	SK 150 (Slovakia)	8	69
Aggregate result of all studies[e]	875		3.8	71

Notes: a = Percentage of equal splits, b = Only observations of the final period, c = Observations of all 10 periods, d = Percentage of offers below 0.25, e = excluding Kahneman *et al.* (1986).

Source: Fehr and Schmidt (1999).

kind (high-wage) or unkind (low-offer). Here we want to highlight that the perceived kindness of an action depends not only on its consequences but also on the *intention* underlying that action. To illustrate the role of intentions consider the two games in Figure 9.2.

Both games in Figure 9.2 are *reduced ultimatum games*. In the left game (henceforth *UG1*) the proposer is asked to divide 10 dollars between himself and a responder. He has only two choices, either to offer 2 dollars to the responder and to keep 8 dollars or to offer an equal split. The responder can either accept or reject the offer. A rejection leads to zero incomes for both players. Assume the proposer chooses to offer 2 dollars. If the responder is a reciprocal player she may consider this choice to be unkind; and she may prefer to reject the offer in order to punish the proposer, rather than to accept it. After all, the proposer *could have chosen* an equal split by offering 5 dollars.

Consider now the second game, which we call *UG2*. Again, the proposer's task is to divide 10 dollars and the responder may either accept or reject the offer. The *alternatives* available to the proposer are *different*, though. In the *UG2* game, the opportunity to reach an equal split is removed. Instead the proposer can offer either 2 dollars (and keep 8 dollars) or offer 8 dollars (and keep 2 dollars).[3]

Suppose the proposer offers 2 dollars and keeps 8 dollars for himself. Would you as a responder consider this particular offer as equally unkind as in the *UG1* game? Experimental subjects do not. Even though the *consequences are exactly the same*, responders consider it as *less unkind* to get the same disadvantageous offer in the *UG2* game. They reject the 2-dollar offer significantly less often than in the *UG1* game (compare Falk, Fehr, and Fischbacher (forthcoming)). The reason for the different rejection rates is that responders care about *why* the proposer chose a particular offer, i.e. they care about the proposer's intentions. In *UG1* it

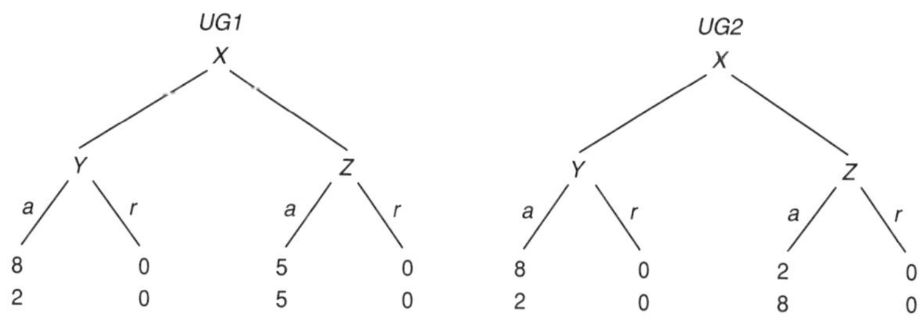

Figure 9.2 The game trees of two reduced ultimatum games with different alternatives for the proposer

is evident that the proposer did not want to reach a fair allocation between himself and the responder. He *could have* chosen an equal split, but he did not. This refusal clearly signals unkind intentions to the responder. This signalling of unkind intentions is less clear in *UG2*. Choosing the 2-dollar offer does not express the refusal to reach a fair allocation: since the proposer has *no opportunity* to offer a fair share, the responder cannot infer that he does not *want* to offer a fair share. In order to infer another person's intentions, subjects look at the opportunity set of the other person. At the extreme, if a person has nothing to decide, e.g. if a person is forced to perform a particular action, or if someone else decides for her, an action does not signal any intentions.

Experimental examples for this extreme situation are reported in Blount (1995), Charness (1996), Falk, Fehr and Fischbacher (forthcoming) and Falk, Fehr and Fischbacher (2001). Blount (1995) compares a 'regular' ultimatum game with a degenerated ultimatum game in which the first mover's offer was determined by a random device. In this treatment the first mover has no choice to make. A low offer, therefore, does not signal any (bad) intentions and is consequently not interpreted as an unkind treatment. In fact, second movers in the random treatment accept much lower offers compared to the 'regular' ultimatum game. However, even if a random device determines the outcome, i.e. even when the action of a first mover does not signal any intention, people still experience the *outcome per se* as either advantageous or disadvantageous compared to some reference. As a consequence subjects reject extremely disadvantageous outcomes even in the absence of intentions (see Falk, Fehr and Fischbacher (2001) for a detailed discussion on intentions). Summing up, perceived kindness contains both (i) the concern for the consequences *per se* and (ii) the underlying intention.

2.4 Does *homo economicus* exist at all? Individual heterogeneity

So far we have argued that reciprocity is an important motivation that shapes aggregate behaviour in many circumstances. This does not mean, however, that *homo economicus* does not exist at all. In fact in the experiments one usually observes a lot of individual heterogeneity. At the one extreme some subjects are extremely reciprocal. On the other extreme, some are purely selfish as suggested in the standard model. Table 9.3 shows for a variety of different experiments the fraction of people who behave like *homo economicus*, and reveals that *homo economicus* exists but is by no means omnipresent.

Table 9.3 Reciprocal and selfish subjects coexist

Study	*Country*	*Game*	*MP*	*No. subj.*	*Selfish*	*Non-selfish (non-recip.)*
Andreoni and Miller (1993)	US	Prisoner's dilemma	S	14	35.7	64.3
Berg, Dickhaut and McCabe *et al.* (1995)	US	Investment game	1	28	42.8	39.3 (17.9)
Cooper *et al.* (1996)	US	Prisoner's dilemma	S	40	35.0	65.0
Fehr and Tougareva (1995)	RUS	Gift exch. posted bid – high stakes	M	35	14.3	85.7
Fehr and Tougareva (1995)	RUS	Gift exch. posted bid – high stakes	M	36	11.1	89.9
Gächter and Falk (forthcoming)	A	Bilateral gift exch.	S	30	20.0	53.3 (26.7)
Falk, Gächter and Kovács (1999)	H	Bilateral gift exch.	S	20	20.0	55.0 (25.0)
Abbink, Irlenbusch and Renner. (2000)	D	Moonlighting game	1	40	37.5	63.5
Miller (1997)	D	Investment game	1	97	21.6	78.4
Dufwenberg and Gneezy (1997)	NL	Trust game	1	30	40.0	60.0
Fischbacher, Gächter and Fehr. (2001)	CH	Public goods	1	44	29.5	50.0 (20.5)
Fehr and Gächter (2000)	CH	Public goods	S	72	22.0	78.0
Keser and van Winden (1998)	NL	Public goods	S	120	20.0	80.0
Bolle (1998)	D	Trust game	1	32	16.0	84.0
Gunnthorsdottir, McCabe and Smith. (1998)	US	Trust game	1	64	45.3	54.7
Fehr and Falk (1999)	CH	Gift exch. double auction	M	44	22.7	77.3

Note: Column 'MP' describes the matching procedure: '1' means 'one-shot', i.e. that the respective game was played exactly once. The games indicated with 'S' (sequences of one-shots) are games where the constituent game was played repeatedly with (randomly) changing opponents. In games indicated with 'M' (one-shot markets) the trading institution was a market. In all games of this table – at least for players in one role – selfishness is unambiguously defined as playing a dominant strategy with respect to the material payoffs. 'Selfish' are subjects who play the dominant strategy. The number of subjects indicated in Table 9.3 relates to the second movers in sequential games and to all players in simultaneous move games. In some studies reciprocal behaviour at the individual level can be unambiguously identified, whereas in others this is hard to achieve. In studies where subjects' non-selfish behaviour can be categorized as 'reciprocal' or 'non-reciprocal', the first number is the percentage of reciprocal behaviour and the number in brackets refers to the percentage of behaviour that is neither selfish not reciprocal. Nevertheless, at the aggregate level, data are highly regular and confirm the importance of non-selfish behaviour.
(*Source*: Fehr and Gächter (1999)).

3 Modelling reciprocity

In this section we sketch out how reciprocity can be modelled in a game theoretic model.[4] The purpose of the presentation in this section is only expositional. We restrict our presentation to the key aspects of our model and omit all technical details. The technically interested reader is referred to Falk and Fischbacher (1999).

According to our model, reciprocity consists of a kind (or unkind) treatment by another person (represented by the *kindness term* φ) and a behavioural reaction to that treatment (represented by the *reciprocation term* σ). Our procedure is to transform the standard game (e.g. the ultimatum game) into a so-called 'reciprocity game'. In this new game the players' utility depends not only on the material payoffs of the original standard game (denoted by π_i) but also on the kindness and the reciprocation term. The utility function for player i is given by the following definition:

> **Definition** Let player i and j be the two players of the game. We define player i's utility U_i in the transformed reciprocity game as:[5]
>
> $$U_i = \pi_i + \rho_i \varphi \sigma \tag{1}$$

According to the definition player i's utility in the reciprocity game is the sum of the following two terms: the first summand is simply player i's **material payoff** π_i. This material payoff corresponds to the payoffs discussed in the ultimatum and the gift-exchange games. The second summand – which we call **reciprocity utility** – is composed of the following terms:

- The positive constant ρ_i is called the **reciprocity parameter**. This constant is an individual parameter which captures the strength of player i's reciprocal preferences. It captures the fact that individuals are very heterogeneous with respect to their reciprocal inclination (compare Table 9.3). The higher ρ_i, the more important is the reciprocity utility compared to the utility arising from the material payoff. Note that if ρ_i equals zero, player i's utility is equal to his material payoff. Put differently, if $\rho_i = 0$, the player has *homo economicus* preferences just as assumed in standard game theory. If, in addition, ρ_j also equals zero, the reciprocity game collapses into the standard game.
- The **kindness term** φ measures the kindness player i experiences from j's actions. As outlined in Section 2, the perceived kindness depends on the *consequences* of an action and its underlying *intention*:

- The consequences determine the sign and (partly) the size of the kindness term. In order to determine the sign and the size of φ, player i needs to compare the payoff consequences of player j's action with a given reference standard. In principle, there are many possible reference standards against which subjects can compare a particular outcome. From many experiments we know, however, that an *equitable* share of payoffs is a salient and commonly held standard.[6] We therefore implemented an equitable outcome share as reference standard. Given this equitable reference standard, player i can either be favoured in an exchange (positive kindness term) or player i can be in a disadvantageous position (in which case the kindness term is negative). If φ is positive, player j is considered as kind. This holds, e.g. in the gift-exchange game if the firm offers a generous wage. The higher the wage, the greater is the kindness term. Of course, φ can also be negative, meaning that the action of player j is considered as unkind. This holds, e.g. in the ultimatum game if the offer is low. The lower the offer, the more negative is φ.
- Notice that the kindness term comprises consequences *and* intentions. Our model takes intentions into account by looking at player j's alternatives. An action by player j is induced intentional if player j has reasonable alternatives to choose from. The more an action is caused intentionally the stronger it is weighted in the kindness term. For example, if player j has been *forced* to perform a particular action the size of the kindness term is smaller compared to a situation where player j has *chosen* the action.

• The **reciprocation term** σ measures the effect of the reciprocal action. It is basically player j's payoff.

• The product of the *kindness* and the *reciprocation term* measures the reciprocity utility. If the kindness term is greater than zero, player i can *ceteris paribus* increase his utility if he chooses an action which increases player j's payoff. This is the case in the gift-exchange game if a high wage is answered by a high-effort choice. The opposite holds if the kindness term is negative. In this case, player i has an incentive to reduce player j's payoff. As an example take the ultimatum game. If the offer was very low, a reciprocal player i can increase his utility by rejecting the offer, which reduces player j's payoff.

Several other attempts to model other-regarding preferences have been made. Most recently, Bolton and Ockenfels (2000) and Fehr and Schmidt (1999) have suggested theories which emphasize equity considerations for the evaluation of kindness. These models are purely outcome-oriented in the sense that they do not account for the role of intentions. Consequently, they ignore an important aspect of the psychology of reciprocity. Moreover, the models fail to predict important experimental results (see below).

Other fairness models explicitly account for the role of intentions (Rabin (1993), Levine (1998), and Dufwenberg and Kirchsteiger (1998)). However, these models do not predict the behaviour of experimental subjects where intentions cannot play any role, as e.g. in the dictator game.

4 Applications of the model

In Section 3 we have outlined the basic structure of our model. In this section we discuss some of our model's predictions. We will concentrate on the gift-exchange game, the ultimatum game and a comparison of the reduced ultimatum games presented in section 2. Additionally, we will restrict the analysis to the second mover behaviour. In Falk and Fischbacher (1999) we present a full characterization of our predictions, with all formal propositions and proofs.

4.1 The gift-exchange game

The gift-exchange game has been introduced above. Contrary to the standard prediction (i) wages and effort levels clearly exceed the lowest possible wage and (ii) there is a positive wage-effort relation. These two stylized facts are predicted by our model. In the following let $w \in [0, 1]$ and $e \in [0, 1]$. We normalize v to 1 and write the convex effort cost function as $c(e) = \alpha e^2$ with $\alpha \leq 1/4$.

The main predictions of our model are illustrated with the help of Figures 9.3–9.5. In Figure 9.3 we depict how – in equilibrium – a worker's effort choice depends on the wage paid by the firm given her reciprocal motivation, ρ_W. Figure 9.3 captures the essence of *positive reciprocity*. From the worker's perspective, the higher the wage paid by the firm, the higher is the kindness term φ (compare Section 3). A reciprocal worker (with a sufficiently high reciprocity parameter ρ_W) improves her utility if she responds in kind, i.e. if she provides more than the minimum effort. As a result, reciprocal workers provide higher effort levels the higher the wage paid by 'their' firm. Moreover, workers will – for a given wage – choose higher effort levels, the stronger their reciprocal inclination. This is depicted in Figure 9.4. The upper graph shows the equilibrium effort choice according to our model for a wage $w = 0.5$, whereas the lower graph depicts the optimal effort for a lower wage ($w = 0.3$). Note that the effort level is zero if $\rho_W = 0$ or $w = 0$.

4.1.1 *Intentions*

Concluding our discussion of the gift-exchange game we present our predictions for the treatment reported by Charness (1996). In his experiment wages are not determined by the firm. Rather, a third party or a random mechanism determines the wage. Compared to the 'regular' treatment, this leads to a *weaker* correlation between wages and effort levels. The reason is that in Charness' treatment a high wage does not signal any (kind) intentions. Our model captures this difference. Since the kindness term captures both, the concern for outcomes *and*

Figure 9.3 Effort choice dependent on the wage paid for a given ρ_W and a given α ($\rho_W = 2$ and $\alpha = 0.2$)

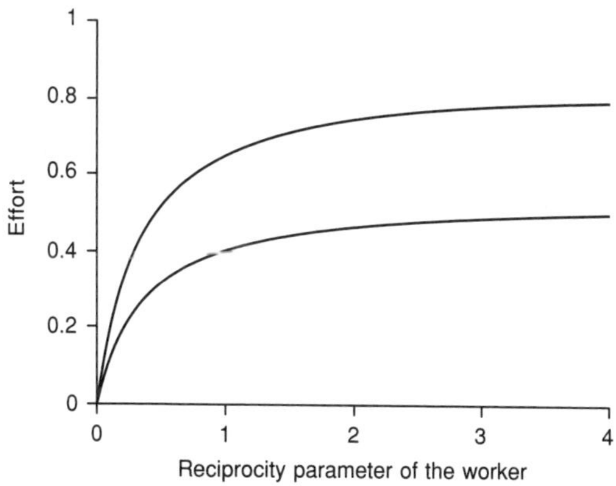

Figure 9.4 Equilibrium effort choice dependent on the worker's reciprocity parameter ρ_W, a given α and two wage levels ($\alpha = 0.2$, $w = 0.3$, and $w = 0.5$)

Figure 9.5 Equilibrium effort as a function of the wage: in the upper graph, the wage is chosen by a human being, in the lower graph by a random device

intentions, the kindness term is smaller in this situation. As a consequence the reciprocal action is weaker as well. For a given reciprocal motivation of the worker ρ_W the model predicts a weaker correlation between wages and effort levels. Put differently, the *same* worker will supply a lower effort for a particular wage in the random treatment compared to the 'regular' treatment. Figure 9.5 shows that result.

4.2 The ultimatum game

Remember that given the standard assumptions, the outcome in the subgame perfect Nash equilibrium is to offer the smallest possible c, which is accepted by the responder. However, low offers are rejected and – as a consequence – most offers are in between 0.4 and 0.5 of the total pie. Thus, the standard subgame perfect prediction is strongly refuted by the data. With the help of Figures 9.6–9.8 we show that our model does a much better job to organize the data.

The most important finding in the experiments is the fact that responders are more likely to accept an offer the higher it is. In our model this is expressed by an acceptance probability p. Figure 9.6 depicts this acceptance probability as a function of the level of the offer and for a given reciprocal inclination of the responder. The figure neatly captures the essence of *negative reciprocity*: a low offer is an unkind act, which results in a negative kindness term. A utility-maximizing responder who is sufficiently reciprocally motivated improves his utility by rejecting the offer. As a result, the lower the offer, the higher is the willingness of a reciprocally motivated responder to punish the proposer by rejecting the offer. Note that as the responder's reciprocity concern ρ_R gets higher (lower), the acceptance curve shifts to the right (left). This means that a person who is more strongly motivated by reciprocity than another person will accept a low offer with a lower probability than the person who is less reciprocal. However, no matter how strongly a responder is reciprocally motivated she will always accept an offer with probability one if the offer is equal or higher than half of the pie (i.e. $c \geq 1/2$). This captures the experimental finding that offers with $c \geq 1/2$ are practically always accepted.

What does this mean for the proposer? In order to guarantee that his offer will be accepted with certainty he must at least offer c_0, i.e. c_0 is the smallest offer that just guarantees an acceptance probability of 1 (compare Figure 9.6). Obviously, the responder's concern for reciprocity is

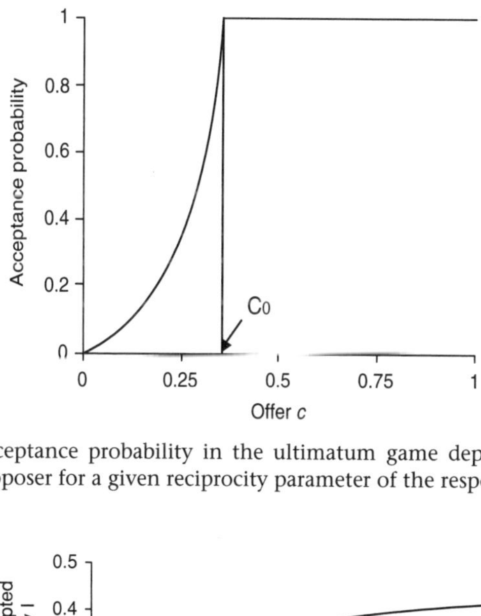

Figure 9.6 Acceptance probability in the ultimatum game dependent on the offer of the proposer for a given reciprocity parameter of the responder of $\rho_R = 2$

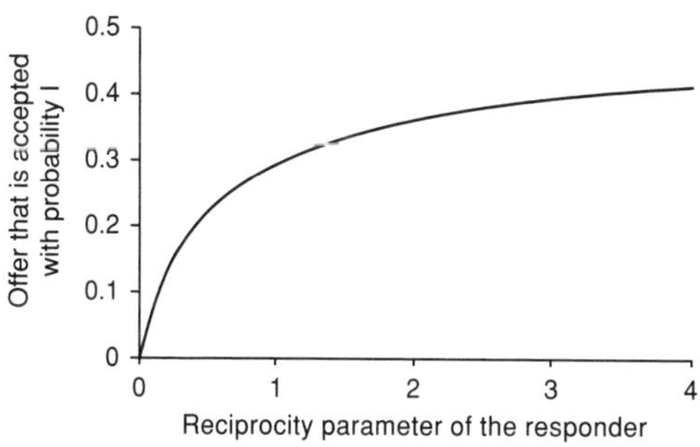

Figure 9.7 Offers in the ultimatum game that guarantee an acceptance probability of 1, dependent on the reciprocity parameter of the responder (ρ_R)

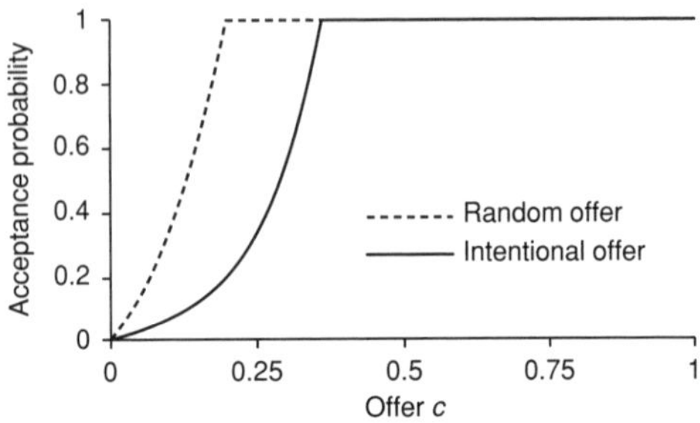

Figure 9.8 Acceptance probabilities in the ultimatum game with intentions (lower graph) and without intentions (upper graph) dependent on the offer (for a given parameter ρ_R)

crucial for the value of c_0. For example, if the responder is selfish (with $\rho_R = 0$) the value of c_0 is equal to zero. The higher the responder's concern for reciprocity, i.e. the higher ρ_R, the higher the value of c_0. As ρ_R gets very large, c_0 approaches 1/2. The dependence of c_0 on ρ_R is shown in Figure 9.7. It is remarkable that even for small values of ρ_R the proposer is 'forced' to make a rather generous offer in order to avoid a rejection.

4.2.1 *Intentions*

Here, we briefly discuss the role of intentions in the ultimatum game. We compare the predictions of our model with the data reported in the 'non-intentional' experiment by Blount (1995). Remember that in her treatment the proposers' offers were randomly selected, i.e. a low offer did not signal any (bad) intentions. As the data of Blount's experiment reveals, the acceptance rate for a given offer is *higher* than in the 'regular' treatment. However, even in the absence of intentions many subjects reject very disadvantageous offers.

Our model predicts exactly these stylized facts. Figure 9.8 depicts the predicted acceptance probabilities in the 'regular' ultimatum game and in Blount's treatment for a given ρ_R. The upper graph corresponds to the Blount experiment whereas the lower graph shows the acceptance behaviour in the 'regular' treatment. As can be seen in Figure 9.8, a responder's acceptance probability for low offers is higher if intentions are absent. The reason for this is that the experienced unkindness and thus the (negative) kindness term is smaller. As a result the reciprocal response is smaller as well. Put differently, the same person may accept a particular offer if generated by a random device and may reject it when offered by a human being.

4.3 A comparison between the reduced ultimatum games

In Section 2.3 we motivated the role of intention with a comparison between two reduced ultimatum games (see Figure 9.2). As Figure 9.9 shows, our model predicts a higher acceptance probability for the unkind offer (8,2) in the reduced *UG2* game, compared to the *UG*1 game. The upper graph shows the acceptance probability of the unkind offer in the *UG2* game, the lower shows that of the *UG1* game. In both games, we see that the acceptance probability of the unkind offer decreases in the responder's concern for reciprocity, i.e. in ρ_R. We also see, however, that for a given ρ_R the acceptance probability is lower in the *UG*1 game compared to the *UG2* game.

Thus, in the *UG2* game a reciprocal responder is willing to accept a higher degree of inequity. The reason is that in the *UG2* the responder does not find it very unkind if he gets the 'unkind' offer, because she cannot infer very bad intentions from this offer. Things are quite different in the *UG1* game. Here, the first mover has the alternative to choose an equitable outcome. Consequently, it *does* signal bad intentions and is considered as quite unkind if this alternative is not chosen. Thus, dependent on the first mover's alternatives the *same* offer will be perceived differently, which leads to a different kindness term. As a consequence, the acceptance rates differ as well. This difference is confirmed in the experimental study by Falk, Fehr, and Fischbacher (forthcoming): The rejection rate of the (8,2) offer is 27 per cent in the *UG2* and 44 per cent in the *UG1*.

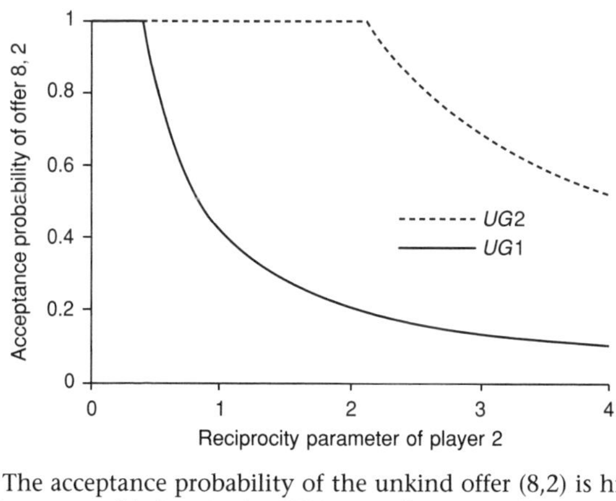

Figure 9.9 The acceptance probability of the unkind offer (8,2) is higher in the *UG2* game (upper graph) than in the *UG1* game (lower graph)

5 Reciprocity in markets?

In the previous sections we reviewed much empirical evidence in favour of the importance of reciprocity. In this section we discuss experimental evidence that is seemingly incompatible with reciprocal preferences: it is a well-established fact in experimental economics that in competitive markets outcomes converge towards the outcome predicted by standard economic theory (Smith (1982), Davis and Holt (1993)). This holds even in markets where the equilibrium outcome is very 'unfair' in the sense that almost the whole surplus is reaped by one side of the market. Put differently, it seems that in a competitive environment subjects behave as if they were completely selfish.

How can a model of reciprocity possibly account for this fact? As it turns out, our model predicts that in competitive markets players will accept a much higher degree of inequity compared to bilateral exchange situations (see Falk and Fischbacher (1999) for details). The intuition behind this striking result is that in competitive markets players have no chance to achieve a 'fair' outcome. We saw that in the *ultimatum game* a responder can 'force' the proposer to make a 'fair' offer by credibly threatening to reject very low offers. This punishment device is ineffective in competitive markets because there may be other traders in the market who accept low offers. Anticipating that low offers will be accepted induces even a reciprocal responder to accept low offers as well. Thus, our fairness theory not only explains why in bilateral institutions outcomes tend to be 'fair' but also why in markets reciprocal subjects' behaviour gives rise to equilibria with an extremely uneven distribution of the gains from trade.

6 Implications of reciprocity

In the previous sections we hare argued that reciprocity is an important behavioural motivation. In this section we will briefly sketch some economic implications and point to fields where reciprocity can give some new explanations to economically relevant questions.

6.1 Voluntary provision to public goods and the interaction between selfish and reciprocal types

Free riding incentives are a pervasive phenomenon in social life. In fact, standard economic theory predicts that in case of private and voluntary provisions of public goods these incentives lead inevitably to an inefficient underprovision. Does reciprocity provide a mechanism to overcome the predicted underprovision? The answer to this question is more subtle than it may seem. It requires a discussion on the interaction of different types of motivation. To answer it, we will refer to two experiments: a standard public goods experiment and an experiment with punishment opportunities.

The strategic structure of a public goods experiment is very similar to that of a prisoner's dilemma. The major difference is that in a public goods game players have more strategies than just to cooperate or to defect. In a typical public goods game each player is provided with an endowment of 20 tokens, say, that can be allocated to a public good or that can be kept for private consumption. The marginal *per capita* return of an investment into the public good is usually smaller than one, i.e. providing zero tokens to the public good is a dominant strategy (whereas it is in the common interest to fully cooperate). In repeated public goods experiments three stylized facts are important: *first*, during the early periods contribution levels are higher than predicted by standard theory and vary between 40 and 60 per cent of the endowment. *Second*, cooperation rates decline to low levels towards the final rounds of the experiment. In a meta study, Fehr and Schmidt (1999) report that in the final periods of 12 different public goods experiments 73 per cent of all individuals ($N = 1{,}042$) chose contributions of zero tokens and many of the remaining players chose contribution levels close to that. *Third*, despite the fact that the dominant strategy is to provide zero tokens, subjects on average contributed more, the higher the contributions of the other group members (Fischbacher, Gächter, and Fehr (2001)).

Thus, even in the presence of reciprocity cooperation cannot be sustained at a high level. The explanation has to do with the heterogeneity of players: the selfish players who always defect and reciprocal players who *conditionally* cooperate (compare Table 9.3). As an example, suppose that in a group of four people there are three reciprocal players and one selfish player. Suppose further that in the first period all three reciprocal players fully cooperate (because they believe everybody does so). Since the selfish player fully defects, the cooperation rate is only 75 per cent. In the next period conditional cooperators will not cooperate fully any more but only at most 75 per cent and so on. Eventually, the average group contribution will approach a low level. Put differently, if there are no further institutional features selfish types are 'decisive' in that they induce the reciprocally fair types to behave noncooperatively.

Therefore it is of great interest whether – given the heterogeneity of reciprocal and selfish people – there are institutional set-ups that can also lead to stable cooperative outcomes. Put differently: what are the interaction structures which enable the reciprocally fair types to force or induce the selfish types to behave cooperatively? In view of the fact that reciprocally fair types are willing to punish unfair behaviour it seems likely that the presence or absence of *punishment opportunities* is crucial here. As Fehr and Gächter (2000) have shown, this is in fact the case. They introduce a slightly different public goods game in which players have the opportunity to punish other players. This punishment is *costly* for the punisher, which means that a purely selfish subject will never punish. A cooperating reciprocal subject, however, is willing to punish a defecting subject because the defection is likely to be viewed as unfair. Therefore, if the selfish subject anticipates that a defection will be punished she has an incentive to cooperate. The experiments show that – even though punishing is costly – subjects punish quite often. Moreover, punishment follows a clear pattern. The big majority of punishments are imposed by the cooperators on the defectors. The punishment a subject receives is the higher the more his contribution falls short of the average contribution of the other group members. As a consequence of the punishment regularities, contribution rates dramatically increase. Contribution rates are significantly higher in the punishment condition compared to public goods games without a punishment opportunity.

The big difference in cooperation rates across conditions suggests that in the presence of punishment opportunities the reciprocally fair types can force the selfish types to cooperate while in the absence of such opportunities the selfish types induce the reciprocally fair types to defect, too. Thus, interaction structures that have theoretically identical implications if there are only selfish types generate fundamentally different behavioural patterns in the presence of reciprocal types.

6.2 Labour relations

An important application of reciprocal motivation is *labour relations*. As pointed out in our discussion of the gift-exchange game, the existence of reciprocity may generate a positive wage–effort relationship, which in turn may explain the existence of *downwardly rigid wages*. The underlying efficiency wage argument was theoretically derived by Akerlof (1982). Empirical support for this hypothesis comes from laboratory experiments (see above) as well as from questionnaire studies (Blinder and Choi (1990), Bewley (1995), Agell and Lundborg (1995), and Campbell and Kamlani (1997)). In these studies owners and managers of firms were asked about their wage setting policies. They suggest that employers are unwilling to cut wages in the presence of unemployment. According to these studies a major reason for firms' refusal to cut wages is the fear that pay cuts will adversely affect work morale. Summarizing this literature Agell (1999, p. 144) concludes that '[r]ecent field surveys on wage rigidity, and laboratory studies of reciprocal behaviour, strongly suggest that persistent social norms are an independent and important cause of wage rigidity'.

Moreover, it has been shown that reciprocity may account for *non-compensating wage differentials* (Fehr, Gächter and Kirchsteiger (1997)) and for firms' *refusal to employ underbidders* (Agell and Lundborg (1995) and Fehr and Falk (1999), Falk and Gächter (2000), Dufwenberg and Kirchsteiger (2000)). In Agell and Lundborg (1995, p. 299), it is shown that although unemployed workers frequently seem to be willing to work for less than the going wage firms report that they refuse to employ underbidders. They conclude: 'While unemployed workers knock on the factory gates to a surprising extent, . . ., firms keep them locked.'

6.3 Economic policy

Traditional economic policy is based on the assumption that *all* people act like *homo economicus*. In the light of the presented evidence, one might ask whether this is really appropriate. Consider the following example in the field of *economics of crime*. The standard economic conception of crime deterrence is exclusively built on the 'price' people have to pay if they break the law. This price is determined by the severity of the punishment weighted by the probability of detection. If people are reciprocal, however, there might be other channels that affect criminal activities (compare Kahan (1997)). One immediate consequence of reciprocity is that people are expected to commit more crimes the more criminal activity is thought to be widespread. If I believe, e.g., that other people cheat on their insurance companies or do not pay their taxes, why should I be the 'sucker' who pays for their free rider behaviour? It follows that if beliefs about the behaviour of others are important, there is a potential utility for belief management. Policies that shape the beliefs that social norms and their enforcement are intact can positively contribute to people's willingness to behave according to these social norms, i.e. to refrain from criminal activities. Kahan (1997), for example, argues in favour of 'policies aimed at suppressing public disorder and visible gang activity, forms of behaviour that can generate social-influence pressure to engage in crime' (p. 365).

In a more general perspective the existence of reciprocal types challenges the standard way economists look at institutional designs. In their analysis of the future of egalitarian politics Bowles and Gintis (1998, p. 3) argue that 'egalitarian policy-making, no less than the grand projects of constitutional design, risk irrelevance if they ignore the irreducible heterogeneity of human motivations'. We agree with Bowles and Gintis (1998, p. 3) that '[t]he problem of institutional design is not, as the classical economists thought, that selfish individuals be induced to interact in ways producing desirable outcomes, but rather that a mix of individuals – selfish, reciprocal, altruistic and spiteful – interact in ways that prevent the selfish and spiteful from exploiting the goodness of others and hence unravelling cooperation when it is beneficial'.

A final implication of the importance of reciprocity and intentions for the institutional design concerns the merits of procedural justice. Our argument is that distributive conflicts in societies can be mitigated if the people who are disadvantaged by a distributional change know that at least the *procedure* that led to the new distribution was fair. The point is that if an unfair outcome is not intentionally caused by the favoured person, negative reciprocity and hence destructive resistance will less likely occur. Institutions that guarantee procedural fairness may achieve this. If an outcome is the result of a fair procedure, nobody assumes bad intentions from the other people's behaviour. Therefore, if an outcome turns out to be 'unfair', the unfavoured person will have fewer negative emotions compared to a situation where the same outcome is caused intentionally by the favoured person. Thus, social welfare is higher. Moreover, societies that ensure procedural justice are better equipped to deal with structural changes and are more likely to reach socially desirable outcomes.

Notes

1 Bowles and Gintis (1998) introduced 'strong reciprocity' and 'weak reciprocity' to differentiate the concept of reciprocity from 'reciprocal altruism'.

2 Notice that we used the functional form $\pi_F = (v - w)e$ instead of the more familiar form $\pi_F = ve - w$. This was done to avoid losses in the experiment. The game theoretic predictions remain the same, however.

3 The *UG2* game is a very stylized version of the so-called best-shot game studied by Prasnikar and Roth (1992).

4 The full model is in detail explained and discussed in Falk and Fischbacher (1999).

5 This formula is only expositional. For the correct utility function see Falk and Fischbacher (1999).

6 On the concept of equity as a reference standard compare Adams (1965) and Walster and Walster (1978). See also Güth, Marchand and Rullière (1997), Loewenstein, Thompson and Bazerman (1989) and Selten (1978).

References

Abbink, K., B. Irlenbusch and E. Renner (2000) 'The Moonlighting Game. An Experimental Study on Reciprocity and Retribution', *Journal of Economic Behavior and Organization*, vol. 42, no. 2 pp. 265–77.

Adams, J. S. (1965) 'Inequity in Social Exchange', in L. Berkowitz (ed.), *Advances in Experimental Psychology, 2* (New York: Academic Press), pp. 267–99.

Agell, J. (1999) 'On the Benefits from Rigid Labour Markets: Norms, Market Failures, and Social Insurance' *Economic Journal*, vol. 109, pp. 143–64.

Agell, J. and P. Lundborg (1995) 'Theories of Pay and Unemployment: Survey Evidence from Swedish Manufacturing Firms', *Scandinavian Journal of Economics*, vol. 97, pp. 295–307.

Akerlof, G. (1982) 'Labor Contracts as a Partial Gift Exchange', *Quarterly Journal of Economics*, vol. 97, pp. 543–69.

Andreoni, J. and J. Miller (1993) 'Rational Cooperation in the Finitely Repeated Prisoner's Dilemma: Experimental Evidence', *Economic Journal*, vol. 103, pp. 570–85.

Bewley, T. (1995) 'A Depressed Labor Market as Explained by Participants', *American Economic Review*, vol. 85, *Papers and Proceedings*, pp. 250–4.

Berg, J., J. Dickhaut and K. McCabe (1995) 'Trust, Reciprocity, and Social History', *Games and Economic Behaviour*, vol. 10, pp. 122–42.

Blinder, A. S. and D. H. Choi (1990) 'A Shred of Evidence on Theories of Wage Stickiness', *Quarterly Journal of Economics*, vol. 105, pp. 1003–16.

Blount, S. (1995) 'When Social Outcomes Aren't Fair: The Effect of Causal Attributions on Preferences', *Organizational Behaviour and Human Decision Processes*, vol. 63, pp. 131–44.

Bolle, F. (1998) 'Rewarding Trust: An Experimental Study', *Theory and Decision*, vol. 45, pp. 83–98.

Bolton, G. and A. Ockenfels (2000) 'ERC – A Theory of Equity, Reciprocity and Competition', *American Economic Review*, vol. 90, pp. 166–94.

Bowles, S. and H. Gintis (1998) 'Is Equality Passé?', *Boston Review*, vol. 23, no. 6, pp. 1998–9.

Cameron, L. (1999) 'Raising the Stakes in the Ultimatum Game: Experimental Evidence from Indonesia', *Economic Inquiry*, vol. 37, pp. 47–59.

Campbell, C. M. and K. Kamlani (1997) 'The Reasons for Wage Rigidity: Evidence from a Survey of Firms', *Quarterly Journal of Economics*, vol. 112, pp. 759–89.

Charness, G. (1996) 'Attribution and Reciprocity in a Simulated Labor Market: An Experimental Investigation', University of California, Berkeley, mimeo.

Cooper, R., D. DeJong, R. Forsythe and T. Ross (1996) 'Cooperation without Reputation: Experimental Evidence from Prisoner's Dilemma Games', *Games and Economic Behaviour*, vol. 12, pp. 187–218.

Davis, D. and C. Holt (1993) *Experimental Economics* (Princeton: Princeton University Press).

Dufwenberg, M. and U. Gneezy (1997) 'Efficiency, Reciprocity, and Expectations in an Experimental Game', CentER for Economic Research, University of Tilburg, mimeo.

Dufwenberg, M. and G. Kirchsteiger (1998) 'A Theory of Sequential Reciprocity', CentER for Economic Research, University of Tilburg, mimeo.

Dufwenberg, M. and G. Kirchsteiger (2000) 'Reciprocity and Wage Undercutting', *European Economic Review*, vol. 44, nos 4–6, pp. 1069–78

Falk, A. and U. Fischbacher (1999) 'A Theory of Reciprocity', IEW Working Paper, no. 6, University of Zürich.

Falk, A., E. Fehr, and U. Fischbacher (2001) 'Testing Theories of Fairness, IEW Working Paper', no. 63, University of Zünch.

Falk, A., E. Fehr, and U. Fischbacher (forthcoming) 'On the Nature of Fair Behaviour', *Economic Inquiry*.

Falk A. and S. Gächter (2000) 'Why Firms Refuse to Hire Underbidders', in P. de Gijsel, R. Olthoff and T. Zwick (eds), *The Unemployment Debate: Current Issues* (Marburg: Metropolis Verlag), pp. 125–54.

Falk, A., S. Gächter and J. Kovács (1999) 'Intrinsic Motivation and Extrinsic Incentives in a Repeated Game with Incomplete Contracts', *Journal of Economic Psychology*, vol. 20, pp. 251–84.

Fehr, E. and A. Falk (1999) 'Wage Rigidities in a Competitive, Incomplete Contract Market', *Journal of Political Economy*, vol. 107, pp. 106–34.

Fehr, E. and S. Gächter (1999) 'Reciprocal Fairness, Heterogeneity, and Institutions', University of Zürich, mimeo.

Fehr, E. and S. Gächter (2000) 'Cooperation and Punishment in Public Goods Experiments', *American Economic Review*, vol. 90, no. 4, pp. 980–94.

Fehr, E., S. Gächter and G. Kirchsteiger (1997) 'Reciprocity as a Contract Enforcement Device: Experimental Evidence', *Econometrica*, vol. 65, pp. 833–60.

Fehr, E., G. Kirchsteiger and A. Riedl (1993) 'Does Fairness Prevent Market Clearing? An Experimental Investigation', *Quarterly Journal of Economics*, vol. 108, pp. 437–60.

Fehr, E. and K. Schmidt (1999) 'A Theory of Fairness, Competition, and Cooperation', *Quarterly Journal of Economics*, vol. 114, pp. 817–51.

Fehr, E. and D. Tougareva (1995) 'Do High Stakes Remove Reciprocal Fairness – Evidence from Russia', University of Zürich, mimeo.

Fischbacher, U., S. Gächter and E. Fehr (2001) 'Are People Conditionally Cooperative? Evidence from a Public Goods Game', *Economics Letters*, vol. 71, pp. 397–404.

Forsythe, R., J. Horowitz, N. Savin and M. Sefton (1994) 'Fairness in Simple Bargaining Experiments', *Games and Economic Behaviour*, vol. 6, pp. 347–69.

Gächter, S. and A. Falk (forthcoming) 'Reputation and Reciprocity: Consequences for the Labour Relation', *Scandinavian Journal of Economics*.

Gunnthorsdottir, A., K. McCabe and V. Smith (1998) 'Identifying Player Types in a Bargaining Game', University of Arizona, mimeo.

Güth, W., N. Marchand and J. L. Rullière (1997) 'On the Reliability of Reciprocal Fairness – An Experimental Study', Humboldt-University Berlin, mimeo.

Güth, W., R. Schmittberger and B. Schwarze (1982) 'An Experimental Analysis of Ultimatum Bargaining', *Journal of Economic Behaviour and Organization*, vol. 3, pp. 367–88.

Hoffman, E., K. McCabe and V. Smith (1996) 'On Expectations and Monetary Stakes in Ultimatum Games', *International Journal of Game Theory*, vol. 25, pp. 289–301.

Kahan, D. M. (1997) 'Social Influence, Social Meaning, and Deterrence', *Virginia Law Review*, vol. 83, pp. 349–95.

Kahneman, D., J. Knetsch and R. Thaler (1986) 'Fairness as a Constraint on Profit-Seeking: Entitlements in the Market', *American Economic Review*, vol. 76, no. 4, pp. 728–41.

Keser, C. and F. van Winden (1998) 'Conditional Cooperation and Voluntary Contributions to Public Goods', *Scandinavian Journal of Economics*, vol. 102, no. 1, pp. 23–39.

Kreps, D., P. Milgrom, J. Roberts and R. Wilson (1982) 'Rational Cooperation in the Finitely Repeated Prisoner's Dilemma', *Journal of Economic Theory*, vol. 27, pp. 245–52.

Ledyard, J. (1995) 'Public Goods: A Survey of Experimental Research', in J. Kagel and A. Roth (eds), *Handbook of Experimental Economics* (Princeton: Princeton University Press), pp. 114–94.

Levine, D. (1998) 'Modelling Altruism and Spitefulness in Experiments', *Review of Economic Dynamics*, vol. 1, pp. 593–622.

Loewenstein, G. F., L. Thompson and M. H. Bazerman (1989) 'Social Utility and Decision Making in Interpersonal Contexts', *Journal of Personality and Social Psychology*, vol. 57, pp. 426–41.

Milgrom P. and J. Roberts (1992) *Economics, Organization and Management* (Englewood Cliffs: Prentice-Hall).

Miller, S. (1997) 'Strategieuntersuchung zum Investitionsspiel von Berg, Dickhaut und McCabe', Diploma thesis, University of Bonn.

Prasnikar, V. and A. E. Roth (1992) 'Considerations of Fairness and Strategy: Experimental Data from Sequential Games', *Quarterly Journal of Economics*, vol. 107, pp. 865–88.

Rabin, M. (1993) 'Incorporating Fairness into Game Theory and Economics', *American Economic Review*, vol. 83, pp. 1281–1302.

Roth, A., V. Prasnikar, M. Okuno-Fujiwara and S. Zamir (1991) 'Bargaining and Market Behaviour in Jerusalem, Ljubljana, Pittsburgh, and Tokyo: An Experimental Study', *American Economic Review*, vol. 81, pp. 1068–95.

Selten, R. (1978) 'The Equity Principle in Economic Behaviour', in H. Gottinger and W. Leinfellner (eds), *Decision Theory and Social Ethics. Issues in Social Choice* (Dordrecht: Reidel).

Slonim, R. and A. Roth (1997) 'Financial Incentives and Learning in Ultimatum and Market: An Experiment in the Slovak Republic', *Econometrica*, vol. 66, pp. 569–96.

Smith, V. L. (1982); 'Microeconomic Systems as an Experimental Science', *American Economic Review*, vol. 72, pp. 923–55.

Trivers, R. (1971) 'The Evolution of Reciprocal Altruism', *Quarterly Review of Biology*, vol. 46, pp. 35–57.

Walster, E. and G. W. Walster (1978) *Equity – Theory and Research* (Boston: Allyn & Bacon).

10

Globalization and Redistribution: Feasible Egalitarianism in a Competitive World

Samuel Bowles
University of Massachusetts, USA

1 Introduction

For well-known reasons, a reduction of impediments to international flows of goods, and factors of production – commonly termed globalization – may enhance allocative efficiency both globally and within national economies, and the associated competition among nation states may contribute to governmental accountability.[1] However, globalization is also thought to raise the economic costs of programmes by the nation state to redistribute income to the poor and to provide economic security for their populations. Among the reasons is the fact that the more internationally mobile factors of production – capital and professional labour – tend to be owned by the rich, and a nation-specific tax on a mobile factor induces national output-reducing relocations of these factors. Similar reasoning demonstrates the high cost of attempting to alter the relative prices of factors of production, for example, by raising the wage relative to the return to capital through trade union bargaining. Even Pareto-improving insurance-based policies are compromised, as cross-border mobility of citizens allow the lucky to escape the tax costs of supporting the unlucky, thereby reintroducing the problem of adverse selection plaguing private insurance and which public insurance was thought to avoid.

The result is a generalization of what Arthur Okun (1975) called redistribution in *leaky buckets*: the net benefit to the recipient may fall considerably short of the loss to those paying the costs. In a democracy, leaky buckets thus make it more difficult to secure governmental support for egalitarian redistribution, and thus compromise both the ethical appeal and the political viability of redistributive programmes. By exacerbating the generalized leaky bucket problem, trade liberalization and other aspects of globalization are thus thought to restrict the range of redistributive policy which is politically sustainable in democratic nation states.[2]

But some of the more politically and economically successful redistributive policies – for example, Nordic social democracy and East Asian land reform – have been implemented in small open economies which would, on the above account, seem to provide a prohibitive environment for egalitarian interventions (Huber and Stephens (1998), Moene (1998), Moene and Wallerstein (1993), Putzel (nd), Yager (1980) and Yang (1970)). Other cases of open-economy egalitarianism include the Costa Rican welfare state (Mesa-Lago (1989), Rosenberg (1981), Yashar (1995)), egalitarian distribution of health services and nutrition in Sri Lanka (Anand and Kanbur (1991), Isenman (1980)) and wage compression in Singapore (Lim (1984)) and the public health policies and dramatic reduction in infant mortality under the socialist government of the Seychelles Republic.[3]

Particularly striking are the cases of two Indian states, Kerala and West Bengal. Goods and factors of production move freely across their boundaries, and their state governments have limited control over the legal and fiscal environment of their state economies. But investments in health, schooling, and other human capacities in Kerala and land tenure reform in both states (especially West Bengal), have substantially redistributed income and improved the well-being of the poor (Ramachandran (1996), Sengupta and Gazdar (1996), Banerjee and Ghatak (1996), Besley and Burgess (1998)). The leftist governments credited with these policies have been repeatedly returned to office in democratic elections.

As even this brief description of cases of relatively successful egalitarian redistribution suggests, the reasons for the policies, as well as their design and the mechanisms by which they worked, have differed substantially. Some owe their existence to electoral competition in polities with substantial majorities of poor voters; others have been implemented to forestall populist political successes. Each case exhibits serious shortcomings; but I will not dwell on these as my point is not to elevate them as models but rather is more modest: unless the cases are entirely idiosyncratic they suggest that the commonplace opposition between globalization and egalitarianism may be overdrawn.

In this chapter I present a model of globalization and redistribution seeking to answer the following question: in a globalized world economy, what programmes of egalitarian redistribution and social insurance are implementable by democratic national states acting independently? A programme is implementable if its desired outcome is a stable Nash equilibrium of the appropriately defined game.[4] An implementable programme must therefore be economically and politically sustainable: not susceptible to being undone either by the electorate or by private exchange.[5]

My response, drawing on recent work of many authors, is that in the absence of international coordination, globalization indeed makes it difficult for national states to affect the relative (after tax) prices of mobile goods and factors of production, and for this and other reasons may limit the effectiveness of some conventional strategies of redistribution. But globalization does not rule out all egalitarian interventions. There remains a large class of governmental and other collective interventions leading to substantial improvements in the wages, employment prospects, and economic security of the less well-off. Included are redistributions of assets which are productivity enhancing, namely those which provide efficient solutions to incentive problems arising in principal–agent relationships such as wage employment, farm and residential tenancy, and the provision of environmental and social public goods in local commons situations.[6]

Because the model I present depicts a deliberately exaggerated version of global openness, a caveat on empirical realism is necessary. A number of empirical studies beginning with Gordon (1998) have stressed that while cross-border flows have increased in recent years, by these measures the degree of both trade and investment openness is quite limited in recent decades compared to a century earlier.[7] The measure of globalization crucial to the above argument, however, refers not to the aggregate quantities on which these studies focus, but to *microeconomic* responses. The relevant indices should measure the impact of globalization on the elasticity of demand for labour with respect to the real wage (openness possibly raising the employment costs of wage increases) as well as the possibly heightened responsiveness of national investment to own-country wage levels and tax rates relative to the rest of the world. There is little hard evidence that by these microeconomic measures openness has increased in recent years, but it seems plausible to think that it has, or at least will.[8] In any case given the widespread view that these aspects of globalization will thwart attempts at egalitarian redistribution, it is worth finding out if this is indeed the case, under admittedly extreme globalization assumptions. Whether the model illuminates real (if very long-term) tendencies operating in the world, or alternatively is a more hypothetical exercise (how the world would work if it were like that) cannot be determined on the basis of existing empirical information.

In Section 2 I present a highly abstract model of a national economy embedded in a globally competitive environment. Section 3 addresses a range of conventional state and trade union policy measures. I then turn in Section 4 to asset redistributions before concluding in Section 5 with a discussion of policies and institutions.

2 Globalization

The model presented below seeks to illuminate the opportunities for egalitarian redistribution in a national economy integrated into a world economy characterized by minimal impediments to capital mobility among nations. To focus on the contribution of globalization *per se* to the leaky bucket problem (and because the problems constituted by corruption and other forms of governmental malfeasance and unaccountability are well-known) I assume that governments are not self-serving leviathans (as in the public choice literature) but rather seek to improve the living standards of the less well-off.

Redistribution takes the form of increases in the living standards of a homogeneous class of workers, either by raising their income or improving their prospects of being employed. Its focus is not on inequality *per se* but on labour market outcomes affecting two important aspects of workers' well-being, jobs and pay. It abstracts from differences among workers, and much else of importance, but seeks to explore the ramifications of two important empirical regularities. The first is that investment relocates globally in response to differences in expected after-tax profit rates, and the second is that under a wide range of institutional conditions real wages covary with the level of employment.[9]

The basic assumptions of the model follow. All markets are perfectly competitive, but labour (which is homogeneous within countries) is not mobile between countries. The global economy is thus modelled as if it were a national economy with a single capital market but segmented labour markets; the difference, of course, is that each labour market segment is represented by an autonomous government. There is a single good which is both consumed and used as capital (corn is eaten and planted as seed). At the end of each period, after the payment of wages, wealth holders (those who own the corn surplus, if it exists) may either consume corn or allocate it as an investment good among many national economies in response to national differences in expected after-tax profit rates.

Actors differ by wealth level: the wealthy are risk neutral while those without assets (workers, employed and unemployed) are risk averse. Neither work effort nor the promise to repay a loan is contractible, so the relations between employers and workers and between lenders and borrowers are principal–agent relationships. Employers use monitoring and the threat of dismissal to induce workers to provide satisfactory levels of effort. For this reason (and perhaps others), the equilibrium of the labour market in each national economy is characterized by involuntary unemployment. Thus labour suppliers are quantity constrained in labour markets. Lacking wealth they are unable provide collateral or other means of attenuating the incompleteness of the credit contract, they are also quantity constrained in credit markets.

The competitive equilibria of this model for the single global markets in capital goods (corn) and credit support a common rate of expected profit and rate of time preference globally (and hence the risk-free interest rate). By contrast, nation-specific institutions and cultures concerning labour relations, government policies, and security of property rights give rise to national differences in equilibrium wages and employment. There are thus $n+1$ prices in this model: each of n nations' real wage (price of an hour of labour relative to the price of corn) and the global risk free interest rate (price of goods now relative to goods later). As I investigate just a single national economy, I do not give national subscripts to the relevant variables.

Because firms use a single production function and are otherwise identical, we can analyse production and wage setting as if it took place in a single (competitive) firm. Aggregate output, Q, is simply total labour effort times average output per unit of effort, y, with a fixed capital (seed) requirement k per hour of labour. Total effort is the average effort level per hour, e, of those employees (the directly productive workers) not engaged in monitoring multiplied by their hours of work, $h(1-m)$, where h is the total (productive and monitoring) hours of work and m is the fraction of total work time accounted for by the monitors. So:

$$\begin{aligned} Q &= yeh(1-m) \text{ for } K \geq kh(1-m) \\ &= 0 \text{ for } K < kh(1-m) \end{aligned} \tag{1}$$

I normalize national labour supply at unity (given exogenously); so $h \in [0,\ 1]$ is the level of employment. Effort is determined by workers in response to the incentives and sanctions devised by the employer. As these include monitoring and the threat of job termination, the worker's optimal effort choice varies inversely with his or her fallback position, namely expected utility if employment is terminated which depends on the expected duration of a spell of unemployment, *a*, and the level of support conditional on being unemployed, *b*. Suppose effort may be either 1 (imposing a disutility of $\underline{a}$ on the worker) or 0, and that the probability of termination if $e = 0$ is τ. Then, with suitable simplifying assumptions, the wage that will just induce workers to choose $e = 1$ equates the expected utility of the two effort choices, which gives:

$$w^* = \underline{a}/\tau(1 - h) + b \tag{2}$$

as the 'no shirking wage'.[10] Of course τ and $\underline{a}$ depend on the institutional structure governing labour relations (the costs to the employer of firing a non-working employee, the perceived fairness of the wage determination process, the degree of effectiveness of the monitoring system, and the like). Along with $e = 1$ which it ensures, (2) implements both the firms' and the employees' first-order conditions, describing the feasible combinations of *w*, *h*, and total effort supplied to firms; it is thus the *labour supply equilibrium condition*. The model underlying equation (2) is quite particular, but it gives a convenient analytical form to the much more general empirical regularity mentioned earlier, namely $w_h > 0$, the covariation of wages and the employment level.[11] (For simplicity I assume monitors are paid the same wage as other employees and I do not address the problem of their incentives to work.) It will be important later to note that because employees do not shirk, they are not fired, and so bear no risk. There is therefore a group of $1 - h$ permanently unemployed.

Labour demand (and hence the level of unemployment) depends on the allocation of the global capital stock among national economies in response to differences in the expected after-tax profit rate. Recalling that the capital good is an intermediate input, the profit rate before tax is just:

$$r = \{(y - k)h(1 - m) - wh\}/kh(1 - m)$$

or expressed in per hour of employment (by eliminating *h*) the profit rate is net output per hour of labour minus the wage rate, divided by the capital input required to employ an hour of labour. Suppose that to finance its activities the national government levies a linear tax, *t*, on profits so the after tax profit rate is:

$$\pi = r(1 - t) = (1 - t)[(y - k)(1 - m) - w]/[k(1 - m)] \tag{3}$$

Wealth holders finance a project if its expected return exceeds their rate of time preference, which I assume is globally equal to the return on some risk-free instrument, ρ. Projects are exposed to a risk of 'confiscation' or other unexpected reduction in their value, the probability of which, $c \in [0,\ 1]$, varies among countries, reflecting national differences in macroeconomic policy, political stability, criminality, and the like. (In a less abstract model with distinct national currencies, risk includes adverse changes in foreign exchange rates.) Suppose the return is zero in the period of the confiscation: wages are paid but the expected costs of contestation occasioned by the confiscation exactly exhaust the profits. The expected profit rate is thus $\hat{\pi} = \pi(1 - c)$. Writing the insecurity premium, $\mu = 1/(1 - c)$, the national economy's level of corn investment is stationary if expected after-tax profit rates are equated across nations and are jointly equal to the risk-free interest rate ($\hat{\pi} = \rho$) or:

$$\pi = \rho\mu \tag{4}$$

Because r is monotonically declining in w, there is just one wage rate which will satisfy (4); using (3) to rewrite (4) we find that this wage $\underline{w}$ is given by:

$$\underline{w} = (1 - m)[y - k(1 + \rho\mu)/(1 - t)] \tag{5}$$

When (5) obtains, the level of the capital stock, and hence employment is stationary; it is the *equilibrium labour demand equation* (conditional on $e = 1$).[12]

Because $w^*(h)$ is monotonic, there is just one h consistent with $\underline{w}$. The general equilibrium of the national economy (taking ρ as exogenous) is defined by:

$$w^* = \underline{w} \tag{6}$$

satisfying the condition for stationarity of both the employment rate and the wage rate.[13] Their determination may be described as follows: the nation's specific institutions which influence the net after tax productivity of labour and the risk premium determine the national wage rate consistent with optimizing by the owners of mobile investment resources, and the nation's institutions concerning labour markets and work organization determine what national level of aggregate employment makes that wage consistent with individual optimizing by firms and workers. Figure 10.1 illustrates the equilibrium of this model for a

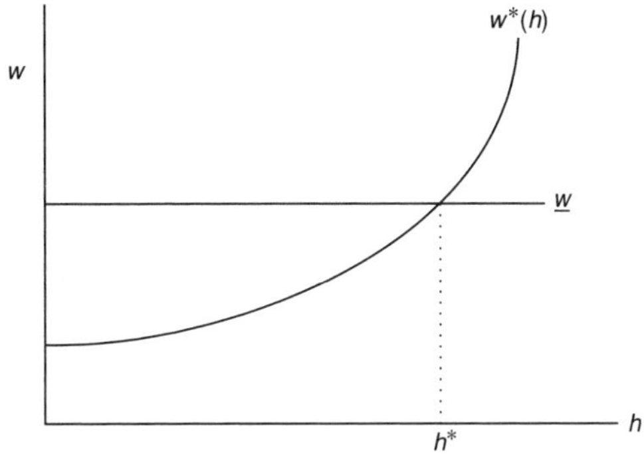

Figure 10.1 Equilibrium employment and wages

given national economy. (Notice that for any wage less than w^*, $e = 0$, so $dh/dt < 0$ for $w < w^*$ or $w > \underline{w}$.)

Finally, the global supply and demand for corn as an investment good together with the above conditions determine the risk-free interest rate, ρ. Suppose that in every country, production takes place according to the nationally specific versions of (6) and at the end of each period there exists a corn surplus, a given fraction of which is consumed by the wealthy, the remaining fraction, ϕ, being allocated to investment among national economies.[14] As capital (unlike labour) is not nationally specific, I assume ϕ is common across countries. At the end of each period, the corn output net of wages per unit invested is $[\pi(1 - c) + 1]$ and ϕ of this is supplied to the global stock of corn capital in the next period (by contrast, the supply of investment goods available in the country is infinitely elastic at the rate ρ). Call the amount $(\pi(1 - c) - 1)\phi$ the corn surplus. Because in equilibrium $\pi(1 - c) = \rho$ in every country each country supplies an amount to next year's global capital stock equal to $[\rho + 1]\phi$ for every unit of the current period's stock. The rate of growth of the world capital stock is thus $(\rho + 1)\phi - 1$ or $\rho\phi - (1 - \phi)$.

The equilibrium global demand for investment goods is just the amount of corn necessary to provide the capital goods required by the employment fraction of each country's labour force consistent with the zero profit condition (i.e. that given by (6)). Thus market clearing (and stationarity of ρ) requires that the global corn surplus (the global supply of capital goods) grow at the same rate as the world labour supply, v. The ρ which equates the growth rates of capital goods supply and labour supply is given by:

$$v = \rho\phi - (1 - \phi), \text{ or} \\ \rho = (v + 1)/\phi - 1 \tag{7}$$

Countries with slower labour force growth will be permanent exporters of corn-capital and conversely. This is because excess supply of investment goods per unit of the current period capital stock (in a given country whose labour force is growing at the rate η) is:

$$\Delta = \phi(\pi(1 - c) + 1) - (1 + \eta) \tag{8}$$

The first term in is the corn surplus available for investment per unit of the current period capital stock and the second is the increase in the capital stock required to sustain the equilibrium level of employment. Using (7) and the fact that $\pi(1 - c) = \rho$ we can see from (8) that $\Delta = v - \eta$. An implication is that when national labour forces all grow at the global average, in equilibrium all investment is domestically financed.[15]

To analyse the determination of global employment, notice that a common global ρ implies country specific $\underline{w}_i(\rho)$s for each of the n national economies; given nation-specific $h_i(w)$s the h_is are determined as well. So we may define global employment, $H(\rho)$, as the horizontal summation of the implied $h_i(\rho)$ functions, giving $H(\rho)$, with $H' < 0$, where the variation in world employment is simply that generated by varying ρ given the equilibrium condition (6). Figure 10.2 illustrates the determination of global employment. In the following analysis of a single national economy I treat ρ as exogenous.

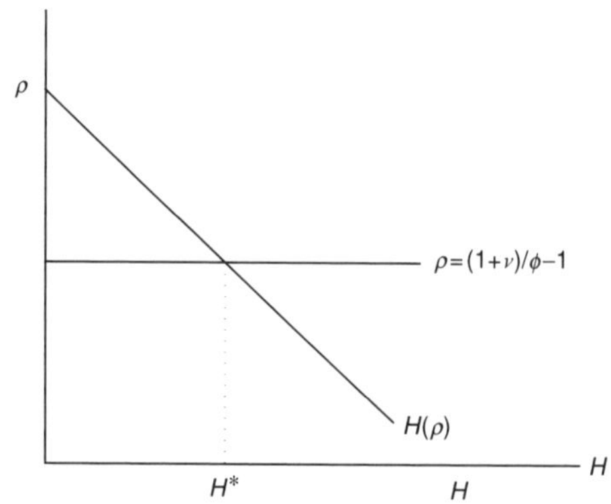

Figure 10.2 World labour demand

3 Increasing wages and employment

Where, as in Figure 10.2 the equilibrium is unique and stable, the effect of country-specific policy interventions may be studied (as I do below) by a comparative static analysis of the displacement of the exogenous terms in $w^*(h)$ and $\underline{w}$. But the more complicated case of multiple equilibria (some of them unstable) cannot be ruled out. To see this, suppose that the confiscation probability c varies inversely with h – high levels of unemployment supporting a populist or criminal environment, for example – so $\mu = \mu(h)$ with $\mu' < 0$. Then $\underline{w}$ is increasing in h, which (because w^* is also increasing in h) means that there may exist many values of h equating the two.[16]

Figure 10.3 illustrates an upward rising equilibrium labour demand function, with the labour market equilibria *a* exhibiting the vicious circle of low employment, low wages, and high insecurity premium ('Nigeria') and *a′* exhibiting the virtuous converse ('Taiwan'). The possibility of multiple stable equilibria enriches the policy analysis considerably, as it allows small one-time interventions to have permanent, non-marginal effects, and it provides a framework for analysing possible divergent growth paths ('high-road' versus 'low-road' wage strategies, for example). A one-time demand expansion, for example, pushing the employment level above the critical value to h'' in Figure 10.3 could permanently shift the equilibrium from the low-wage/high-insecurity poverty trap to its virtuous converse.

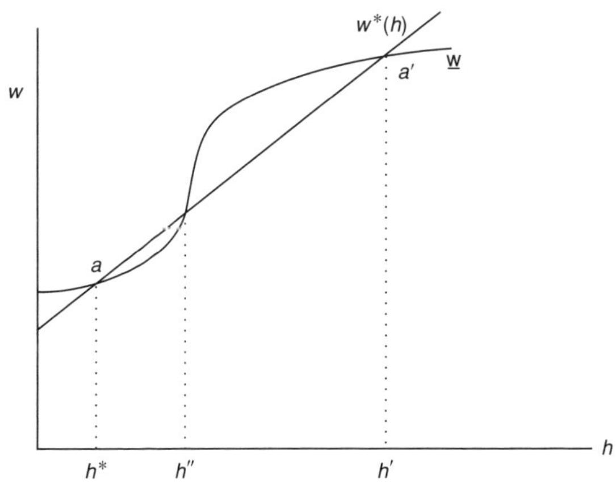

Figure 10.3 Multiple equilibria (endogenous risk)

The impact of strategies to raise wages and employment may now be assessed through their curve-shifting effects in Figures 10.1 or 10.3. For example, enhanced security of property rights by reducing c (for any level of h) lowers μ, hence raises $\underline{w}$, and increases both h^* and w^* (from Figure 10.3, it can be seen that the implied upward shift in $\underline{w}(h)$ might also eliminate the 'low-road' equilibrium, displacing a national economy previously entrapped there to a rapid transition to the 'high road').

The effects of changes in labour relations and labour market structure are equally transparent. Efforts to protect workers from dismissal for cause by reducing τ through job protection strategies shift the $w^*(h)$ function upwards without affecting $\underline{w}$ leaving the wage rate unaffected but reducing employment. Raising b, the magnitude of transfers whose availability is conditional on being out of work, has a similar effect, but unlike a reduction in τ, the welfare implications of an increase in b are ambiguous, as it raises the well-being of the least well-off (the jobless), while increasing their numbers.

Trade unions may increase wages and/or employment in a number of ways, however (Bowles and Boyer (1990b)). First, unions may draw on workers' private information concerning the performance of other workers to improve the disciplinary environment of the workplace (raising τ or lowering m). Second 'union voice' effects (Freeman and Medoff (1984)) may raise productivity and reduce the disutility of labour (the latter would lower the $w(h)$ function, supporting a higher level of employment). Third, collective bargaining agreements to provide well-defined job ladders and security from cyclical job loss provide greater incentives for firm-specific investments by workers (Pagano (1991)). Both union voice and specific investment effects shift $\underline{w}$ upwards and $w^*(h)$ to the right.[17] Fourth, negotiated incomes policies may lower or flatten the $w^*(h)$ function.[18] Finally, if $\underline{w}$ becomes accepted as a fairness norm – perhaps because it is the wage rate that will give the employer a rate of return equal to what other employers receive, or to the marginal disutility of foregoing current consumption – and if, as seems likely, perceived fairness is a determinant of work effort, the $w^*(h)$ function will flatten, thereby increasing the employment gains associated with upward shifts in $\underline{w}$ owing to productivity gains. Because in equilibrium, no employed is working harder as a result of any of these changes, and because the unemployed prefer employment, the welfare gains associated with the implied trade union induced increases in wages and or employment are unambiguous.

The effects of government expenditures and the efficiency of public service delivery may be explored in similar fashion. Suppose the productivity of a unit of effective labour depends on λp, the effectiveness (λ) and level (p) of public expenditure on productivity enhancing complementary inputs (such as nutrition, health care, schooling, and infrastructure) so $y = y(\lambda p, \ldots)$. Assume the government spends all of its tax revenues on p as well as b, the benefit paid to a worker when unemployed, giving the budget constraint (expressed as an equality):

$$b(1 - h) + p = th\{[(1 - m)y(\lambda p) - k] - w\} \tag{9}$$

From (9) it can be seen that for a given tax rate, there is a level of employment such that unemployment benefits exhaust the entire budget, and productivity per effective unit of labour is $\underline{y} = y(0)$.

Above this level of employment, productivity enhancing public expenditures increase, which by (5) then require a higher wage to equilibrate the capital market, yielding the upward rising $\underline{w}$ function in Figure 10.4. The also upward rising $w^*(h)$ function (as drawn) intersects the equilibrium labour demand function twice, suggesting a possible high and low public investment divergence among nations.[19] Because for any level of h, $\underline{w}$ covaries with λ and varies inversely with b, and because (as we have seen) decreasing b also shifts the $w^*(h)$ function to the right, it follows that reallocating expenditure from transfers conditioned on unemployment towards productivity enhancing public investment and increasing the effectiveness of public expenditures will simultaneously raise the (stable) equilibrium wage and employment level.[20] It might appear that this change is unambiguously welfare enhancing, but

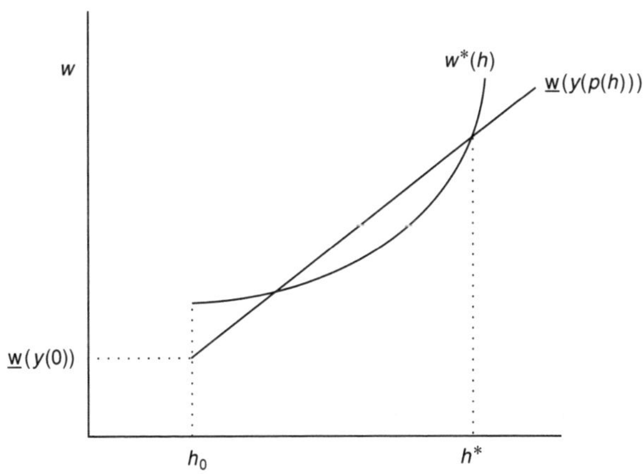

Figure 10.4 Endogenous transfers and public investment

a more realistic model in which the employed periodically lose their jobs would show that for sufficiently high levels of risk aversion among workers, the lost insurance would more than offset the higher expected wage.

Increases in productivity (y), whether owing to public expenditure or exogenous technical change, shift $\underline{w}$ upward allowing increases in equilibrium employment. Differentiating (6) we see that the size of this employment effect depends critically on db/dy, the effect of the change in productivity on the fallback position of employed workers:

$$dh/dy = \{(1 - m) - db/dy\}/w_h \tag{10}$$

which has the same sign as its numerator, as we know that $w_h > 0$. Where productivity gains are shared with the unemployed through increases in b, and where monitoring levels are substantial, the upward shift in the equilibrium labour supply condition (2) may even reverse the potential employment gains. There is thus a policy choice concerning the manner in which productivity increases should be shared with the unemployed through expanding the number of jobs on the one hand, or by raising the average income of those remaining unemployed on the other.

As the examples in this section make clear, opportunities for raising wages and/or employment arise when allocative inefficiencies can be corrected either at minimal cost (as when union voice effects may attenuate the misalignment of incentives arising from the incomplete employment contract) or through expenditures on which the expected social rate of return exceeds $\mu\rho$ (as when credit constraints or other reasons induce workers to acquire inefficiently little schooling). The problems of credit constraints and incomplete contracts may also be addressed more directly by a redistribution of assets, or more precisely by a redistribution of the rights of residual claimancy and control commonly bundled with asset ownership, and by extending to the asset poor the credit market and insurance opportunities of the wealthy.

4 Asset-based redistribution

Suppose at the beginning of each period, a national government borrows corn on the world market at the rate ρ, in turn lends it to teams of producers at the rate $\rho\mu$, who at the end of the period are equal residual claimants on the income of the team, after repaying the government an expected amount of $1 + \rho$ per unit of corn borrowed (accounting for confiscations occurring as before at the rate c).[21] Assume that these cooperatives ('coops') adopt a labour discipline strategy similar to their erstwhile employers (dismissing non-performing team members). Coops are therefore constrained to offer members a level of income equivalent to $w^*(h)$, to deter shirking (as we will see immediately below, because the producers now bear risk, the coop must offer a certainty equivalent income equal to $w^*(h)$). Workmates have private information on each others' work activities, and as residual claimants on the income of the team members are motivated to participate in mutual monitoring, so the monitoring costs of maintaining work effort will be reduced, to $m^- < m$.[22] As before, I assume that the monitors receive the same hourly payment as the directly productive coop producers. Finally, let the implicit tax rate on the use of capital remain unchanged.

The coop's advantage of reduced monitoring may be more than offset by suboptimal risk-taking. The reason is that risk averse members now control the production process and (relaxing the assumption of given production technologies) face a choice among production methods of varying risk and expected output. Recall that as wage employees the producers bore no risk, but as residual claimants they must, given that they are residual claimants on a stream of output which is subject to stochastic variation. For concreteness imagine that corn may be planted at various times, and the expected return and its variance depend on the planting date, with greater risk covarying with higher expected returns over some range.

Suppose that expected output per hour of effective labour is $y(\sigma)$ where σ is the standard deviation of output and y is increasing and concave in its argument, reaching a maximum at σ^*. The risk neutral employer of course selected σ^*, so the analysis of Section 3 assumed a level of expected productivity of $y = y(\sigma^*)$. Utility maximizing risk averse coop members will select some level of $\sigma^- < \sigma^*$ and hence generate a level of expected income $y(\sigma^-) < y(\sigma^*)$. Coop members are thus residual claimants on an income stream generated by this lesser level of risk-taking and, using (5), have an expected income of:

$$\omega = (1 - m^-)\{y(\sigma^-) - k(1 + \rho\mu)/(1 - t)\} \tag{11}$$

Of course the expected value of their residual income $\omega(y(\sigma^-))$ may nonetheless exceed the $\underline{w}$ possible under wage employment, depending on the magnitude of the monitoring savings relative to the reduced expected income occasioned by suboptimal risk-taking. But what matters for them is a comparison of the certain income $\underline{w}$ in wage employment with the certainty-equivalent income associated with the coop's risky income stream, namely $\underline{\omega}(y(\sigma^-), \sigma^-)$.[23]

In order to define the members' certainty-equivalent income, I assume the disturbances in the income stream of the coop are such that one can represent the utility function of the risk-averse members simply as:

$$u = u(\omega,\sigma) \tag{12}$$

where ω is a 'good' and σ is a 'bad'; Figure 10.5 illustrates two of the implied family of indifference loci.[24] Figure 10.5 also indicates the capital market clearing wage rate, $\underline{w}$ defined as before by (5), and the expected residual claim of the coop member $\omega(\sigma)$; the latter, using (5) and (11) is given by:

$$\omega(\sigma) = \underline{w}(\sigma)(1 - m^-)/(1 - m)$$

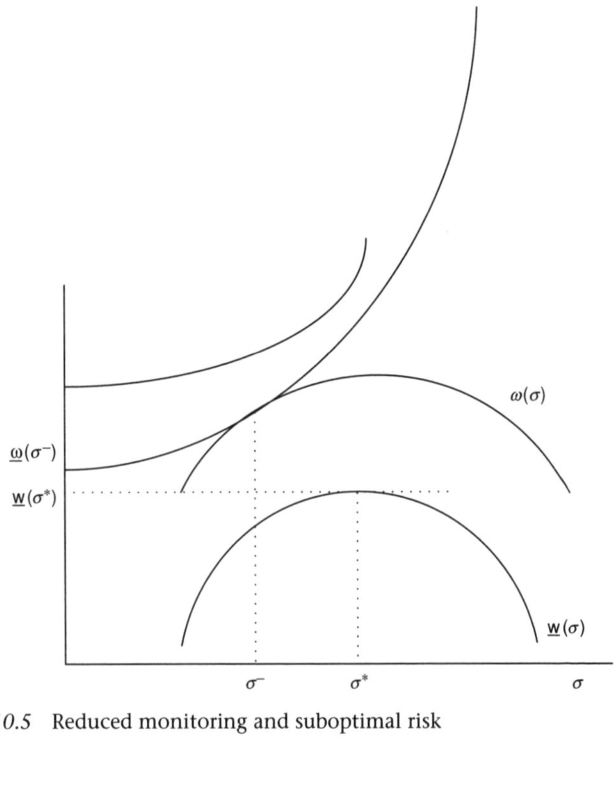

Figure 10.5 Reduced monitoring and suboptimal risk

Risk neutral indifference loci are flat of course, which is why the erstwhile employer selected σ^*. The vertical intercept of an indifference locus is the certainty equivalent of each point making up the locus, so $\omega^\wedge(y(\sigma^-), \sigma^-)$ for example, is the certainty-equivalent income of the expected income and risk level resulting from the coop's choice of σ^-.

For this example, $\omega^\wedge(\sigma^-) > \underline{w}(\sigma^*)$ – producers' certainty-equivalent income would be raised by the formation of coops – and for this reason, coops would proliferate and wage employment would be eliminated. As Figure 10.6 shows, the level of joblessness would fall as a result, though not more than h^- producers can belong to coop work teams as the $1 - h^-$ jobless are required to sustain the no-shirking condition at the certainty-equivalent income consistent with the stationarity of the country's capital stock. If, by contrast, $\omega^\wedge(\sigma^-) < \underline{w}(\sigma^*)$ of course, producers would not accept the government loans, and coops would not form.

Suppose, however, that as in Figure 10.5 the coop is advantageous to the producers; why was the government's intervention required to allow their formation? The obvious answer – that the asset-less producers were precluded from borrowing at economically viable rates of interest – raises a more difficult question. If, as this answer implies, the wealth-poor producers' subjective cost of postponing current consumption exceeds $\rho\mu$, why would they not prefer to use the government loan for consumption purposes? They would; so a successful loan programme would have to embody an enforceable provision restricting the use of the corn to planting rather than eating. But as we will see, this administrative difficulty is an artifact of the simplicity of the model.

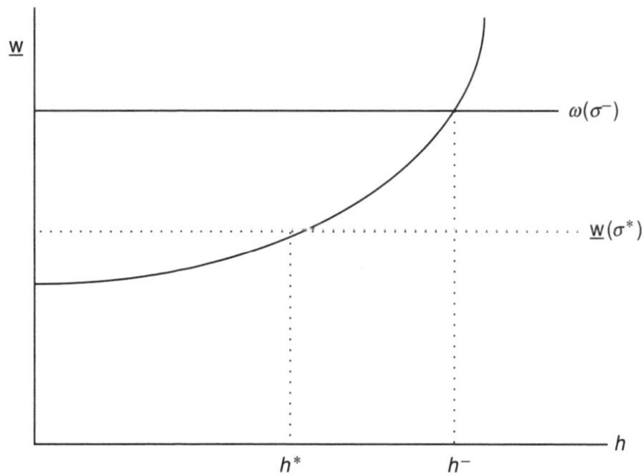

Figure 10.6 Coop income and employment

Bowles and Gintis ((1999b) Theorems 2 and 3) show that a transfer of an asset (rather than a loan) mandated by the government may induce the producer to hold the asset and use it productively even when the transfer of property rights could not have occurred through private contracting. This implies, of course, that both the *ex ante* and the *ex post* distribution of property rights are Nash equilibria. There are two reasons why this is possible. Both stem from the fact that the asset transfer alters the opportunities and constraints of the producer, with the *ex post* situation supporting use of the asset by the producer while the *ex ante* situation precludes it. First, changing the wealth status of the producer also changes his or her credit market status (and hence the subjective cost of delaying consumption), increased wealth lowering the subjective cost of capital. And second, increased wealth may plausibly reduce the degree of risk aversion, so that while the choice of σ by a wealthless producer (say, renting the asset or using borrowed funds) might have precluded the project being viable, the (riskier) choice of the same producer with increased wealth (as owner of the asset) may be viable.[25] For this reason a one-time mandated redistribution of wealth – making the producers owners and residual claimants – may be sustainable in competitive equilibrium and thus have permanent effects.[26]

Whether the peer-monitoring advantages of the coop will outweigh its risk avoidance will depend among other things on the policy environment, of course. More adequate insurance may induce risk adverse producers to choose a higher level of σ (effectively rotating the indifference loci in Figure 10.5 clockwise (Bowles and Gintis (1999b)). Such insurance policies may protect the producer against risk unassociated with the production process (health insurance, insurance against exogenous variation on housing wealth) or against those aspects of stochasticity in the income stream of the production process which are observable and not affected by the actions of the producer (for example, macroeconomic stabilization, Shiller (1993)). Because these insurance policies may be self-financing (fair), the gains to producers constitute Pareto-improvements and the range of egalitarian redistribution of residual claimancy and control of assets (through loans or outright transfers) which is consistent with global competitive equilibrium is expanded.

Egalitarian asset redistribution may have other productivity enhancing effects, for example, supporting more effective governance institutions in communities, firms, and the national level, and in promoting a more growth inducing structure of human capital accumulation.[27]

5 Policies

Of course actual governments and trade unions may fail to implement efficient redistributions for a variety of well-known reasons. But on the basis of the above reasoning, there appears to be ample scope for the implementation of policies capable of raising wages, employment levels, and living standards of the less well-off owners of globally immobile factors of production, even in the empirically unlikely world of hyper-globalization posited in the model. It seems likely that substantial majorities of the relevant populations would benefit from these policies, so the policies might be sustainable in democratic polities.

That these objectives can be furthered by nation states acting singly is suggested by the dramatic national differences in real wage growth that have been sustained over long periods. Figure 10.7 presents data (from Verhoogen (1999)) on real manufacturing wage growth over an 22-year period.[28] Even taking account of the possible importance of productivity catch-up effects (by comparing national economies initially at the same wage level) one finds extraordinary differences: the *annual* rate of change of real wage was 16 percentage points higher in Taiwan and S Korea than in Tanzania and 10 percentage points higher in Barbados and Italy than in Jamaica and Venezuela. Some of the high-wage-growth economies have also experienced very rapid employment growth.

Figure 10.8 confirms what one would expect – that wage growth is closely tied to productivity growth; but even for economies experiencing similar rates of increase in manufacturing value added per worker, the differences in wage growth are substantial. Productivity in Indonesia grew at the same rate as in Italy, for example, but wages grew over 5 per cent faster per annum in the latter. While much of the differences are owing to idiosyncratic events and circumstances – the differing impacts of the two oil shocks, for example – national contrasts of this magnitude suggest that institutional and policy choices do matter, even for small open economies, and that those which shared broadly similar institutions experienced far less variability in subsequent wage growth.)

We know little, it seems, about which institutions and policies account for the success stories. A common opinion in some policy circles is that strong unions and substantial redistributive programmes are counterproductive in attempting to raise living standards of the less well-off. The reasoning behind this view is that these institutions favour the egalitarian division of the pie, rather than more promising long-term strategies of rapid growth in investment and average income. Examples confirming this reasoning are all too easy to produce. (This is consistent

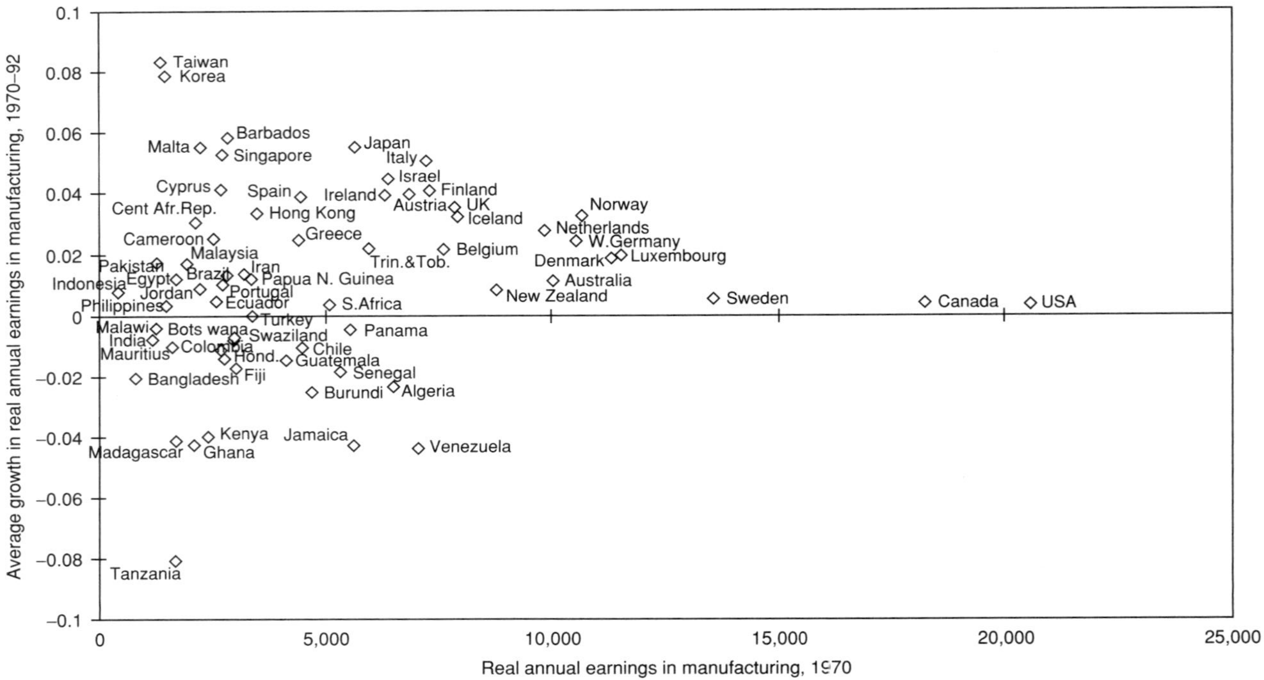

Figure 10.7 Annual rate of change of real wages and initial wage levels, 1970–92

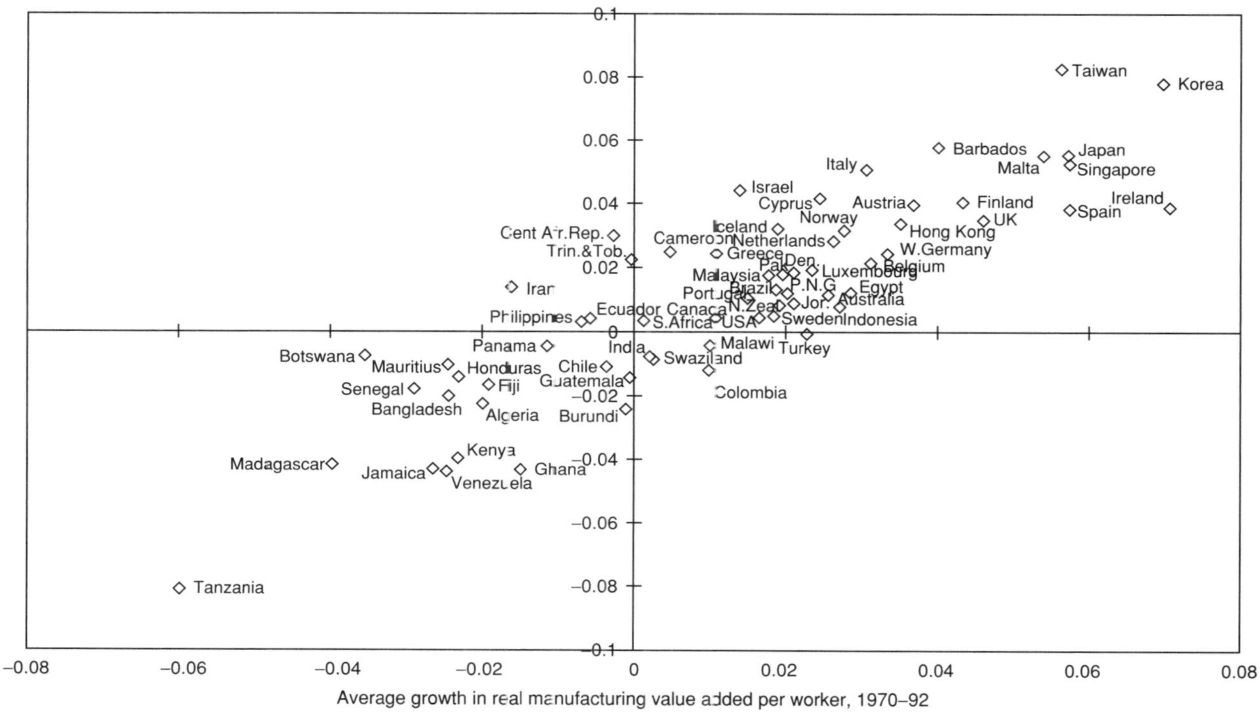

Figure 10.8 Rate of change of real wages and value added per worker, 1970–92

with the fact that economies in which wages exceeded $10,000 in 1972 and which shared broadly similar institutions, experienced far less variability in subsequent wage growth.)

But this view finds little support in the above data. Indeed a long historical perspective suggests the opposite: as Figure 10.9 shows, the golden age of the welfare state and of trade unionism in the advanced economies witnessed by far the most rapid rates of growth of income *per capita* and investment in the history of capitalism.[29] In most countries, the improvement of living standards of the less well-off was correspondingly rapid.

The model presented here and the empirical evidence suggests three ways that egalitarian redistribution in open economy settings may have succeeded. The first is by increasing productivity (or certainty-equivalent income, where risk-bearing is involved). Examples include the East Asian asset redistributions and the Nordic (especially Swedish) and Singaporean policy of eliminating wage disparities among similar workers, thus putting competitive pressure on low-productivity firms and sectors and driving resources into higher-productivity uses. The second is improving the labour discipline environment and thereby reducing monitoring

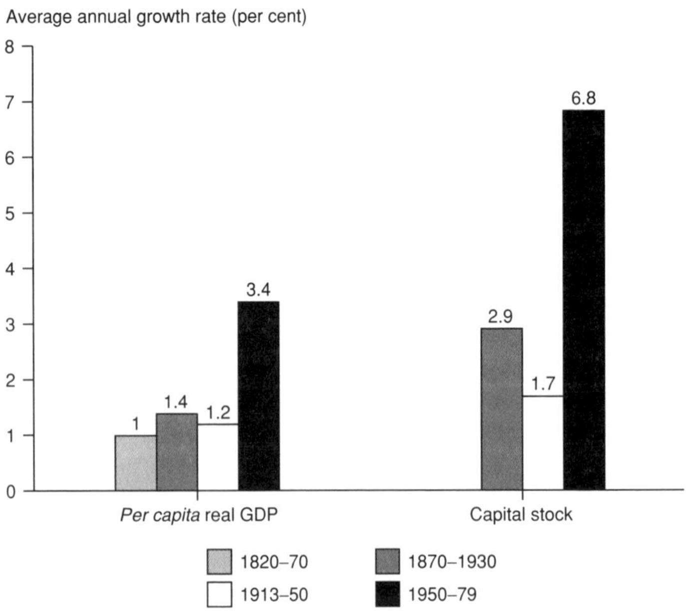

Figure 10.9 Growth and investment, 1820–1979

costs and shifting the equilibrium labour supply condition to the right. Examples include the effect of wage increases, the disutility of effort (through the fair wage effect), trade union and work team participation in monitoring, and the effect of centralized wage bargaining on flattening the labour supply function. The fact that supervisory labour input is strikingly lower in countries with more egalitarian earnings distributions (Sweden, Japan) may reflect these and related effects (Gordon (1994)).

The third strategy is simply to redistribute labour income in a more egalitarian manner without eroding effort incentives. Suppose, instead of providing income conditional on unemployment, the government gave all adult members of the population an unconditional grant β and financed the grant by a tax on wages supplemented by the general revenue savings occasioned by setting $b = 0$. Assume the government sought to do this while maintaining the status quo work incentive situation, as modelled in Bowles (1992). As $b = 0$ the equilibrium labour supply condition (no shirking condition) is now:

$$w^* = a/\tau(1 - h) \qquad (2')$$

a flat tax on wage income of b would restore the equilibrium labour supply condition. As the labour demand equation has not been altered, the employment and (before tax) wage level would thus remain at the status quo levels. The unconditional grant would be financed from tax revenues of hb plus savings on the elimination of the previous transfers of $(1 - h)b$. All adults would thus receive an unconditional grant of $\beta = bh/N$, where N is the adult population. The effect would be a redistribution from the employed and the unemployed to those not in the labour force, obviously favouring the old, the young, women, and other groups sometimes called 'excluded'. It might be thought that the effects of the unconditional grant would be slight because family structure and other sharing arrangements allow income pooling. But even in the empirically implausible case that all of the differentially affected groups were paired in pooling arrangements so that the expected income of each was unaffected by this policy, dispersion of unconditional income claims to those not in the labour force would predictably alter the intra-family bargaining power and possibly also the credit market status of the previously relatively poor and powerless. This appears to be the case, for example of the quite generous transfers to the elderly in South Africa (Ardington and Lund (1995)). Of course the grant β need not take the form of a cash transfer but could rather be dedicated claims on health, education, recreation, and other services.

As this last example suggests, in the design and implementation of policies consistent with the supply-side egalitarian approach surveyed here, the heuristic distinction between the asset redistribution approach of Section 4 and the wage and employment policies of Section 3 will lose some of its salience. Where labour contracts embody both job security and group- or firm-level gain sharing, for example, employees may become *de facto* residual claimants on a substantial fraction of the income streams they generate. Trade union bargaining can thereby capture some of the peer monitoring advantages of outright asset distribution to coops. This is particularly likely to be the case where the monitoring labour effort by outsiders is ineffective (as in many information-based and other service activities), where firm-specific human resource investments are important, and where the capital required is either limited in amount or general (rather than transaction-specific) and not subject to depreciation through misuse. The land tenure reform in West Bengal mentioned at the outset embodied exactly this logic: the outright transfer of assets to farmers was precluded by the property clauses in the Indian constitution. Rather, the farmer's share of the crop was increased from a customary one-half to three-quarters, and tenants were given protection from eviction as long as they granted the landlord the stipulated reduced share. The result was a substantial increase in the rights of residual claimancy due not only to the increased share, but also to the reduced threat of eviction and hence the greater likelihood that the farmer would enjoy the future returns to land improvements and other investments.

6 Conclusion

Does globalization impede egalitarian redistribution? What globalization does is to make it quite costly and possibly politically infeasible to depress the expected after tax rate of return to capital, or to alter the relative prices of tradable goods and services. But while globalization – at least in the *hyper* form illustrated here – fixes the relative prices of some productive services, it precludes neither an egalitarian redistribution of the tangible and human assets from which those services flow, nor the enhancement of the assets currently owned by the less well-off, nor the improvement of the institutionally determined flow of services from labour assets. Thus, gain-seeking competition does restrict the range of economically and politically sustainable relative prices, but it does not preclude egalitarian redistribution. The fundamental theorem of welfare economics defines conditions under which *any* technically feasible and Pareto optimal distribution of welfare can be attained by *some* redistribution of assets followed by perfectly competitive exchange. The theorem is not intended as a guide to policy, but it does underline an important truth: to the extent that globalization heightens competitive pressures it may reduce the attractiveness of redistributive approaches which rely on altering relative prices, but this hardly exhausts the set of egalitarian strategies.

An implication of the above is that the traditional vehicles of egalitarian aspirations – trade unions and states – have a different but no less important role to play in a highly competitive world than in closed economies. The scope for conventional governmental and trade union measures which reduce the after-tax expected rate of profit is indeed restricted. But policies to implement Pareto-improving productivity gains may in some respects require a greater rather than lesser degree of collective interventions in atomistically competitive outcomes. Examples include an expanded role for publicly provided insurance to improve the trade off between peer monitoring gains and suboptimal risk-taking losses entailed by more extensive residual claimancy and control of assets by the non-wealthy, and greater involvement of collective bargaining in more closely aligning the incentives of employers and employees with respect to both working and learning on the job.

A notable effect of globalization, unremarked thus far, is that (in the extreme form assumed here) it makes the non-wealthy members of a national population residual claimants on the results of both their productive efforts and their success in solving productivity dampening coordination failures. It thus inverts the more common relationship in which the wealthy are the residual claimants on the income streams generated by the efforts of the less well-off. While in competitive equilibrium the wealthy cannot get *less* than ρ, they also cannot get *more*, so productivity improvements are fully captured by the non-wealthy. To the extent that conditions approximate those assumed in this model, then, the globalization may reduce the collective action problems confronting would-be coalitions of the non-wealthy seeking to enhance productivity by attenuating coordination failures.[30]

The theoretical results presented here, as well as the data in Section 5, suggest that efforts to raise the living standards of the less well-off may succeed where they attenuate the incentive problems arising when property rights are ill-defined or insecure, contracts are incomplete, and wealth is highly concentrated. The rationale for the egalitarian supply side interventions summarized here – in contrast to policies restricted to pie-dividing or demand expansion – is dramatized by globalization, but it is no less compelling for closed economies.[31]

This is not to say that globalization makes no difference. Even in the very long-run perspective taken here, the effect of globalization on the out-of-equilibrium dynamics may be decisive. A one-time aggregate demand expansion may be crucial, for example, in permanently displacing an economy from a 'low-road' to a 'high-road' equilibrium of the type illustrated in Figure 10.3, but the effectiveness of the necessary macroeconomic policies may be reduced by greater openness.

Appendix: The Model and Notation

Equations

(1)	$Q = yhe(1 - m)$ for $K \geq kh(1 - m)$	Production
	$= 0$ for $K < kh(1 - m)$	Capital requirement
(2)	$w^* = a/\tau(1 - h) + b$	Labour supply equilibrium condition
(3)	$\pi = r(1 - t) = (1 - t)[(y - k)h(1 - m) - hw]/[kh(1 - m)]$	After tax profit rate
(4)	$\pi = \rho\mu$	Stationary K
(5)	$w = (1 - m)[y - k(1 + \rho\mu)/(1 - t)]$	Labour demand equilibrium condition
(6)	$w^* = w$	Equilibrium in national economy
(7)	$\rho = (v + 1)/\phi - 1$	Global rate of return
(8)	$\Delta = \phi(\pi(1 - c) + 1) - (1 + \eta)$	
	$\Delta = v - \eta$	Excess national supply of k
(9)	$b(1 - h) + p = th\{[(1 - m)y(\lambda p) - k] - w\}$	Government budget constraint
(10)	$dh/dy = \{(1 - m) - db/dy\}/w_h$	Employment effects of Δ productivity
(11)	$\omega = (1 - m^-)\{y(\sigma^-) - k(1 + \rho\mu)/(1 - t)\}$	Expected residual claim of coop members
(12)	$u = u(\omega, \sigma)$	Coop members risk averse $u()$

Notation

- y Output per unit of effort
- h hours employed (labour demand)
- m monitoring (fraction of labour time)
- k capital per hour of productive labour
- w^* no shirking wage
- a disutility of effort
- τ probability of detection (shirker)
- c Probability of confiscation
- ρ risk free interest rate
- ϕ fraction of corn surplus invested
- v rate of change of world labour supply
- η rate of change of nation's labour supply
- λ effectiveness of public expenditure
- p level of public investment

b terminated workers fallback
π after tax profit rate
t profits tax rate
μ risk premium ($= 1/(1 - c)$)
ω expected residual claim (coop)
σ sd of members' income stream
u coop members utility

Notes

1 Thanks for research assistance by Bridget Longridge, Yongjin Park, and Lawrance Evans, helpful contributions from Pranab Bardhan, Daniel Bromley, Helena De Letourdis, Steven Durlauf, Maurizio Franzini, Ugo Pagano, Fabio Petri, Eric Verhoogen, and Elisabeth Wood, and to the MacArthur Foundation for financial support.

2 Globalization can work powerfully to reduce inequalities, both between countries, and even within them, where it may induce more competitive product markets (reducing the discrepancy between prices and marginal costs and thus raising real wages) and providing greater accountability for state and parastatal institutions often dominated by elites. It is in part for these reasons that centre-left parties such as the African National Congress (ANC) in South Africa and the former Communist Party in Italy have supported trade liberalization. On the basis of available data, however, one cannot conclude that either recent or long-term globalization tendencies have on balance favoured greater equality in world income. The period of increased liberalization from 1988 to 1993, for example was marked by a substantial increase in world inequality (Milanovic (1999)). See also Zimmerman (1962) and Schultz (1998).

3 The nature of the openness which characterizes these cases differs of course; all have relatively large trade flows while some have (or had) relatively restricted capital flows.

4 More stringent requirements might be imposed, namely that the changes needed to enact the transition from the status quo to the desired programme (not just the programme itself) be implementable, or that the underlying preferences be stationary. I do not explore these problems here.

5 The cases of open economy egalitarianism cited above fail to meet some criteria of democracy over the relevant years (especially alternation of parties in power for South Korea, Taiwan, and Singapore) but none were outright dictatorships and most were exemplary democracies (Przeworski *et al.* (2000)).

6 A review of these cases is provided in Bardhan, Bowles, and Gintis (2000). Asset-based redistribution is also stressed in Birdsall and Londoño (1997). Atkinson (1999) and Franzini and Milone (1999) likewise view the constraints thought to be posed by globalization as exaggerated.

7 See also Glyn and Sutcliffe (1999), Taylor (1999) and the works cited there.

8 Slaughter's (1999) estimate of an impact of openness on the wage elasticity of demand in the US economy cannot be distinguished from a time trend, and the same is true of Heintz and my estimates showing a secular increase in the elasticity of demand for labour in South Africa (Heintz and Bowles (1997)). Gordon, Bowles and Weisskopf (1998) found some evidence of a substantial negative 'rest-of-the-world-profit-rate' effect on US investment, but while Koechlin (1992) also found a statistically significant negative effect of other countries' profit rates on domestic investment in the US this was true in none of the six other countries for which he estimated investment functions.

Epstein (1996) found little evidence of convergence of profit rates among nations.

9 Econometric evidence of profit-led investment is presented in Bashkar and Glyn (1995), Bowles, Gordon and Weisskopf (1989), Bowles and Boyer (1995), Catinat *et al.* (1988), Clark (1979), Feldstein (1982), Gordon, Weisskopf and Bowles (1998), Kopcke (1985) and the works cited there. Evidence concerning the covariation of real wages and employment is found in Bowles (1991) and Blanchflower and Oswald (1994).

10 A bare bones model is this. Workers commit to a level of effort at the beginning of each period at which point with some probability they will be monitored and detected if they are shirking. The utility of providing effort is just $u(w)$-$\underline{a}$ while for providing none is $(1-\tau)u(w)+\tau[(1-h)u(b)+hu(w))]$ where the second term gives the consequences of termination, namely a probability $(1-h)$ of remaining unemployed and receiving b, and a probability (h) of finding work at the going wage. The assumption that those who are terminated and then find work will not be monitored again until the beginning of the next period allows a particularly simple no-shirking condition: $u(w)-u(b)=a/\tau(1-h)$. See Shapiro and Stiglitz (1984) and Bowles (1985); Bowles (1991) provides empirical estimates of the resulting wage function. The equation in the text lets $u(w)=w$ and $u(b)=b$, thus abstracting from workers' risk aversion. Endogenizing the employers' choice of the desired effort level and monitoring intensity would complicate the model but not alter the results.

11 An alternative formulation yielding similar qualitative results would make the wage level and effort level the outcome of a collective bargaining process, with the (Nash) bargain struck depending on the fallback position of the two parties, and labour's fallback rising with h.

12 Nothing of substance depends on the assumption that k is exogenous. If firms using a production function with the conventional properties chose an optimal level of k depending on the wage rate so that $k=k(w)$ with $k'>0$ and $y=y(k)$ with $y_k>0$ the unique wage rate consistent with world capital market equilibrium (and independent of h) would exit as in (5) but with the production technology endogenous; (5) would represent the wage satisfying both the firm's first-order conditions for the choice of inputs and the global capital market equilibrium consistent with those inputs. Thus making the dependence of y and k on w explicit does not alter the fact that there exists just one national wage rate consistent with equalized expected wage rates among nations. The invariance of w with respect to h results not from exogeneity of k but from the assumption that there are constant returns to scale at the national level and no factors are in fixed supply.

13 The equilibrium exists as long as $w^*(0;b)<\underline{w}<w^*(1;b)$. The equilibrium is stable and unique under current assumptions but, as we will see presently, need not be.

14 The invariance of ϕ with respect to ρ may be motivated in a number of ways, for example it results from an intertemporal utility function of the wealthy of the form $u=ux^{1-\phi}g^{\phi}$ where x is this period's consumption and g is a bequest to the next generation equal to the returns on the invested corn, given next period. Nothing of substance would be altered if ρ and the investment share of the surplus were jointly determined.

15 Note that in this 'hyper-globalized' economy, there are no investment or trade flows in equilibrium, underlining the importance of distinguishing between aggregate flow-based and microeconomic response-based measures of openness.

16 I here provide no reason to expect multiple equilibria – they are not difficult to imagine – but simply note that their possibility may help explain the pattern of divergence among apparently similar national economies (Nigeria's *per capita* income exceeded that of Taiwan, for example, in 1950 (Summers and Heston (1984)) and more generally what Quah (1996) calls the 'twin peaks' pattern of divergence in income levels among countries.

17 In a multi-period context, a reduction in the probability of job loss for reasons other than insufficient effort (protection from cyclical layoffs, for example) reduces the no-shirking wage because it increases the value of not shirking.

18 Where, as in the Nordic social democratic countries and especially Sweden, collective bargaining explicitly sought to implement wages consistent with successful competition in global markets, the $w^*(h)$ function came to approximate the $\underline{w}$ function itself (the latter defining the target wage in the above bargaining model), with firm- and industry-specific wage drift accounting for discrepancies between the two functions. Perhaps surprisingly, negotiated incomes policies can lower the labour supply equilibrium condition (for all values of h) even if $w^*(h)$ represents a conventional efficiency wage no-shirking condition; for the competitive equilibrium wage in that case will exceed that which would minimize the cost of an effective unit of labour if implemented by collusion among employers. The reason (explained in Bowles and Boyer (1990a)) is that each worker's fallback position includes the prospect of a job at *other* employers' wages, so employers face a coordination problem resulting in their overpaying relative to their joint profit maximum. Thus there exists a lower wage which colluding employers would prefer, and which might be implemented through negotiated incomes policies.

19 There is no 'low-road' equilibrium in this case, as h_0 violates (6) while lower levels of employment violate the budget constraint.

20 For a given level of b, λ and h, there exists a tax rate that maximizes $\underline{w}$ (and hence both employment and wages); for obvious reasons it varies inversely with b (if taxes were spent only on b, the optimal rate would be zero) and covaries with λ and h (where h is high little tax revenue goes to unemployment benefits and more to productivity enhancement, so as long as the rate of return of public investment exceeds ρ it raises $\underline{w}$.)

21 The simpler case in which individual producers use the corn to produce independently is transparent, but not empirically relevant where team production is required by economies of scale or for other reasons. I assume that there is no rental market in corn.

22 Bowles and Gintis (1999a) present a model of this process and point to a number of empirical cases in which reassigning residual claimancy to members of even very large teams has substantially increased output per worker hour.

23 To ensure that the loan is repaid with certainty, I must assume either that in those presumably rare cases where their realized residual claim is negative (realized gross income $= y^r < k(1+\rho\mu)/(1-t)$) coop members have con-

sumption smoothing opportunities, or that these cases are sufficiently unlikely that they may be ignored.

24 A sufficient assumption is that risk is generated by a linear class of disturbances which would arise, for example, if the realized output level is defined by $y^r = \sigma z + y(\sigma)$ where z is a random variable with mean zero and standard deviation unity. This treatment draws on Bowles and Gintis (1999) and the works by Sinn (1990) and Meyer (1987) cited there.

25 Evidence for an inverse relationship between wealth and risk aversion is presented in Saha, Shumway, and Talpaz (1994) and the studies cited there.

26 Technically, the distribution of wealth is governed by a non-ergodic dynamical process in which initial conditions (or one-time exogenous interventions) determine which of many possible equilibria will obtain. Galor and Zeira (1993) and others have shown that where credit constraints face the asset-poor, and where there is a minimum economically viable project size (accounting for the necessity of team production in this case) the wealth distribution process may be non-ergodic.

27 Examples are given in Engerman and Sokoloff (1997), Engerman, Sokoloff and Mariscal (1998), Bowles and Gintis (1999a), and Birdsall and Londoño (1997).

28 The data (for Figures 10.7 and 10.8) are from the United Nations Industrial Development Organization Industrial Statistics Database. The wage measure is average annual earnings in manufacturing. The subsequent productivity measure is value added per employee in manufacturing.

29 The data refer to 13 economies comprising most of world output over the period covered and are from Glyn *et al.* (1990) based on Maddison's (1982) data set. The measure of capital accumulation is based on the tangible reproducible non-residential fixed capital stock.

30 The argument is not that the non-wealthy have identical interests, but simply that the difficulty of securing mutually beneficial cooperative solutions with mobile wealth owners may be circumvented.

31 Abstracting from different national rates of population growth, equilibria of a closed economy version of this model are identical with the open economy version (though the out of equilibrium dynamics are quite different and may be critically important). To see why this is true, consider the supply of investment goods in a closed economy: the national surplus remaining after the consumption of the wealthy, in the open economy case, is the contribution of the nation to the global supply of investment goods; in the closed economy case this becomes the supply function for capital goods in that country (the open economy supply function is infinitely elastic at the rate ρ). Thus country-specific supply and demand for corn as an investment good are as indicated in (8) (supply is increasing in ρ, as expected while demand is invariant). If $\eta = v$ there are no out of equilibrium flows of corn among countries. As before there is a single interest rate $\rho = (1+v)/\phi - 1$ that clears the market in corn-for-investment, and (by the zero profit condition) this ρ determines w and therefore h. Thus the closed and open economy equilibria are identical. Of course, closed economies in which populations are growing more rapidly than the world average support higher equilibrium rates of expected profit and interest and thus experience lower wages and employment (because this years workers must produce a larger surplus to employ a constant fraction $(h)^*$ of the relatively more numerous workers of the next period).

References

Anand, S. and R. Kanbur (1991) 'Public Policy and Basic Needs Provision: Intervention and Achievement in Sri Lanka', in J. Drèze and A. Sen (eds), *The Political Economy of Hunger: Vol III: Endemic Hunger* (Oxford: Clarendon Press), pp. 59–92.

Ardington, E. and F. Lund (1995) 'Pensions and Development: Social Security as Complementary to Programmes of Reconstruction and Development', *Southern Africa*, vol. 12, no. 4, pp. 557–77.

Atkinson, A. (1999) 'Equity Issues in a Globalizing World: The Experience of the OECD Countries', IMF, mimeo.

Banerjee, A. and M. Ghatak (1996) 'Empowerment and Efficiency: The Economics of Tenancy Reform', MIT, mimeo.

Bardhan, P., S. Bowles and H. Gintis (2000) 'Wealth Inequality, Credit Constraints, and Economic Performance', in A. Atkinson and F. Bourguignon (eds), *Handbook of Income Distribution* (Dordrecht: North-Holland).

Bashkar, V. and A. Glyn (1995), in G. Epstein and H. Gintis (eds), *Macroeconomic Policy after the Conservative Era: Research on Investment Savings and Finance* (Cambridge: Cambridge University Press).

Besley, T. and R. Burgess (1998) 'Land Reform, Poverty Reduction and Growth: Evidence From India', The Suntory Centre, mimeo.

Birdsall, N. and Londoño, J. (1997) 'Asset Inequality Matters: An Assessment of the World Bank's Approach to Poverty Reduction', *American Economic Review*, vol. 87, no. 2, pp. 32–7.

Blanchflower, D. G. and A. J. Oswald (1994) *The Wage Curve* (Cambridge, MA: MIT Press).

Bowles, S. (1985) 'The Production Process in a Competitive Economy: Walrasian, Marxian, and Neo-Hobbesian Models', *American Economic Review*, vol. 76, no. 1, pp. 16–36.

Bowles, S. (1991) 'The Reserve Army Effect on Wages in a Labour Discipline Model: US, 1954–1987', in T. Mizoguchi (ed.), *Making Economies More Efficient and More Equitable: Factors Determining Income Distribution* (Oxford: Oxford University Press), pp. 385–406.

Bowles, S. (1992) 'Is Income Security Possible in a Capitalist Economy? An Agency Theoretic Analysis of an Unconditional Income Grant', *European Journal of Political Economy*, vol. 8, pp. 557–78.

Bowles, S. and R. Boyer (1990a) 'A Wage-led Employment Regime: Income Distribution, Labour Discipline, and Aggregate Demand in Welfare Capitalism', in S. Marglin and J. Schor (eds), *The Golden Age of Capitalism. Reinterpreting the Postwar Experience* (Oxford: Clarendon Press), pp. 187–217.

Bowles, S. and R. Boyer (1990b) 'Labour Market Flexibility and Decentralization as Barriers to High Employment? Notes on Employer Collusion, Centralized Wage Bargaining and Aggregate Employment', in R. Brunetta and C. Dell'Aringa (eds), *Labour Relations and Economic Performance* (London: Macmillan–now Palgrave), pp. 325–52.

Bowles, S. and R. Boyer (1995) 'Wages, Aggregate Demand and Employment in an Open Economy: A Theoretical and Empirical Investigation', in G. E. and H. Gintis (eds), *Macroeconomic Policy after the Conservative Era: Research on Investment, Savings and Finance* (Cambridge: Cambridge University Press), pp. 143–71.

Bowles, S. and H. Gintis (1999a) *Recasting Egalitarianism: New Rules for Markets, States and Communities* (London: Verso).
Bowles, S. and H. Gintis (1999b) 'Risk Aversion, Insurance, and the Efficiency Equality Tradeoff', University of Massachusetts, mimeo.
Bowles, S., D. M. Gordon and T. E. Weisskopf (1989) 'Business Ascendancy and Economic Impasse', *Journal of Economic Perspectives*, vol. 3, no. 1, pp. 107–34.
Catinat, M. *et al.* (1988) 'Investment Behaviour in Europe: A Comparative Analysis', *Recherches Economiques de Louvain*, vol. 4, no. 3, pp. 277–324.
Clark, P. (1979) 'Investment in the 1970s: Theory, Performance, and Prediction', *Brookings Papers on Economic Activity*, vol. 1 pp. 73–113.
Engerman, S. L. and K. L. Sokoloff (1997) 'Factor Endowments, Institutions, and Differential Paths of Growth Among New World Economies: A View from Economic Historians of the United States', in S. Haber (ed.), *How Latin America Fell Behind* (Palo Alto: Stanford University Press), pp. 260–304.
Engerman, S., K. Sokoloff and E. Mariscal (1998) 'Schooling, Suffrage, and the Persistence of Inequality in the Americas, 1800–1945', mimeo.
Epstein, G (1996) 'International Profit Rate Equalization and Investment: An Empirical Analysis of Integration, Instability and Enforcement', in G. Epstein and H. Gintis (eds), *Macroeconomic Policy After the Conservative Era* (Cambridge: Cambridge University Press), pp. 308–31.
Feldstein, M. (1982) 'Inflation, Tax Rules, and Investment: Some Econometric Evidence', *Econometrica*, vol. 50, pp. 825–62.
Franzini, M. and L. Milone (1999) 'I dilemmi del welfare state nell'epoca della globalizzazione', in N. Acocella (ed.), *Globalizzazione e stato sociale* (Bologna: II Mulino).
Freeman, R. and J. Medoff (1984) *What Do Unions Do?* (New York: Basic Books).
Galor, O. and J. Zeira (1993) 'Income Distribution and Macroeconomics', *Review of Economic Studies*, vol. 60, no. 1, pp. 35–52.
Glyn, A., A. Hughes, A. Lipietz and A. Singh (1990) 'The Rise and Fall of the Golden Age', in S. M. and J. B. Schor (eds), *The Golden Age of Capitalism; Reinterpreting the Postwar Experience* (Oxford: Clarendon Press), pp. 39–125.
Glyn, A. and R. Sutcliffe (1999) 'Still Underwhelmed: Indicators of Globalization and their Misinterpretation', *Review of Radical Political Economy*, vol. 31, no. 1, pp. 111–32.
Gordon, D. (1994) 'Bosses of Different Stripes: A Cross-National Perspective on Monitoring and Supervision', *American Economic Review*, vol. 84, no. 2, pp. 375–9.
Gordon, D. (1998) 'The Global Economy: New Edifice or Crumbling Foundations?', *New Left Review*, vol. 68, pp. 24–64.
Gordon, D., S. Bowles and T. Weisskopf (1998) 'Power, Profits and Investment: An Institutionalist Explanation of the Stagnation of US Net Investment After the Mid-1960's', in S. Bowles and T. Weisskopf (eds), *Economics and Social Justice: Essays on Power, Labor and Institutional Change* (Cheltenham: Edward Elgar), pp. 130–5.
Heintz, J. and S. Bowles (1997) 'Wages and Employment in the South African Economy', University of Massachusetts, mimeo.
Huber, E. and J. Stephens (1998) 'Internationalization and the Social Democratic Model', *Comparative Political Studies*, vol. 31, no. 3, pp. 353–97.
Isenman, P. (1980) 'Basic Needs: The Case of Sri Lanka', *World Development*, vol. 8, no. 3, pp. 237–58.

Koechlin, T. (1992) 'The Determinants of the Location of USA Direct Foreign Investment', *International Review of Applied Economics*, vol. 6, no. 2, pp. 203–16.
Kopcke, R. (1985) 'The Determinants of Investment Spending', *New England Economic Review*, vol. , pp. 19–35.
Lim, C. (1984) *Economic Structuring in Singapore* (Singapore: Federal Publications).
Maddison, A. (1982) *Phases of Capitalist Development* (Oxford: Oxford University Press).
Mesà-Lago, C. (1989) 'Costa Rica: A Latecomer Turned Boomer', in C. Mesà-Lago (ed.), *Ascent to Bankruptcy: Financing Social Security in Latin America*, (Pittsburgh: University of Pittsburgh Press), pp. 0–0.
Meyer, J. (1987) 'Two-Moment Decision Models and Expected Utility', *American Economic Review*, vol. 77, no. 3, pp. 421–30.
Milanovic, B. (1999) 'True World Income Distribution, 1988 and 1993: First Calculation Based on Household Surveys Alone', Washington, DC: World Bank, mimeo.
Moene, K. O. (1998) 'Feasibility of Social Democracy', University of Oslo Conference on Decentralised Development, Calcutta.
Moene, K. O. and M. Wallerstein (1993) 'The Decline of Social Democracy', in K. G. Persson (ed.), *The Economic Development of Denmark and Norway since 1879* (Cheltenham: Edward Elgar), pp. 385–403.
Okun, A. (1975) *Equality and Efficiency: The Big Trade-Off* (Washington, DC: Brookings Institution Press).
Pagano, U. (1991) 'Property Rights, Asset Specificity, and the Division of Labour under Alternative Capitalist Relations', *Cambridge Journal of Economics*, vol. 15, no. 3, pp. 315–42.
Przeworski, A. M. E. Alvarez, J. A. Cheibub and F. Limongi (2000) *Democracy and Development* (Cambridge: Cambridge University Press).
Putzel, J. (nd) 'The Politics of Agrarian Reform in South Korea', London School of Economics, mimeo.
Quah, D. (1996) 'Twin Peaks: Growth and Convergence in Models of Distribution Dynamics', *Economic Journal*, vol. 106, pp. 1045–55.
Ramachandran, V. K. (1996) 'On Kerala's Development Achievements', in J. Drèze and A. Sen (eds), *Indian Development: Selected Regional Perspectives* (Oxford: Oxford University Press), pp. 205–356.
Rosenberg, M. (1981) 'Social Reform in Costa Rica: Social Security and the Presidency of Rafael Angel Calderon', *Hispanic American Historical Review*, vol. 61, no. 2, pp. 278–96.
Saha, A., R. C. Shumway and H. Talpaz (1994) 'Joint Estimation of Risk Preference Structure and Technology Using Expo-Power Utility', *American Journal of Agricultural Economics*, vol. 76, no. 2, pp. 173–84.
Schultz, T. P. (1998) 'Inequality in the Distribution of Personal Income in the World: How It Is Changing and Why', *Journal of Population Economics*, vol. 11, pp. 307–44.
Sengupta, S. and H. Gazdar (1996) 'Agrarian Politics and Rural Development in West Bengal', in J. Drèze and A. Sen (eds), *Indian Development: Selected Regional Perspectives*, (Oxford: Oxford University Press), pp. 129–204.
Shapiro, C. and J. Stiglitz (1984) 'Unemployment as a Worker Discipline Device', *American Economic Review*, vol. 74, no. 3, pp. 433–44.

Shiller, R. J. (1993) *Macro Markets: Creating Institutions for Managing Society's Largest Economic Risks* (Oxford: Clarendon Press).

Sinn, H.-W. (1990) 'Expected Utility, mu-sigma Preferences, and Linear Distribution Classes: A Further Result', *Journal of Risk and Uncertainty*, vol. 3, pp. 277–81.

Slaughter, M. (1999) 'International Trade and Labour-Demand Elasticities' (Dartmouth College), NBER, mimeo.

Summers, R. and A. Heston (1984) 'Improved International Comparisons of Real Product and its Composition, 1950–1980', *Review of Income and Wealth*, vol. 30, pp. 207–71.

Taylor, A. (1999) 'International Capital Mobility in History', NBER, mimeo.

Verhoogen, E. (1999) 'Trade Pressures and Wage Convergence', University of Massachusetts, Amherst and the Brookings Institution, mimeo.

Yager, J. (1980) *Transforming Agriculture in Taiwan: The Experience of the Joint Commission on Rural Reconstruction* (Ithaca and London: Cornell University Press).

Yang, M. (1970) *Socioeconomic Results of Land Reform in Taiwan* (Honolulu: East–West Center Press).

Yashar, D. J. (1995) 'Civil War and Social Welfare: The Origins of Costa Rica's Competitive Party System', in S. Mainwaring and T. Scully (eds), *Building Democratic Institutions: Party Systems in Latin America* (Stanford: Stanford University Press), pp. 0–0.

Zimmerman, L. J. (1962) 'The Distribution of World Income, 1860–1960', in E. De Vries (ed.), *Essays in Unbalanced Growth: A Century of Disparity and Convergence*, (The Hague: Mouton), pp. 28–47.

11
Distributed Information and the Role of the State in the Economy

Kenneth J. Arrow
Stanford University, USA

1 Introduction

I intend to make here some reflections on the role of the state in the government of the economy. More specifically, I want to draw the implications of the fact that knowledge in the economy is very widely dispersed. Neither the state nor any other entity has ready access to any more than a small portion of the myriad of facts, generalizations, and judgements, explicit and implicit, which are known somewhere in the economic system and affect its outcome. This perception is classic among economists, as seen in Adam Smith, if not before. In recent times, there is a prevailing consensus that the government is in a poor position to make economic decisions since its knowledge is such a small part of that scattered through the economy, a position especially associated with the name of Friedrich von Hayek (1945). This view is manifested in practice in the strong current trend towards privatization and towards deregulation even of natural monopolies. I want to re-examine the argument and show that the inference from dispersed information to absence of government intervention is valid only for some cases but not for others. The generalizations common in current rhetoric are too sweeping.

In this analysis, I want to call upon the fact that modern economic theories since the 1960s have increasingly been stressing the implications of dispersed information. I am referring to the study of asymmetric information and incentive-compatible contracts, where a whole panoply of implications for the nature of economic equilibrium is driven by the fact that economic agents know different things and know that they know different things.

To focus the discussion, I confine myself to the role of the state in improving the efficiency of the economy. Richard Musgrave (1959) gave a much-cited classification of government roles as allocative (improvement of efficiency), redistributive, and stabilizing. I consider the redistributive role as of the greatest importance, politically and ethically, and much of government expenditure in all countries is devoted to that end. Indeed, redistribution was one of the major themes of the Buenos Aires Congress. But I set it aside to keep the discussion within bounds. The stabilizing role seems to me more properly part of the allocative, as indeed is implied by Robert Solow's address to the Congress; the fact that markets and, in particular, labour markets frequently fail to clear may imply a role for the government.

I am not going to be very precise about the meaning of efficiency. It suffices to think of Pareto-efficiency or of maximization of total output, defined somewhat arbitrarily. Comparison of states of affairs neither of which Pareto-dominates the other has well-known difficulties. In fact, any such comparison must fail some reasonable criteria for good measurement, as was shown for the Kaldor–Hicks (potential Pareto-improvement) test by Scitovsky (1941) and more generally by the impossibility theorem of social choice (Arrow (1963)).

To outline briefly the rest of the chapter, I review in section 2 the history of economic thought and practice as relevant to my theme. In Section 3 I indicate the newer aspects of economic theory to which I have alluded, the emphasis on asymmetric information and its implications for economic organization. In Section 4, I discuss how and why information is dispersed and how the dispersion should affect the choice of the decision-maker to achieve efficiency, with particular stress on the role of the state.

2 A review of the history of thought and practice

2.1 *Laissez-faire* and its cyclical fluctuations

The idea that decentralization of decision-making is efficient because information is dispersed has been central to economic thinking since Adam Smith spoke of the 'natural system of liberty' and 'the invisible hand'. This concept has the concomitant implication that government policy has little appropriate scope. The strength of this tradition among economists and among the forces that influence decision-making has shown cyclical fluctuations comparable to those in gross domestic product (GDP). *Laissez-faire* is not an easy doctrine to establish; it defies common sense in many ways.

If we look at changes in practice, we see a triumph of *laissez-faire* in the middle of the nineteenth century in Great Britain, exemplified grimly by its application to the Irish potato failure and consequent famine. But this period was followed by attacks and erosion on a number of different fronts. The countries that began to compete with Great Britain in manufacturing all used tariffs to protect their industries; Germany, France and, most conspicuously, the US did not accept free trade doctrines. The regulation of natural monopolies began towards the end of the nineteenth century. Social insurance was instituted in Germany in the 1880s and gradually spread to other countries, Great Britain in 1911 and the US only in the 1930s.

In the immediate post-Second World War period, economic planning became an ideal in most of Europe and in virtually all of the developing countries. There are many reasons why this happened, but certainly the economic failures of the interwar period, especially the Great Depression, were important motivations. More dramatically, an economic system based on entirely different principles came into being, in the Soviet Union, in China, and – by conquest rather than diffusion of ideas – in eastern Europe. The example of communism, we must remember, was a significant attraction in several western European countries; there were large communist votes, from one-quarter to one-third of the total in France and Italy.

To be sure, much of the swing in ideology and formal policy statements was rhetorical rather than effective. Evidently, comprehensive planning in non-communist countries, at least, proved to have little effect on the course of the economy. But the piecemeal interventions that accompanied planning were pervasive and had effects. There were currency controls, import licences, protective tariffs (which have gradually decreased), limits on international capital movements, and allocation of capital to investors (even in very successful countries, such as Korea). In addition, redistributive measures, such as social insurance, public housing, and welfare systems, were extensive in many countries in the postwar period. There was a widespread view that governments were responsible for macroeconomic stability. Later in the period, environmental regulations became and have remained significant.

More recently, the long cycle of the degree of government intervention has moved to a trough, with increasing attention paid to the use of markets. Fiscal policy plays very little role today, deregulation is in full swing, currency controls and restrictions on international capital movements have been removed or greatly reduced in magnitude, redistributive measures are under attack. Again, it must be said that the rhetoric has changed dramatically, the practice a good deal less. For example, the proportion of national income going to public expenditures, certainly one index of intervention, has changed very little.

2.2 Analytic bases

Let me turn to the evolution of thought among professional economists. I like to think of the evolution as a growth process but, as Solow has reminded us, growth has always been accompanied by cycles, at least in the capitalist era. The history of economic thought, like all history, is a record of winners, and so a lot of trends, some very interventionist, have been lost to view. Let me just take the standard landmarks.

Despite the advocacy of free markets by classicists such as Smith and Ricardo, there was no analytic basis for the argument that free markets produce better results before the appearance of a utility theory of consumption. I cannot see in what sense Ricardo could claim that free trade was superior to protection with his analytic tools.

2.2.1 Marginal cost pricing and increasing returns

However, even before full-fledged utility analysis appeared, Jules Dupuit (1844) saw that it was necessary to have some kind of measure of consumer satisfaction in order to determine the justification for public expenditures to build a canal, a bridge, or a highway; his official position, after all, was Inspector of Bridges and Highways. Dupuit argued that the area under the demand curve measured consumer gain, to be compared with cost, and this was a criterion for government intervention. But one immediate observation of his was that the price charged for any service, public or private, should be marginal cost. This proposition held even for increasing returns industries, and he advocated pricing railway services in this way. The implications of this policy would certainly be losses and therefore government ownership (or at least subsidy). Further analysis of railroad pricing is due to Dionysius Lardner (1850).

2.2.2 The idea of externalities

Increasing returns was thus one great argument for government intervention. The second was the notion of externalities, first given real weight by Alfred Marshall ((1890; see the distinction between external and internal economies, p. 310, 8th edition (1948)). He recognized that there were direct interactions among economic agents which were not mediated through the market. Marshall certainly had interventionist leanings ('*Laissez-faire:* Let the State be up and doing' (Marshall (1907), p. 19)), which were taken up by most of his successors, such as Arthur C. Pigou (1929).

However, the economy has many interrelations among economic agents; distinguishing which are externalities is somewhat subtle. Pigou (1912) attempted a systematic exposition of the grounds for intervention under the title, *Wealth and Welfare*. Allyn Young in his review of this book (1913) gave the first clear definition of an externality; further clarification was due to Frank Knight (1924). These papers made the crucial distinction between what Jacob Viner (1931) later called *technological* and *pecuniary* externalities; only the former call for intervention to increase efficiency (a point developed much further by Scitovsky (1954)). The entrance of a new competitor can reduce the profits of existing firms, a pecuniary externality, but has no effect on efficiency. The later editions of Pigou's book, by then retitled *The Economics of Welfare* (1929), elaborated many cases of true externalities.

2.2.3 *Welfare economics theorems and externalities as market failure*

The basic theorems which identified more clearly the requirements for efficient pricing were first set forth with precision and generality by Harold Hotelling (1938) and Abram Bergson (Burk) (1938), with later clean-up jobs by Gerard Debreu (1951) and Kenneth Arrow (1951). A more general definition of externalities as essentially the failure of appropriate markets to exist developed in the 1950s; see William Baumol (1952), Francis Bator (1958), and Kenneth Arrow (1969). The basic idea is simple. If there are markets for all goods and if these markets are in competitive equilibrium, then the outcome is efficient. Hence, under competitive conditions, it is the failure of a market to exist that constitutes an externality.

2.2.4 *Failure of futures markets and indicative planning*

There is one implication of this reason that attracted some practical and theoretical attention. In the formulation of intertemporal equilibrium due to Erik Lindahl (1929; English translation, 1939, Part III) and John R. Hicks (1939), future deliveries are among the goods existing today. The failure of an adequate number of futures markets to exist should constitute a market failure. In a world characterized by uncertainty, we also need a large set of state-contingent markets (Arrow (1953)) to achieve efficiency, and again their failure to exist constitutes a set of externalities. This observation supports the views that the government has a role in planning by creating consistent expectations for the future. In practice, the Commissariat au Plan in France, under the direction of Pierre Massé, was engaged in precisely this exercise of 'indicative planning'. There is a very systematic treatment of this approach in James Meade (1972, Part 3).

This line of thought has not gone very far. The French found that indicative planning had no significant effect on the economy. I do not know if there has been any serious research into this failure, but I would surmise that the underlying reason is that the information, even when collected, was much less than the firms had already. The information transmitted was only a small fraction of that available to the firms; for example, it was available only at a level of aggregation too broad for serious use. Hence, the firms found the indicative plans not helpful in their planning.

There is another question raised by the attempted use of planning to serve the function of non-existent futures and contingent markets. If these markets had a social value, why had they not come into being? One very important answer is the presence of transaction costs, and I return to this later.

Another, sophisticated, answer was given by Roy Radner (1968). A contingent market means that a payment is made or goods delivered if some event occurs. But if only one party to the transaction knows whether or not the event occurs, the contract cannot be entered into, since the uninformed party will assume that the other will control the relevant information and can be misleading. This is the case of asymmetric information.

2.3 Summary of the traditional case for allocative intervention

The fact that indicative planning has not been useful suggests that market failure for reasons of transaction costs is deeper or at least more powerful in motivating government intervention than market failure due to asymmetric information. In combination with earlier arguments, we are left with market failure due to transaction costs and increasing returns as the two main arguments in price-oriented economic theory for government intervention to improve efficiency.

The argument for intervention under increasing returns, to be clear, is a consequence of the theorem that perfect competition leads to Pareto-efficiency. Under private ownership and control, increasing returns is viable only under imperfect competition, as already observed by Auguste-Antoine Cournot (1838), and imperfect price competition implies inefficiency.

The argument that market failure and increasing returns both lead to inefficiency in a private ownership economy implies only that an omniscient and omnipotent intervener could make every one better off. Among other problems, it leaves open the question of finding the Pareto-improvement. We have to have some mechanism, such as benefit-cost analysis, to test whether a given change is in fact an efficiency improvement.

I think this fairly summarizes the basic case for intervention before the modern developments in economic theory.

3 Newer considerations in the analysis of the state and the market

Since the 1960s, there has been a considerable reorientation of microeconomics. I stress two points. One is the abandonment of exclusive analytic reliance on the price system. Modern theory relies to a large extent on the broader concept of a contract, in which a given amount of goods is sold against a given amount of money (possibly contingent on external events). Second is the emphasis on the asymmetric information of the parties. The implications of these changes for economic policy have been examined at great length in Joseph Stiglitz's important book (1994), although I do not agree with all of Stiglitz's conclusions.

3.1 Prices and contracts

3.1.1 The centrality of prices in traditional theory

The tradition of economics has emphasized the importance of prices, by which is meant that at least one side of the market can buy (or sell) any amount it chooses at a fixed price per unit. This assumption is made not only for perfect competition but also for monopoly and even oligopoly (under either Cournot or Bertrand (1883) assumptions). The one step away from this was the theory of price discrimination (see Joan Robinson (1933, Chapter 15), but even here any given buyer was operating at given prices, though the prices differed across market segments. One of the most notable features of post-1960 economics has been the increasing emphasis on non-linear pricing, in effect, contracts rather than prices.

3.1.2 Non-linear price schemes and general contracts

In part, contracts have emerged from the analysis of incentive-compatible relations under asymmetric information. In fact, though, non-linear pricing is always a possibility under increasing returns (non-convexities) even in the absence of informational issues. Let me give one dramatic illustration. Ronald Coase (1960) famously argued that a system which permitted any possible contract exchanging goods for money would lead to efficient allocation. Neither imperfect competition nor monopoly would prevent efficiency if arbitrary contracts were allowed – for example, a monopolist offering a two-part tariff. In fact, the underlying point had been made much earlier, by Francis Edgeworth (1881), in his concept of the contract curve, though admittedly for a different reason. The axiom emphasized by Edgeworth is the same as that underlying Coase's reasoning; if there is an inefficient allocation, then the parties will get together and make themselves all better off, so that no inefficient contract will be entered into. This is an example of a very well-known argument which was not well understood. Marshall, for example, wrote a glowing review of Edgeworth's book, yet never referred to Edgeworth's arguments in the relevant passages in the *Principles*.

Also, John von Neumann and Oskar Morgenstern (1944, Chapter 6), in their study of cooperative games, made the same assumption, almost without argument as being self-evident; no inefficient bargain would be entered into.

This argument would destroy the classic argument for state intervention to meet the problem of increasing returns. A natural monopoly, say an electric power company, will get together with its customers to arrive at an efficient allocation. Similarly, this argument, if fully accepted, could be applied to any externalities, for example, environmental externalities. Suppose a factory can pollute its neighbours, and assume that the gains to the factory from polluting outweigh the losses to the neighbours. It can be agreed that the factory has the right to pollute, and then the neighbours can pay it to refrain, or that the neighbours have the right not to be polluted, and the factory can pay them to waive the right. Similarly, if the gains to the factory are outweighed by the losses to the neighbours, the exercise of whatever property rights are assigned will lead to cessation of pollution. In either case, the efficient outcome is achieved.

3.1.3 Transaction costs and dispersed information

Coase did not regard this argument as realistic. Rather, he used its failure to conclude that transaction costs were very important in the economy. Now the concept of transaction cost is rather vague. In my view, the most important element in transaction cost is dispersed information. The problem with bargaining between the producer and the consumers of an externality is that the producer does not really know what the costs of the consumers are nor do the latter know the costs of the producer. Making the bargain which makes everyone better off depends on common knowledge of benefits and costs, and the absence of the common knowledge prevents achievement of an efficient state.

3.2 The dispersion of information

3.2.1 Local information and global efficiency

We thus come back to the dispersion of information as a central property of the economy. Traditional economics has always emphasized the economy's achievement of a high degree of coordination with relatively little exchange of information. Indeed, it is usually held not only to be a fact but a positive efficiency gain in minimizing the necessary costs of transmitting information. Hayek goes so far as to say that the central economic problem is not the efficient allocation of scarce resources but the efficient utilization of dispersed knowledge. This distinction is certainly not clear to me. He goes on to argue that the price system is a way of disseminating local information. His picture of the world is that knowledge about each specific kind of production or market is held by a fairly small number of people and that prices form a means by which this local information is effectively signalled to others. I cannot really understand how this is accomplished; diffusion of specific technological knowledge cannot be accomplished by prices.

The general doctrine is that a market system should tend ultimately to move resources to those most able to use them and, in particular, to those with the most appropriate information. But this process raises all the questions of asymmetric information that economic theorists have been so much preoccupied with in the last 35 years. The innovator can make profitable use of capital but does not have the capital. The capitalists do not have the same information about the innovation. The incentives on both sides to misrepresent are obvious. Nevertheless, in spite of the theoretical difficulties, we feel the market has done a fairly good though not perfect job. Good ideas often go unfunded. More often, bad ideas, that is, ideas that would be inefficient if judged by all the information in the economy, are funded. Still, bad ideas will not survive, so that successful firms will grow relative to unsuccessful ones, and also good ideas are imitated. Hence, we may expect the market to do well in accommodating problems of asymmetric information.

3.2.2 Specialization in information as efficiency

That information is dispersed is not merely a fact of the economy, it is almost a necessary fact. Since information is costly to acquire, there are grounds for specialization of information. Professional training is a strong example of such specialization. It does not pay everyone to learn medicine, even though everyone can benefit from it.

4 The distribution of information and the distribution of decision

4.1 Collocation of information, decision, and utility in classical economics

There is a very important qualification to the usual interpretations of information dispersal in classical or modern economic analysis or indeed in much popular and political discourse. In standard competitive theory, it is assumed that the individual who makes decisions also both reaps their consequences and has the knowledge needed to evaluate them (to the extent anyone does). When there are externalities, it is recognized that decisions may have consequences for others as well as the self. But it must also be stressed that even when there are no externalities in that sense, another individual may have more knowledge about consequences than the decision-maker. The dispersion of information which arises from economies of specialization can easily lead to this consequence. Medical and other professional knowledge is a clear illustration. The consequences of medical treatment are borne by the patient but best appreciated by the physician (as a rule).

4.2 Information and legal responsibility

Guido Calabresi, a law professor and judge, wrote a very important book (1970) on legal responsibility for accidents. His theme was that the most informed person should bear the responsibility and make the relevant decision. In other words, he wanted to collocate decision and information. The trouble is that from the efficiency viewpoint it is desirable to collocate three properties: information, decision, and utility, and it is frequently not possible to make more than two coincide.

4.3 Dispersion of information as limiting governmental efficiency

Typically, the dispersion of information implies that government will not be well informed, even when there is a potential social gain owing to externalities or increasing returns. and this fact would certainly argue in favour of privatizing decisions, moving them to the place where the information is greatest.

4.3.1 Increasing returns reconsidered

In a period of rapid technological change, even natural monopoly may not be a sufficiently good justification for government intervention. The lack of knowledge by the government may make intervention so inefficient as to outweigh the value of reducing monopoly. The increasing returns argument for intervention can thus become weak.

4.3.2 Classical externalities

Here, government intervention may be practically unavoidable. The classic case is that of *fugitive resources*, to use the term introduced by S. Ciriacy-Wantrup (1945), goods which are so mobile by nature that they cannot be made property. Examples are air and flowing water (including ground water). Still, it must be recognized that the policies adopted will display considerable inefficiencies because of the dispersion of the relevant information on benefits and costs. It is true that by judicious uses of the price system in environment regulation, such as transferable permits, we may exploit private information so as to minimize the cost of achieving any given degree of environmental control, e.g. sulphur dioxide levels in the atmosphere. But to use benefit-cost analysis to determine what degree of regulation is desirable requires information which is hard to acquire. Professor Solow and I had some joint experience in trying to improve the process of collecting information on non-use values of environmental amenities by questionnaires (a process called *contingent valuation*) and found grave obstacles; see National Oceanic and Atmospheric Administration (1993).

4.4 Delegating decision in the direction of information

Even in the private economy, one response to dispersion of information is for one individual to delegate voluntarily decisions to another with greater information. Medicine and the other professions provide outstanding examples, but principal–agent relations are pervasive. The government will frequently serve for many reasons as an appropriate agent. Consider, for example, building codes, requirements imposed on the building of houses to achieve such aims as fire resistance and safety against natural disasters such as earthquakes (a local concern of mine) and tropical storms. There are a vast number of qualities important to a house of which those cited are but a few. The average consumer is in no position to know even what the possible problems are, let alone the ways of dealing with them, even though he or she has the greatest incentive to take care of them. It is simply too costly to transmit the information to each potential buyer. Knowledge can be specialized and collected by the government, which will use the same information over and over again.

4.5 Dispersion of information as increasing the role of the government

This argument is indeed a defence of paternalism in certain circumstances. Education provides another example. Even those who advocate subsidies for students to go to private schools have to agree that the private schools have to be regulated and standards have to be set for them. This position implies that the ultimate responsibility for assembling information on behalf of the students and their parents lies in the hands of the government. One reason for this responsibility is the presence of scale economies in the assembly of information. A great deal of knowledge comes from statistics, gathering of information from many cases. For many products, the experience of a single consumer is frequent enough so that he or she can gather meaningful statistical information. I would prefer not to rely on my own experience to judge medical interventions or, for that matter, industrial accidents.

4.6 The alternative of information dissemination

One alternative to regulation is the dissemination of the information assembled by the government. This policy clearly improves freedom of choice, as well as permitting the individual to use his or her private information to supplement that provided. But there can be a high cost. Receiving information, even information already created by others, can be very costly in time and displacement of other activities. Clearly, information dissemination may be superior in some cases but not in others.

4.7 Conclusion

I leave here the argument that dispersion of information may lead to the government's having an active role. When the information needed for decision is too costly for the individual but can be used repeatedly for many individuals, the government can have a considerable role in assembling the information and, in many cases, making the decision for the individual.

References

Arrow, K. J. (1951) 'A Reconsideration of the Basic Theorems of Classical Welfare Economics', in J. Neyman (ed.), *Proceedings of the Second Berkeley Symposium on Mathematical Statistics and Probability* (Berkeley and Los Angeles: University of California Press), pp. 507–32.

Arrow, K. J. (1953) 'Le rôle des valeurs boursières dans la répartition la meilleure des Risques', in *Econometrie, Colloques Internationaux*, vol. 11 (Paris: Centre National de la Recherche Scientifique), pp. 41–7.

Arrow, K. J. (1963) *Social Choice and Individual Values*, 2nd edition (New Haven and London: Yale University Press).

Arrow, K. J. (1969) 'The Organization of Economic Activity: Issues Pertinent to the Choice of Market vs. Nonmarket Allocation', in Joint Economic Committee,

United States Congress, *The Analysis and Evaluation of Public Expenditures: The PPB System* (Washington, DC: Government Printing Office), vol. 1, pp. 47–64.

Bator, F. (1958) 'The Anatomy of Market Failure', *Quarterly Journal of Economics*, vol. 72, pp. 351–79.

Baumol, W. J. (1952) *Welfare Economics and the Theory of the State* (Cambridge, MA: Harvard University Press).

Bergson, A. (Burk) (1938) 'A Reformulation of Certain Aspects of Welfare Economics', *Quarterly Journal of Economics*, vol. 52, pp. 310–34.

Bertrand, J. (1883) 'Théorie des Richesses', *Journal des Savants* (September), pp. 499–508.

Calabresi, G. (1970) *The Costs of Accidents: A Legal and Economic Analysis* (New Haven and London: Yale University Press).

Ciriacy-Wantrup, S. (1945) 'International Cooperation in Conservation Policy', *World Economics* (March–June), pp. 83–102.

Coase, R. (1960) 'The Problem of Social Cost', *Journal of Law and Economics*, vol. 3, pp. 1–44.

Cournot, A.-A. (1838) *Recherches sur les Principes Mathématiques de la Théorie des Richesses* (Paris: Rivière).

Debreu, G. (1951) 'The Coefficient of Resource Utilization', *Econometrica*, vol. 19, pp. 273–92.

Dupuit, Jules (1844) 'De la mesure de 1'utilité des travaux publics', *Annales des Ponts et Chaussées*, 2ième Série, vol. 8, pp. 332–75.

Edgeworth, F. Y. (1881) *Mathematical Psychics: An Essay on the Application of Mathematics to the Moral Sciences* (London: C. Kegan Paul).

Hayek, F. von (1945) 'The Use of Knowledge in Society', *American Economic Review*, vol. 35, pp. 519–30.

Hicks, J. R. (1939) *Value and Capital* (Oxford: Clarendon Press).

Hotelling, Harold (1938) 'The General Welfare in Relation to Problems of Taxation and Railway and Utility Rates', *Econometrica*, vol. 6, pp. 242–69.

Knight, Frank H. (1924) 'Some Fallacies in the Interpretation of Social Cost', *Quarterly Journal of Economics*, vol. 38, pp. 582–606.

Lardner, D. (1850) *Railway Economy* (London: Taylor, Walker & Maberly).

Lindahl, E. (1929) 'Prisbildungsproblemets Uppläggning från Kapitalteorisk synpunkt', *Ekonomisk Tidskrift*, vol. 31, no. 2, pp. 31–81.

Lindahl, E. (1939) *Studies in the Theory of Money and Capital* (London: George Allen & Unwin).

Marshall, A. (1890) *Principles of Economics*, 1st edition (London: Macmillan), 8th edition (London: Macmillan, 1948).

Marshall, A. (1907) 'The Social Possibilities of Economic Chivalry', *Economic Journal*, vol. 17, pp. 7–29; reprinted in A. C. Pigou (ed.) *Memorials of Alfred Marshall* (London: Macmillan, 1925), pp. 323–46.

Meade, J. E. (1972) *The Controlled Economy* (Albany, NY: State University of New York Press).

Musgrave, R. (1959) *The Theory of Public Finance: A Study in Public Economics* (New York: McGraw-Hill).

National Oceanic and Atmospheric Administration (1993) Report of Panel on Contingent Valuation, *Federal Register*, vol. 58, no. 10 (15 January), pp. 4602–14.

Neumann, J. von and O. Morgenstern (1944) *Theory of Games and Economic Behavior* (Princeton: Princeton University Press).
Pigou, A. C. (1912) *Wealth and Welfare* (London: Macmillan).
Pigou, A. C. (1929) *The Economics of Welfare* (London: Macmillan).
Radner, R. (1968) 'Existence of Equilibrium of Plan, Prices and Price Expectations', *Econometrica*, vol. 36, pp. 31–58.
Robinson, J. (1933) *Economics of Imperfect Competition* (London: Macmillan).
Scitovsky, T. (1941) 'A Note on Welfare Propositions in Economics', *Review of Economic Studies*, vol. 9, pp. 77–88.
Scitovsky, T. (1954) 'Two Concepts of External Economies', *Journal of Political Economy*, vol. 17, pp. 143–51.
Stiglitz, J. (1994) *Whither Socialism?* (Cambridge, MA: MIT Press).
Viner, J. (1931) 'Cost Curves and Supply Curves', *Zeitschrift für Nationalökonomie*, vol. 3, pp. 23–46.
Young, A. (1913) 'Pigou's Wealth and Welfare', *Quarterly Journal of Economics*, vol. 27, pp. 672–86.